SEA WOLF

John D. Bulkeley, USN, "The Sea Wolf." (U.S. Navy)

SEA WOLF

A Biography of John D. Bulkeley, USN

William B. Breuer

★

PRESIDIO

Published by Presidio Press
31 Pamaron Way, Novato, CA 94949

LIBRARY OF CONGRESS
Library of Congress Cataloging-in-Publication Data

Breuer, William B., 1923–
Sea wolf: a biography of John D. Bulkeley/by William B. Breuer
p. cm.
Bibliography: p. 309.
Includes index.
ISBN 0-89141-335-9
1. Bulkeley, John Duncan, 1911– . 2. Admirals—United States—Biography. 3. United States. Navy—Biography. I. Title.
V63.B84B74 1989
359'.0092'4—dc19
[B] 88-21757
CIP

Printed in the United States of America

Dedicated to
ADMIRAL CARLISLE A. H. TROST, USN
Chief of Naval Operations
whose wisdom, vision, and zeal
are keeping the Navy strong
and America at Peace

and to the
Memory of the thirty-seven Navy men who died
for America on the USS *Stark,* Persian Gulf,
May 17, 1987

Doran H. Bolduc
Braddy O. Brown
Jeffrey L. Calkins
Mark R. Caquette
John A. Ciletta, Jr.
Brian M. Clinefelter
Antonio A. Daniels
Christopher W. DeAngelis
James S. Dunlap
Steven T. Erwin
Jerry B. Farr
Vernon T. Foster

Dexter D. Grissett
William R. Hansen
Daniel Homicki
Kenneth D. Janusik, Jr.
Steven E. Kendall
Stephen G. Kiser
Ronnie G. Lockett
Thomas J. MacMullen
Charles T. Moller
Jeffrey L. Phelps
Randy E. Pierce
James Plonsky

Kelly R. Quick
Earl P. Ryals
Robert L. Shippee
Jeffrey C. Sibley
Lee Stephens
James R. Stevens
Martin J. Supple
Gregory L. Tweady
Vincent L. Ulmer
Joseph P. Watson
Wayne R. Weaver
Terence D. Weldon
Lloyd A. Wilson

Contents

Acknowledgments

In creating this book, the author tracked down and interviewed or contacted 236 persons who were involved with Vice Adm. John D. Bulkeley during the fifty-nine years of his extraordinary career. Most of them probed their memories and, in person, by telephone, on tape, and by correspondence, told their candid and often startling and dramatic recollections. These reminiscences, along with those of Admiral Bulkeley himself, form the backbone of this story. Long-forgotten combat diaries, after-action reports, photographs, letters, maps, and media clippings were also made available.

A particular debt of gratitude is owed to Admiral Bulkeley and his wife, Alice. The Sea Wolf, certainly one of the world's busiest men, nevertheless made time for lengthy personal interviews at his Washington home and elsewhere over many months to answer the author's seemingly endless barrage of questions. Alice Bulkeley, an especially meticulous lady, kindly made available to the author a large volume of letters, photographs, telegrams, military orders, and other materials she had lovingly cataloged over her nearly five decades as the Sea Wolf's first mate. In his zeal, the author fears that he may have left her neatly assorted memorabilia in shambles.

Mrs. Alyce Mary Guthrie and Don Rhoads of PT Boats, Inc., the large veterans' association headquartered in Memphis, Tennessee, were most helpful in a variety of ways. Appreciation is also expressed to syndicated columnist Jack Anderson, to Bob Ferrell, who rendered the detailed drawing of the PT boat that appears in these pages, and to

Bruce M. Bachman for permission to draw on his book *An Honorable Profession*.

At the request of the author, reference librarians at the Willowbrook (Illinois) Public Library literally scoured the nation to come up with "impossible-to-find" data and information. They are Debbie Wordinger, Mary Nordstrom, Jane Lydy, and Karen Merritt.

Dr. Dean C. Allard, senior historian, and B. F. Calavante, both of the Naval Historical Center in Washington, D.C., and their staffs provided beneficial materials and information. So did Col. Lyman H. Hammond, Jr., director, MacArthur Memorial, Norfork, Virginia.

Most helpful were Rear Adm. Jimmie B. Finkelstein, navy chief of information, and four of his staff: Comdr. Kendell Pease; L. Comdr. Robert B. Pritchard; Ms. Anna C. Urband, media services division; and Russell D. Egnor, head of the news photo branch. Also Rear Adm. L. Burkhardt, III, Naval Military Personnel Command, and Anita M. Coley, office of the navy judge advocate general.

Thanks go to Gen. P. X. Kelley, commandant, marine corps; Henry I. Shaw, Jr., chief historian, marine corps; and navy Capt. John R. Condon, commander, United States Naval Base, Guantanamo Bay, Cuba.

Finally, a tip of the hat to several men who closely read selected chapters with the critical eye of participants in the events. They flagged technical errors, which were subsequently corrected. They are: retired navy Capt. Robert B. Kelly, chapters about the early PT-boat actions in the Philippines; L. Rumsey Ewing, the chapter on John Bulkeley's second tour of PT-boat duty in the Pacific; Joseph R. Ellicott, Edward W. Slater, and William "Bud" Liebenow, the chapters on the spy-running operations across the English Channel and PT-boat actions during the Normandy invasion; Jack W. Watson, the chapter on the invasion of southern France; Michael L. Infante and retired navy Capt. Lynn C. Cavendish, the chapters on the 1964–1966 confrontation with Fidel Castro and the Kremlin at the U.S. Naval Base, Guantanamo Bay, Cuba; and retired navy Comdr. Samuel J. Alexander, and retired Navy Capt. Alan Cabot, the chapters on the Naval Board of Inspection and Survey.

WILLIAM B. BREUER
Chicago
April 1988

1

The Japanese Ambassador's Disappearing Briefcase

Twenty-four-year-old Ens. John D. Bulkeley strolled into the dining salon of a Wilson Lines coastal steamer plying between Norfolk, Virginia, and Washington, D.C. on a sweltering July evening in 1936. Two years after his commissioning, Bulkeley remained slightly self-conscious of his immaculate white dress uniform with its choke collar and shoulder boards. Bulkeley's ship, the cruiser *Indianapolis,* was docked in Norfolk, so he planned to spend the weekend in Washington and nearby Baltimore.

Standing just inside the door of the salon, Bulkeley spotted four Japanese men seated at a table and talking animatedly. One man was wearing formal clothing; judging from their cropped hair, military bearing, and ages, Bulkeley concluded that the other three Japanese were generals or admirals, even though they were dressed in civilian clothes.

Bulkeley asked a salon steward if he knew the identity of the four Japanese. Yes, indeed, he replied, they made regular round-trips between Washington and Norfolk. The Virginia city was the site of one of the United States Navy's largest and most important bases, and at one time or another, almost every navy vessel afloat put in at Norfolk.

"The distinguished gentleman with the silver hair and the fancy duds is the Japanese ambassador to the United States," the steward pointed out in a conspiratorial tone.

Bulkeley's curiosity peaked. Ever since he had taken a Federal Bureau of Investigation course on counterespionage, he had been ultra security conscious. How odd, he reflected, that a busy ambassador could take time off from his duties to make periodic trips to Norfolk, and take along with him three high-ranking military officers. Bulkeley knew that the scuttlebutt among young officers on the *Indianapolis* was that the Japanese were engaged in widespread spying at the Navy's mainland bases and at Pearl Harbor, in Hawaii.

Bulkeley asked to be seated next to the Japanese party. He wanted to eavesdrop on their conversation, but he was disappointed: they were conferring in their native tongue, and he could not understand a word of it. As he pecked at his food, the ensign caught sight of a bulging briefcase sitting on the deck next to the diplomat. Bulkeley's heart began to pound faster, and his adrenaline started pumping furiously. That *briefcase!* No doubt it was chock-full of United States military secrets concerning the naval base at Norfolk, and therefore a threat to national security.

Instantly, Bulkeley reached a decision. He was convinced that it was his duty as an officer in the United States Navy to "acquire" the Japanese ambassador's briefcase and turn it over to naval intelligence.

ADM. JOHN BULKELEY:
I saw that the Japs at the table had drunk enough tea at dinner to float a battleship. So they would have to use the head during the night, I concluded. The tiny cabins did not have their own heads, so passengers had to use a communal one on deck.

I did a quick recon to locate the Jap ambassador's cabin, then for four or five hours hid in the darkness outside, waiting for him to go to the sandbox. Not long before dawn, it must have been about oh-four-hundred [4:00 A.M.] the ambassador came out and walked down the deck toward the sandbox to heed the call of nature.

Moments later, I scrambled through the hatch of the Jap's cabin, grabbed his briefcase, and barreled back through the hatch. I slipped along the deck to the stern, and then all hell broke loose. The chief Nip had returned to his cabin and found his briefcase gone. He began screaming and hollering and raising holy hell. Then the other Japs joined in the screaming. The racket was so loud, they no doubt heard it in Tokyo.

Bulkeley knew he had to get off the steamer—fast. A short distance to port, the dim contours of land could be seen, and he knew that the vessel had entered the Potomac River on her way to a Washington dock. Silently, he scrambled over the side and dropped into the dark water. Holding the briefcase high overhead, Bulkeley began sidestroking toward the Maryland shore.

Still wearing his dress uniform, complete with shoes, the ensign pulled himself from the water and began walking along a dirt road until he reached a main highway. There he hitchhiked a ride into Washington, where he holed up in a shabby hotel to wait until Monday when the office of naval intelligence would be open.

Early Monday morning, Bulkeley stole out of the hotel and took a taxi to the main navy building on Constitution Avenue. He was directed to the intelligence office, where he banged on the unmarked door for nearly a minute.

> ADMIRAL BULKELEY:
> Some old gent—he must have been 106 years old and going down for the third time—cautiously opened the door. He was stone-faced, and wearing civilian clothes. I found out later that he was a captain in naval intelligence. He never invited me inside. Merely said "Yes?" and stood there while I told him of events on the Norfolk-Washington steamer. Then I proudly held up the Jap ambassador's briefcase. The old bastard turned ashen—I thought he was going to faint. Finally, he asked my name, rank, and duty station, then slammed the door shut in my face.
>
> I was mad as hell and frustrated. Suddenly the door opened again, and the same gent snatched the briefcase out of my hand, told me to report back to the *Indianapolis* immediately, and again slammed the door.

John Bulkeley's venture into international intrigue had rapid ramifications. As soon as he returned to the *Indianapolis,* he was told to report to Capt. H. Kent Hewitt, the skipper. Now, Bulkeley reflected, he would get credit for his counterespionage coup. Instead, Captain Hewitt told him that he didn't want to hear a word about whatever had taken place on the steamer, that Bulkeley was to keep his mouth shut about the affair, and that the ensign was to report immediately to the transport *Chaumont,* also docked at Norfolk.

Bulkeley learned that the Navy was literally shanghaiing him out of the country, for the *Chaumont* would sail in twenty-four hours for Shanghai, China—about as far from Washington as horrified navy brass could send the young upstart without his falling off the earth.

Before dismissing Ensign Bulkeley, Captain Hewitt gave him a parting admonition: "Don't forget to pay your mess and laundry bill."

Bulkeley, who had felt honor-bound not to open the Japanese ambassador's briefcase, would never learn the nature of its contents.

John Duncan Bulkeley was born in New York City on August 19, 1911, to forty-three-year-old Frederick F. Bulkeley, a well-to-do businessman, and his Scottish-born wife, Elizabeth. On that date, William Howard

Taft was president of the United States and a gallon of gasoline cost seven cents, a pound of round steak eighteen cents, and a loaf of bread a few pennies. The most popular song was "Oh, You Beautiful Doll!" and new dance steps were sweeping the country—"The Kangaroo Dip," "The Crab Step," and "The Turkey Trot"—crazes that caused oldsters to cluck that the young generation was going to hell in a hand basket. The first transcontinental airplane flight left New York and, after eighty-two hours of actual flying time and nineteen crashes, arrived on the West Coast forty-nine days later.

John Bulkeley's family originated in Concord, Massachusetts, a town founded in 1635 by the Reverend Peter Bulkeley, who was buried there twenty-three years later. There had never been much doubt that John would choose a career in the Navy, for his family's association with naval history predates the Revolutionary War. One ancestor, Lt. Charles Bulkeley, had been second in command of the *Bonhomme Richard,* flagship of Capt. John Paul Jones, the "Father of the United States Navy," when, on September 23, 1779, she tangled with the much larger and better-armed British warship *Serapis,* in the North Sea. After the two vessels exchanged point-blank gunfire for three hours, the *Serapis*'s mast fell, and she surrendered. But the *Bonhomme Richard* had been so badly damaged that she sank two days later.

Another ancestor, Richard Bulkeley, had served as a midshipman aboard British Lord Horatio Nelson's HMS *Victory* when, on October 21, 1805, Nelson's fleet of twenty-seven warships engaged and defeated a combined French and Spanish armada of thirty-three vessels off Trafalgar, a cape on the southern coast of Spain. Lord Nelson had been mortally wounded in the fight, and Midshipman Bulkeley was said to have been at his side when the admiral died on board.

When a teenager, John Bulkeley's father, Frederick, had joined the United States Navy, gone to sea, and contracted a tropical disease in Panama. Seaman Bulkeley was sent to a New York hospital, where he was nursed back to health by Elizabeth MacCuaig, who worked at the medical center. The couple fell in love and were married.

When Frederick's enlistment ended, he left the Navy and went into business for himself. Despite minimal formal education, Frederick had a knack for commerce, and soon his company was thriving.[1]

In 1918, when John Bulkeley was seven years old, the family moved to Hackettstown, New Jersey, where the boy began his lifelong love affair with the sea. For hours he would sit at his father's knee and listen in fascination as the elder Bulkeley spun tales of his life at sea while a youngster. With a dedication foreign to most boys his age, John taught himself how to navigate by the stars. Many a night he would fall asleep clutching a book containing pictures of sailing schooners.

When John reached the age of twelve his father managed to ship the boy as an ordinary seaman aboard the Colombian freighter *Baracoa.* The wide-eyed youngster could not believe his good fortune: not only would he be doing what he had dreamed about, but Colombia Steamship Lines would pay him a dollar a day. For three successive summers, John traveled on the high seas, mainly in the Caribbean.

During the other months, John attended Hackettstown High School, where he was a halfback on the football team, a member of the track squad, and belonged to the literary society. On Memorial Day 1927, John delivered an oration at the school's observance program and his topic, prophetically, was "The War Inevitable."

At his graduation in 1928, the Hackettstown High School yearbook predicted that John Bulkeley would one day become a sailor—a peak of understatement in light of events in the decades ahead.

MRS. ELSIE LA BAR:

John Bulkeley was in the basic French class I taught at Hackettstown High School during my first year after college graduation. He was always well-groomed, courteous, cheerful, and cooperative. The basic French course could be very tedious at first, and I thought that John was bored and disinterested. But as the momentum picked up, I was glad to see a change in his attitude.

I could not call John studious. But his innate intelligence achieved for him satisfactory grades, with no great effort. His love was math and science, subjects in which he excelled.

John was popular with boys and girls, as well as the faculty. Once the football coach said to me that he often noticed John's ability to *lead,* and that some day he would go far.

In one conversation I had with John after class, I asked what he would like to do after high school. His quick reply: "United States Naval Academy—and I'll make it!" He was cocksure of himself, even then.

Shortly after John Bulkeley graduated from Hackettstown High School, the Great Depression wiped out his father's business. So the family moved to a 360-acre farm in New Jersey, one that Frederick had purchased as a retreat during the years of national prosperity following World

War I. On moving to the farm, the elder Bulkeley told his family: "As long as we can raise our own food, we won't starve to death." But son John had no intention of becoming a lifelong farmer; his focus remained on Annapolis, Maryland, and the Naval Academy.

However, John was confronted by a major obstacle. Candidates for appointment to the Academy are made after recommendations by United States senators or representatives. But Frederick had no high-level political connections to buttonhole about an appointment for his son.[2]

John was only seventeen years of age, but he decided that he himself would go to Washington and coerce some member of Congress into appointing him to the Naval Academy. (Appointments in his own New Jersey district had already been filled for that year.) To pay for his son's trip to the capital, the elder Bulkeley sold off a few of his cattle.

Arriving by train in Washington, the boy from the New Jersey farm began tramping the halls of Congress, entering the office of one legislator after another. None would even talk to him—New Jersey residents could not vote in their states. Undaunted, John kept wearing out shoe leather and finally hit pay dirt.

Congressman Morgan G. Sanders, of the Third District of Texas, had found himself in an awkward predicament: all of his district appointees had flunked the entrance examinations for both the Naval Academy and the Military Academy at West Point. Sanders was willing to talk to his youthful visitor, and the congressman's interest picked up when John explained that his father, despite his acute financial pinch, still had landholdings in Sanders's district. So why, John asked, couldn't the supplicant become an "instant Texan" and be appointed to Annapolis from the Lone Star state?

That made sense to Sanders, who appointed John to the Naval Academy. The boy breezed through his entrance examinations, except for English, a subject that had always given him fits, but he managed to squeak through it. In June 1929, Bulkeley passed through the Annapolis gates as a plebe.

The Texan from New Jersey was mesmerized by the sights and sounds that until now he had only read or heard about. The training school for navy and marine corps officers had been founded by George Bancroft, secretary of the Navy under President James K. Polk, in 1845 and was located on the banks of the Severn River. The academy and adjacent naval facilities occupied about 1,000 acres.[3]

Even the prompt head-shave inflicted on incoming plebes failed to dampen Bulkeley's early ardor. He was fascinated by the great gray eminence of majestic Bancroft Hall, and the reflections cast by the copper dome of the chapel. However, Bulkeley's view soon turned sour as he absorbed the facts of life at the Naval Academy as they were in the year 1929.

Traditionally, plebes were the objects of cruel, even sadistic, hazing, a procedure that would allegedly weed out those who were physically or psychologically incapable of standing up to the pressures of military stress. Plebes who faltered or broke down were dismissed from the academy or resigned, after which they returned home in "disgrace."

ADMIRAL BULKELEY:
We plebes were beaten severely, often with broom handles, for failure to pronounce flawlessly the passages in *Reef Points,* a large collection of navy lore and tales. Often the pain was nearly unbearable. Most of this savagery, which had no relation whatsoever to producing top-notch and dedicated navy officers, was inflicted by a small percentage of first-classmen [seniors]. Three of the first-classmen in the class of 1930 stand out in my mind even today as the cruelest of the whole lot, and they later attained flag rank [admiral]. I do not begrudge their career success, but I damned well hate the manner in which they obtained their personal goals. No doubt, in advancing to the top levels of their profession, these three bastards had often directed their sadistic streaks against junior officers and enlisted men.

Hundredth Night was a tradition at the Naval Academy and marked 100 days before graduation of first-classmen. It was also a time for inflicting pain and humiliation upon the "impudent swine not worthy of crossing a ship's deck"—the plebes. Bulkeley was one of the "swine" selected by a first-classmen "tribunal of sea lords" to be disciplined: he was thrashed with a hundred strokes of a broom handle and lapsed into unconsciousness.[4]

Despite his extreme distaste for many phases of Academy life, John Bulkeley endured. During his four years he had a penchant for acquiring nicknames, and was known variously as Jack, Buck, and Bull.[5]

CAPT. STANLEY M. BARNES, USN (RET.):
In the fifty-eight years I've known John Bulkeley since we were classmates at Annapolis, he's always marched to his own drummer. Neither of us was distinguished to the slightest degree [at Annapolis]. I recall him as

> a quiet, dogged, self-contained individual whose only special interest was engineering. John used to disappear into the machine shop available to midshipmen and do his thing. He once made a poppet valve model engine, which turned up some 10,000 rpms. He also transformed the engine of an old Ford into a diesel.
>
> John had great mechanical talents, but scholastically both of us were way down at the bottom of our graduating class.[6]

The Great Depression, which forced government belt-tightening, played a cruel joke on those in the lower half of the scholastic standings in the class of 1933. (Bulkeley ranked 394th among 431 class members, but 134 others would fail to graduate.) President Franklin D. Roosevelt personally handed a diploma to each graduate, but those in the bottom half of the standings did not receive commissions.[7]

2

A Spy in Shanghai

John Bulkeley had a heaviness of heart over the events that had denied him the ensign's rank he had dreamed of since early childhood. He found himself in a twilight world, a civilian with a Naval Academy diploma. Gaining a military commission remained his consuming passion, so when he was accepted as a flying cadet by the Army Air Corps, Bulkeley eagerly reported to Randolph Field, Texas, in the fall of 1933.

Cadet Bulkeley felt that now he had the world by the tail. He was fascinated by the speed and power and peril involved in flying airplanes, was en route to earning lieutenant's bars, and was making big money—seventy-five dollars a month. Then his bubble burst.

> CAPT. STANLEY BARNES:
> John Bulkeley cracked up an airplane or two at Randolph, and that brought an end to his career as an army pilot. Even in those days, John seemed to lead a charmed life, for he walked away from the accidents. Years later he told me that he had gotten a real hard blow on the head in his last crack-up, and felt that ever after he had become a different person.

Bulkeley's gloom over leaving Randolph Field was quickly lifted. In March 1934, President Roosevelt recalled to active duty the Naval Academy class of 1933 graduates who had not been commissioned. Bulkeley's euphoria was not dampened by the fact that he and the others recalled were given probationary commissions, meaning that the commitments could be revoked at any time, even at the whim of a cantankerous superior officer.

In June 1934, an excited Ensign Bulkeley, decked out in a full-dress white uniform and carrying a ceremonial sword in its scabbard, boarded the cruiser *Indianapolis* at Provincetown, Massachusetts. His navy career began as a junior watch officer, and at this point his loftiest ambition was to become a qualified officer of the deck, a status that would take him three years to achieve.[1]

CAPT. STANLEY BARNES:
Even though I had been a classmate of John Bulkeley at Annapolis, I got to know him well only when we were fellow officers on the *Indianapolis*. He was the ship's F Division [fire control] officer, and was sent to take a course in optical range finders. In no time, he was the only officer taking the course who could take a range finder apart and put it back together again—while blindfolded.

John, through his own initiative, also trained himself to be such a good "spotter" with the range finder that the *Indy* brought home several Es [for battle efficiency] for its five- and eight-inch guns in the navy's annual short-range battle practice competition.

Despite his record of achievement, Ensign Bulkeley's tour of duty on the *Indianapolis* was short-circuited in the wake of his caper with the Japanese ambassador's briefcase, and he arrived in Shanghai aboard the plodding old tub *Chaumont* in December 1936. There he was assigned to the coastal gunboat *Sacramento,* an old coal-burner being held together by bailing wire and chewing gum.

In Shanghai, Ensign Bulkeley found himself in the midst of a savage war that had been raging since September 18, 1931. At that time, Japanese warlords had seized Manchuria (a northern province of China) and made it into a puppet state called Manchukuo. In 1937, the Nipponese cooked up a clash between their troops on maneuvers and a Chinese army outpost on the Marco Polo bridge near Peking (Beijing) and used that as an excuse to launch a massive invasion of China proper. The Chinese Nationalist army under General Chiang Kai-shek was steadily pushed southward, and the Japanese captured the Yangtze River Valley (which included Shanghai). From that point, the Chinese fought mainly guerrilla actions against the Japanese invaders.[2]

John Bulkeley, in the months ahead, witnessed on occasion the atrocities being inflicted on the Chinese people by the invaders, and he developed a deep hatred for the Japanese. He was sickened by the sight of Chinese civilians being terrorized and tortured, of women being publicly raped and murdered, of cities deliberately being burned. Mentally tough though he was, Bulkeley blanched when he saw Chinese male civilians, bound hand and foot, dragged into a town square to have their heads lopped off by swords or beaten to a bloody pulp by rifle butts, while the population was forced to watch.

Official Washington and the American people could stick their heads in the sand and ignore the holocaust that the empire of Japan was inflicting on the Chinese people, Bulkeley reflected. But from the savageries he had seen, the ensign was convinced that the Japanese warlords were bent on conquest in the Pacific, and that Nippon's grand design called for eventual war with the United States.

In February 1937, Bulkeley was presented with a chance to strike back at the Japanese. He was called in by the intelligence officer on the flagship of Adm. Thomas C. Hart, commander of the U.S. Naval Forces in the Far East, and asked if he would take on an undercover assignment against the Japanese. Bulkeley eagerly accepted the challenge to become a "spy." He was to dress in civilian clothes, pose as a foreign sightseer or shopper, conceal a small camera on his person, and snap photographs of tanks, artillery, troops, and Nipponese warships in the Yangtze River.

Shanghai, the world's second largest city at the time with a teeming population in excess of seven million, was a confusing jumble of jurisdictions. It consisted of the International Settlement along the banks of the Whangpoo River, the French concession ("Frenchtown"), and the Chinese City. The municipality of Greater Shanghai surrounded the International Settlement and the French sector, and included the suburban towns of Hongkew, Chapei, and Nantao and the old walled city of Shanghai. Further complicating the hodgepodge of jurisdictions, the Japanese army, which was skirmishing with Chiang Kai-shek's guerrillas in the region, occupied certain sectors of the sprawling community.

John Bulkeley, garbed in casual civilian attire, set out on his mission. His concealed camera had a remote release, and by a movement of his arm the lens would be exposed to snap a picture. Approaching the Garden Gate Bridge leading into suburban Japanese-occupied Hongkew, Bulkeley saw a large sign on which was written in three languages: "All foreigners entering Hongkew must realize that the sentry on duty represents his Imperial Majesty the Emperor of Japan and must bow to him and wish him good morning or good evening."

Bulkeley waved breezily at the sentry, called out "Hi," and walked on into Hongkew, which was crowded with Nipponese troops, weapons, and vehicles.

> ADMIRAL BULKELEY:
> While on this mission, I crossed over into Hongkew many times, and got away with this piece of insolence. As an American, I was not about to stop and take a deep bow before anyone, especially a Japanese son of a bitch. The guards got used to seeing me, and paid no attention. But one day there was a new boy on the block [sentry]. This one thought he was truly a Son of Heaven. I gave him my customary wave and ''hi'' and he responded angrily by lowering his rifle, pointing it directly at me, and gesturing wildly toward the sign.
>
> In Pidgin English, he ordered me to bow to him. I said no way. We had a hell of an argument in Japanese and English, and finally a few other Japs showed up and I was hustled off to the Nip jug. There I was defiant as hell. I identified myself as an American naval officer, and told the Nips that we didn't bow to anyone.
>
> I could not explain away why I had a camera concealed on me, so I was taken to Japanese naval headquarters in Hongkew. There I was confronted by an Admiral Hasgawa, who spoke fluent English and asked me how was ''Tommy Hart.'' Hasgawa was an Annapolis graduate as an exchange student, and had been a classmate of my big boss, Admiral Thomas Hart.

Admiral Hasgawa was pleasant but reserved, stressing that he understood American customs, but Hongkew was a Japanese sector, so Japanese customs would have to be observed by all foreigners. So wouldn't the stubborn Bulkeley go back to the Garden Gate Bridge, bow to the sentry, and all would be forgiven—including his carrying a hidden camera. Again the ensign refused, so he was returned to the Japanese brig.

Bulkeley was summoned again by Admiral Hasgawa the next morning. If the American would write out a thousand times, ''I must bow before sentries who represent the Imperial Majesty the Emperor of Japan,'' he would be released. Bulkeley refused. On the following day, Hasgawa made the same offer. Again the ensign said no.

On about the fifth day of his incarceration, Bulkeley once more was taken before the admiral, who expressed a desire to reduce his terms. If the American would write the requested wording a hundred times, he could leave Hongkew. By now Bulkeley was fed up with the food at the Nipponese brig, his bug-infested straw bed, the stinking water that ran in the toilet. So he agreed to Hasgawa's terms.

Ensign Bulkeley returned to uniformed duty aboard the *Sacramento,* but his venture into the cloak-and-dagger field had been successful, discounting the five days he had spent in a vermin-infested and filthy Japanese brig. He turned over to the fleet intelligence officer a few hundred clandestinely taken photos. Now Bulkeley vowed revenge against the Japanese, and that opportunity soon surfaced.

At the turn of the century, a Chinese secret society, known to foreigners as the Boxers, fomented a bloody rebellion in which they murdered 231 foreigners and countless Chinese Christians. In 1900, an armed international force, representing seven nations, arrived in Shanghai and snuffed out the Boxers' uprising. Five of the intervening countries—including the United States and Japan—set up a Shanghai peacekeeping force to guard against further violence by armed Chinese.

ADMIRAL BULKELEY:
The rule was for the ships of the five nations enforcing the Boxer Rebellion Treaty to mutually guard against any armed reprisal from the Chinese, just as it had been for thirty-seven years. At this time, the Japs had twenty-two warships in the Whangpoo River bombarding the Chinese guerrillas and rebels. Each day one ship of the five nations, excepting the Japanese, would take the "watch," and if anything suspicious was seen—frogmen or other methods of potential attack—a whistle was to be blown six times to alert other ships in the Whangpoo of possible attack.

The Chinese had sneaked two small boats with stern-launching torpedo tubes to the town of Nantao, up the Whangpoo from Shanghai. So I was on watch this night when the pair of Chinese torpedo boats came roaring along the river, and I knew instinctively that they were going to conduct a torpedo attack on Admiral Hasgawa's flagship, which was anchored a short distance away. I knew that I was supposed to warn the remainder of the ships that something suspicious was underway on this cold, rainy, and foggy night—but, curiously, there was no steam in the ship's whistle.

So I stood on the platform of the accommodation ladder and cheered on the Chinese torpedo boats with a "Go, man, go!" When the boats got opposite Hasgawa's flagship, they turned 180 degrees and fired four torpedoes and at least two of them hit the target. After dawn we could see that the Jap admiral's flagship had sunk—right up to the gunwales in the mud of the Whangpoo River. What a joyous sight! That was my revenge.

Admiral Hasgawa called on his "old pal" Admiral Tom Hart to complain bitterly about the lack of warning when the Chinese boats struck. I believe that Hart knew the whole story, but he said nothing.

Ensign Bulkeley missed no opportunity to bedevil the Japanese in the Shanghai region, and he took a fiendish delight in playing tricks on them, especially antics that would cause them to lose face. It had long been a naval courtesy practice for the boarding officer of a station ship to call on the skipper of a newly arrived warship and present his own captain's personal card. So when the Japanese cruiser *Yubari* anchored in the Whangpoo River, Bulkeley, as boarding officer of the *Sacramento,* hopped into his captain's gig and carried out a scenario that he had honed to perfection during earlier visits to Nipponese warships.

Bulkeley headed down the Whangpoo and pretended that he had no interest in the *Yubari*. Then, when he was convinced that the *Yubari*'s officer of the deck had ceased watching the gig, he darted back to the heavy cruiser and quickly tied up at her accommodation ladder. It was the Japanese practice to put two sailors at the bottom of the ladder, and most of them wore no shoes unless a foreign naval officer was calling.

Bulkeley dashed up the ladder before the officer of the deck knew that he was aboard and could get shoes on his two seamen. The flustered officer of the deck was taken by total surprise, but he escorted the visitor to the commander of the *Yubari,* who was both angry and embarrassed over the loss of face he had suffered through barefoot seamen and a deck officer who had been caught with his epaulets down.

The American ensign paid his respects to the cruiser's captain, then made it a point to slip along the deck once more to catch the officer of the deck by surprise. He arrived just in time to see the Japanese officer belting the pair of sailors who had been without shoes while receiving aboard a foreign navy officer. Faces had been lost all around.

On the first day of July 1937, the *Sacramento* was anchored at the port of Foochow, and nearby was the *Diana,* a British warship. Ensign Bulkeley was instructed by his skipper to call on the captain of the *Diana* and invite him to be the *Saccy* commander's guest for a celebration of American Independence Day, on July 4. Bulkeley boarded the *Diana* and extended the invitation.

"American Independence Day?" the Royal Navy officer repeated with raised eyebrows. "Wasn't that one of those Indian wars in the colonial days?"

"Why, you son of a bitch!" the angry Bulkeley snapped, "do you remember the battle of Bunker Hill?" [3]

The American was hustled off the *Diana* by two British ratings.

That fall of 1937, the HMS *Diana* and the USS *Sacramento* were again anchored near to each other, this time at Swatow, a port 200 miles north of Hong Kong. The *Diana* was to sail for England in a few days, so her captain invited the officers of the *Saccy* to a farewell reception. On the evening of October 12, the American officers reached the *Diana*'s accommodation ladder, and Ensign Bulkeley, being last in the pecking order of rank, stepped aside to go aboard last.

While he was waiting, a group of British civilian guests arrived and filed up the ladder. One of the guests caught his eye, an attractive young woman he judged (correctly) to be twenty-five years of age. On board, Bulkeley arranged an introduction, and found that the object of his affection was Hilda Alice Wood, a British subject who had been born in Swatow, where her father, Cecil H. Wood, had a pilotage business and was also a marine surveyor for the British government. Alice, as she was known to friends, held a degree from the University of Hong Kong, and she had won many medals as a star athlete in track and field. At the time, Alice was a confidential secretary for the manager of Butterfield & Swire, a shipping firm at Swatow.

Almost at once, cupid fired his quiver of arrows at John Bulkeley and Alice Wood, but soon the *Sacramento* sailed away. However, Bulkeley returned to Swatow on occasion in the months ahead and the romance blossomed.

Meanwhile, back in the States, there was public and governmental indifference to Japan's warlike actions. Even the deliberate bombing and sinking of the American gunboat *Panay* by the Japanese while she was patrolling the Yangtze River on December 12, 1937, and the machine-gunning of survivors floundering in the water, aroused but a few feeble protests. President Roosevelt accepted Japanese apologies and dropped the matter.[4]

But in China, John Bulkeley was far from ready to forgive and forget. The *Panay* was not far from the *Saccy* at the time of the sinking, and Bulkeley later saw the riddled bodies of American sailors who had been killed while trying to swim to safety from the mortally wounded *Panay*. His hatred of anything Japanese intensified.

After a 13-month romance, on November 10, 1938, John Bulkeley and Alice Wood were married by Special Judge Nelson F. Lurton of the United States Court for China at the American consulate in Shanghai. It was now late afternoon, and the newlyweds took a boat 20 miles down the Whangpoo River to where the *Sacramento* was tied up at docks of the Standard Oil Co. They ate with ship's officers, took a few photos of the occasion, then the new Mrs. John D. Bulkeley was initiated into the capricious lifestyle of a navy wife. Her husband explained that he was duty officer on the *Saccy* that night.

Bulkeley and a few officers escorted the bride to a nearby house that had been the home of a Standard Oil manager. The structure was vacant because most American families had been evacuated to the States due to the war that had become more intense around Shanghai. Alice was shown to the basement, where there was a cot and a washroom. Here she would spend her wedding night—alone.

Before departing, the groom handed Alice his .45 Colt and said, "You may need this." When he had closed the door shut behind him, the bride stood there for long moments with the pistol in her hand, wondering what she would do with it. She had never fired a shot in her life and didn't know how.

Finally the new Mrs. Bulkeley stuck the weapon under her pillow; somehow she felt safer knowing that John's Colt was there. She closed her eyes and dozed off, awakened on occasion through the night by the sound of gun shots.

Two months after the couple had tied the marital knot, the *Sacramento* was ordered to return to the United States for a badly needed overhaul. It would be an 18,000-mile trek, by way of Europe, to the Brooklyn Navy Yard. Cynical *Saccy* crewmen were making bets on whether the old tub would reach Brooklyn, and how many miles she would chug before her engines gave out—or she sank.

Alice Bulkeley was not an American citizen, despite her marriage to a United States citizen, so she would have to remain behind until her husband reached Brooklyn and could send for her.

Early one spring morning in 1939, fog blanketed Shanghai harbor as the *Sacramento* sailed toward the open sea. After a circuitous cruise that took her halfway around the globe, the old gunboat huffed and wheezed into New York harbor in mid-May—much to the astonishment of John Bulkeley, her chief engineer, and all hands. The *Saccy* promptly began resting her ancient bones in drydock.

Bulkeley sent word for Alice to join him, and before departing she traveled to Swatow to bid good-bye to her father and mother. The Japanese army was closing in on Swatow, and Alice would never again see Captain Wood.

Meanwhile, John Bulkeley's career was moving forward, albeit snail-like, in a Navy to which Congress was ladling out funds with a tiny spoon. His rank changed from probationary to temporary ensign, and then he reached permanent status when promoted to lieutenant, junior grade. At the same time, war clouds were gathering over the world. The Japanese invaders now occupied most of the important coastal regions as well as major cities in the interior of China, and the warlords in Tokyo were rattling their samurai swords and growing steadily more hostile toward Uncle Sam. In Europe, on September 1, 1939, Adolf Hitler sent his booted German legions storming into Poland, and in a startling six-week blitzkrieg overran that tormented country.

Lieutenant Bulkeley remained with the *Sacramento* until December, when he was ordered to report for duty aboard one of the Navy's largest and most powerful ships, the aircraft carrier *Saratoga,* now undergoing an overhaul at the Bremerton Navy Yard in the state of Washington. Bulkeley was awed by the immenseness of the *Sara;* his old gunboat could nestle comfortably on one end of her flight deck.

When the *Sara* reached her base at Long Beach, California, she anchored near a merchant dock. There Bulkeley (and most other navy officers) noticed the almost constant presence of Japanese shipping. It was a rare day when a Nipponese freighter was not loading scrap iron. Japanese tankers came in regularly to haul oil back to their homeland. And part of the fishing fleet working out of nearby San Pedro was manned by Japanese.

The empire of Japan and the United States had been on a collision course as far back as the sinking of the *Panay*. Bulkeley, who had long been convinced that Japan's warlords planned to eventually fight America, and his fellow officers often conjectured if American scrap iron would one day return in the form of bombs, shells, and bullets.

3

"The Situation Is Tense Out Here!"

The carrier *Saratoga* and her sister, the *Lexington,* were the largest warships in the world. And they had power to match their size—185,000 horsepower. Neither ship was designed to be a carrier, but started as battle cruisers and were converted under the terms of the Washington Disarmament Conference of 1922. Along with the *Sara* and the *Lex,* the United States Navy had but three more carriers.[1]

Despite his modest rank, Lt. John Bulkeley was assigned to be second division officer, a post that put him in charge of about one-fourth of the *Saratoga*'s crew. As the months rolled past he was gripped by an urge to become a navy pilot. Zooming off the flight deck of a sometimes bucking aircraft carrier, tangling with hostile fighter planes 200 to 300 miles from the ship, returning to the carrier that may be 50 miles from where the pilot left it (there are no landmarks or signposts on the ocean), and using split-second timing to cut through often gusty, shifting winds to come aboard—all sounded like great fun to Bulkeley. A carrier pilot was a special breed of cat.

The *Sara*'s skipper, Capt. Albert T. Read, a skilled pioneer in navy aviation, had taken a personal interest in his eager lieutenant and had encouraged him to fly, declaring that aircraft carriers would be decisive in a future war involving the United States. So the *Sara*'s captain approved Bulkeley's request to transfer to the naval flight school at Pensacola, Florida.

In February 1941, Lieutenant Bulkeley departed the *Saratoga* for Pensacola, but en route he made a stopover in Washington. There he was asked by navy brass if instead of flight school he would like to join up with an exciting new branch of the service—patrol-torpedo boats—PT boats, for short. Knowing that to refuse such an ''offer'' would squash future promotions, Bulkeley agreed to the assignment.

On his arrival at the Brooklyn Navy Yard a week later, Bulkeley was given command of Submarine Chaser Division Two, an experimental unit whose PT boats were specially equipped to detect and then sink hostile underwater craft. Known as PTCs, the modified boats were seventy-footers and had been built by the Elco Naval Division of the Electric Boat Company, at Bayonne, New Jersey. Depth-charge racks had been installed; they were Rube Goldberg–type devices that launched explosives from the stern. Each PTC had three powerful Packard engines that could drive it through the water at fifty-five knots (about sixty land miles per hour), without four torpedoes aboard. Four of Bulkeley's boats were equipped with sonar—sophisticated gear that protruded its head underwater to provide ''ears'' with which to detect and pinpoint the location of submarines.

CAPT. ROBERT R. GREEN, USN (RET.):

I came to John Bulkeley's command in the spring of 1941 from duty as an ensign on a destroyer in the Pacific. Things were very confused in the new PT-boat service. No one really knew what he was doing.

Bulkeley was always hopped up on security. To some extent, there was good reason for concern about sabotage to the PT boats, for there were plenty of pro-Nazi types around New York harbor. He often got us out on the dock and gave us demonstrations and lectures on how to approach a suspected saboteur or spy. We held antisabotage drills, and Bulkeley would go out at night and try to creep up on guards without being detected.

I'm sure other people at the Brooklyn Navy Yard thought we were nuts.

In March, Lieutenant Bulkeley took his four sonar-equipped PTCs to Key West, Florida, to conduct antisubmarine trials. The results proved to be disastrous. When racing through the Caribbean Sea, the boats' motion was so violent that the sonar heads were broken off or torn loose and fell to the ocean floor. Not a single sonar head survived.

Meanwhile, historic events had taken place. Adolf Hitler's mighty Wehrmacht had smashed France's once-vaunted army in a dazzling six-week blitzkrieg, and Britain now stood alone and in peril of defeat. So at 3:51 P.M. on March 11, 1941, President Roosevelt signed into law the lend-lease bill that he had ramrodded through Congress in record time. Lend-lease was an ingenious method to supply ships, tanks, airplanes, weapons, and munitions to beleaguered England in return for nominal payments.

Three weeks after Roosevelt signed on the dotted line, Lieutenant Bulkeley was told to rush back to New York, where his PTCs, along with most of the other PT boats, would be turned over to the British.

Bulkeley's four boats set out on the 1,300-mile run to New York with all throttles wide open. The skipper wanted to find out how much pounding the wooden boats could take on extended open-ocean runs and still be ready to fight. Dashing through the water at full speed, a PT boat was a thing of beauty. Its bow lifted clear of the water and the boat glided gracefully over the surface, throwing out a great wave to either side and a rooster tail of foamy white astern. But the men who rode the PTs roundly cursed their personal discomfort, claiming that to be aboard at high speed was akin to being inside a revolving concrete mixer.

So on arrival at the Norfolk naval base to refuel for the last leg of the run, John Bulkeley and his four crews were exhausted after a long day of incessant pounding in particularly rough seas. All hands sprawled about the decks, eating cold sandwiches and drinking lukewarm Coca Colas. The men were wet, dirty, unshaven, and wearing dungarees and oil-stained T-shirts.

Bulkeley was unaware that the PTs had moored in front of the quarters of Adm. Ernest J. King, commander of the Atlantic Fleet, who had a reputation in the Navy as one who ate people for breakfast. Less than thirty minutes after the PTs were made fast, Admiral King's flag lieutenant appeared on Bulkeley's boat. Immaculate in his dress white uniform with high collar, the aide told Bulkeley, "Admiral King wants you to report to him immediately—in the uniform of the day." (That is, dress whites.)

Bulkeley knew that the strict disciplinarian King had spotted what appeared to be a band of pirates on the PT boats, and was going to raise holy hell with their chief. Bulkeley had no dress uniform. Those conducting speed trials through heavy seas certainly did not carry formal garb with them. The aide had not asked the skipper for his name, so Bulkeley told his men, "To hell with that old bastard King!"

The four PT boats slipped out of Norfolk and raced off to New York, leaving Admiral King behind and no doubt furious over the fact that the bedraggled band of buccaneers had escaped his clutches.

Based on the ill-fated experiments with sonar, Lieutenant Bulkeley recommended to navy brass that efforts to convert PT boats into subchasers be jettisoned, a suggestion that was accepted. However, one notable success had been scored. On the return high-speed-and-endurance trip back to New York, Bulkeley's boats had roared through choppy waters at an average speed of 41.3 knots, with only two refueling stops en route. That feat impressed the navy gold braid: it proved that the presumably fragile PT boats could withstand prolonged pounding on the open ocean, and therefore could be deployed almost anywhere in the world.

While John Bulkeley and other PT-boat skippers were making practice runs in waters around New York harbor, J. Edgar Hoover, director of the Federal Bureau of Investigation, dropped a bombshell. On July 2, 1941, Hoover announced that seventy-two hours earlier FBI agents had swept up thirty-three Nazi spies in New York City and suburban towns in the greatest espionage roundup in American history.

Among Adolf Hitler's spies peeking through bars were several whose beat had been the New York waterfront, where they had reconnoitered vessels targeted for sabotage and relayed to German U-boats lurking offshore the sailing dates of ships taking accoutrements of war to Great Britain.

"This is one of the most active and vicious gangs we have ever had to deal with," Hoover told the press. "Their sinister game was to snatch important national defense secrets and transmit them to a foreign power [Germany]." [2]

Suddenly, attitudes toward security did a drastic flip-flop all over New York harbor, with its U.S. naval yards and hundreds of docks and mooring berths. Where there had been total apathy toward the threat of enemy sabotage, now spy-mania erupted.

LT. COMDR. C. JOE VIOLETTE, USN (RET.):

In the navy yard's main powerhouse was a master switch, and John Bulkeley's boats would hook up to this power source when at the dock to save their battery systems. When we wanted to get underway, it was my job, as radioman first class, to get into the powerhouse and pull the switch, then run back to my PT boat and disconnect the "shore line."

One day they were doing repair work in the powerhouse and moved things around. So I accidentally threw the wrong switch—and caused the base's entire communications system to go dead.

Well, the base commander was mad as hell. Wanted to court-martial me. He reasoned that I was of French descent, and therefore I must have been an agent of the Vichy French, who were collaborating with the Germans, and had tried to sabotage the base communications system.

Bulkeley had asked me what happened, and went along with me that afternoon when I was called to the base commander's office. I was left outside the door of the captain's office, guarded by an armed marine and scared to death. I could hear the base commander shouting to Bulkeley . . . kept hearing the word "saboteur."

Finally, Bulkeley came out and said, "Okay, Joe, let's go." As we walked back to our boat, he grinned and remarked, "It's a damned good thing that I'm a great sea lawyer, Joe—that captain wanted to hang you!"

Meanwhile, a crisis with Japan was brewing in the Pacific. On July 21, 1941, Secretary of War Henry L. Stimson called out of retirement a famed American hero, Douglas MacArthur, and appointed him commanding general, United States Army Forces in the Far East, with headquarters in Manila. When he had retired in 1935, MacArthur sailed for the Philippines, where he had been made a field marshal by President Manuel Quezon with the mission of shoring up the commonwealth's defenses.[3]

Now General MacArthur launched an eleventh-hour struggle to build up enough force to repel a Japanese invasion of the Philippines. He begged Washington for airplanes, ships, munitions, and men. Washington had little to send, but in August reinforcements began to trickle toward the Philippines. Among these were the six PT boats of Lt. John Bulkeley's Squadron 3.

COMDR. HENRY J. BRANTINGHAM, USN (RET.):
After the subchaser squadron was dissolved in New York, John Bulkeley went to its officers and men, seeking volunteers for a new PT-boat squadron that was to be deployed in "an exciting secret place." This approach produced sufficient eager volunteers, including myself.

Squadron 3 boats were loaded on a tanker and set sail for our unknown destination. En route through the Panama Canal and past Pearl Harbor, Bulkeley conducted skull sessions on strategy and tactics, which had to be improvised for there was no established doctrine for the tactical deployment of PT boats in combat.

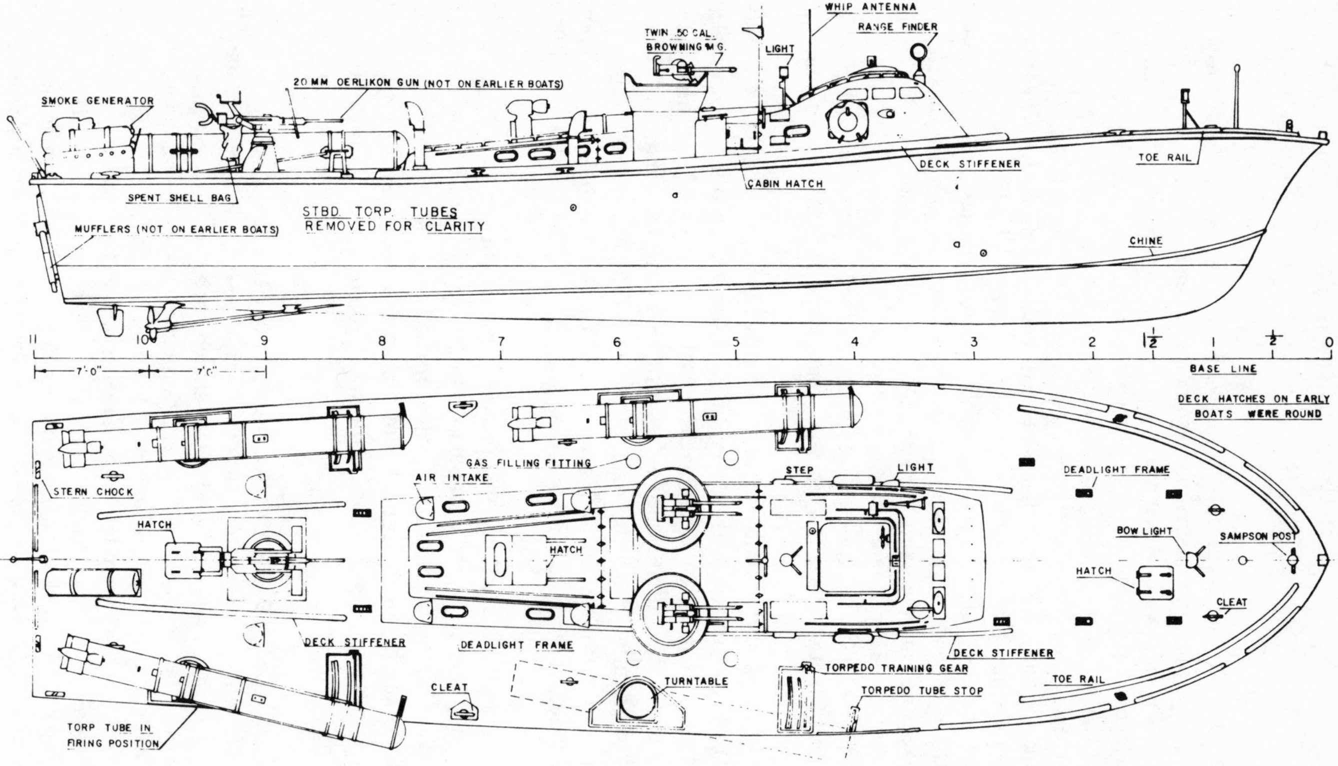

(Drawing by Bob Ferrell, courtesy PT Boats, Inc.)

77-foot Elco PT boat used by John Bulkeley's squadron in Philippines.

Bulkeley was an eagle-eyed inspector, I soon found out, as he checked our boats frequently for condition and conformity during the long trip. I had added some chrome-plated wood screws to hold down the corners of rubber mats at various places on the deck of my boat, and he spotted them. He did not make me remove the unauthorized screws, but made me buy screws for all six boats—a fair punishment for my violation of *conformity*.

John Bulkeley and his men were heading for the Far East with patrol-torpedo boats of a new design. Each was longer (seventy-seven feet) than were the PTCs he had taken to Key West, and, in relation to their size, carried heavier armament than any naval vessel—four torpedoes in tubes, two pairs of .50-caliber machine guns in power turrets, and two .30-caliber automatic weapons on fixed mounts.

Motor Torpedo Boat Squadron 3 reached Manila on September 28, 1941, and its craft were off-loaded and moored at city piers. A few days later, the squadron set up shop at Cavite Navy Yard, ten miles south of the Philippines capital, on the eastern shore of Manila Bay.

CHARLES DI MAIO:
Those of us in Squadron 3 [I was chief torpedoman] knew that John Bulkeley was a leader with great foresight. We had brought along with us nine spare engines and spare parts, but instead of storing these in the warehouse at Cavite, where they might be destroyed by enemy bombing or sabotage, Bulkeley hid them in private garages scattered around Manila. Only he and a few of his officers knew where he had stashed them. Events would bear out his vision.

On November 6, John Bulkeley wrote wife Alice that he had "taken up the filthy habit of smoking cigars," but more significantly he observed casually that "I don't think it will be too long before we get into war for keeps—we have certainly prepared ourselves the best we can." And three weeks later the "squad dog," as the Navy called squadron commanders, wrote: "Boats are OK—but plagued with engine troubles. . . . The situation is tense out here—and no fooling! Our decks are cleared. If Japan wants war, we are ready. It sure seems to me very close. We [the PT-boat crews] are all saving our strength for when it hits." [4]

In the dark early morning hours of December 8, 1941, only the faint snores of sleeping men disturbed the silence inside the officers' quarters at Cavite Navy Yard. Suddenly the telephone jangled impatiently. John Bulkeley flipped on a bedside lamp and glanced at his watch: it was 3:20 A.M.*

Sleepily, Bulkeley picked up the instrument. "We're at war!" a voice straining to remain calm blurted out. "The Japs are bombing Pearl Harbor!" The grim voice added, "The Old Man wants you over here, right away." The Old Man was tall, graying Rear Adm. Francis W. Rockwell, commander of the 16th Naval District and the Cavite Navy Yard.

Bulkeley shook awake one of his officers, Ens. Anthony B. Akers, a lanky, soft-spoken Texan, and told him the news. Akers thought his boss was joking. "This is a hell of a time to be declaring war!" he grunted.

Rapidly throwing on some clothes, Bulkeley drove off to the Commandantia, the thick-walled old Spanish structure that served as Admiral Rockwell's headquarters. The squadron skipper was not surprised by the grim news except for the Japanese target: Pearl Harbor, Hawaii, 5,123 miles and four time zones to the east. He had expected the first Nipponese blow to strike the Philippines.

Dawn was starting to break when Lieutenant Bulkeley walked into the Commandantia, where Rockwell and his chief of staff, Capt. Harold G. Ray, were dressed and waiting for more information to arrive. Gazing into the dark sky, the admiral remarked evenly, "They should be here any time." "They" were Japanese bombers.

Admiral Rockwell was calm and collected, even though he was fully aware that General MacArthur and Adm. Thomas Hart, naval commander in the Far East, did not have the muscle to beat off a full-blooded Japanese invasion of the Philippines.

Rockwell issued Lieutenant Bulkeley his first wartime orders. The skipper was to take his six PT boats westward across Manila Bay to Mariveles Harbor, at the tip of the Bataan Peninsula. If the Nipponese air force were to strike Cavite Navy Yard, Rockwell didn't want the PT boats smashed before they could go into action.

As he rushed to his boat moorings, Bulkeley had no way of knowing that he, a lowly navy lieutenant, had learned that the United States had been bombed into war before General MacArthur had been advised of that fact. Admiral Hart had received a radio signal from Adm. Husband

* The Philippines are on east longitude time. At 8:00 A.M., December 7, 1941, at Pearl Harbor, Hawaii, it was 3:00 A.M. December 8 in Manila.

E. Kimmel in Honolulu within minutes of the first Pearl Harbor bomb explosion. But Hart and most other admirals had been feuding with MacArthur for years, and relations between the two American military leaders in the Philippines had become so strained that Hart did not pass on the shocking news to MacArthur.

At 3:40 A.M., about the time that Bulkeley was leaving the Commandantia, General MacArthur was replacing the telephone on the table next to his bed in his family penthouse in the Manila Hotel. An on-duty corporal had picked up word of the sneak Japanese attack on Pearl Harbor over an English-language radio station, and he told a headquarters officer who quickly telephoned MacArthur.

"Pearl Harbor!" the general muttered in amazement. "That should be our strongest point!" MacArthur dressed, read the Bible for ten minutes (as was his daily custom), and hurried off to his office. There a knot of grim-faced officers had gathered. No one knew what was going on in the Pacific. Rumors abounded.[5]

John Bulkeley and his men required most of the day to load on board and arm torpedoes, haul in machine-gun ammunition, and prepare the boats for battle. He decided to break his command into two sections, three boats in each. Just before 5:00 P.M. three boats led by the squadron executive officer (second in command), lanky New Yorker Lt. Robert B. Kelly, were ready to depart for Mariveles. Bulkeley's orders to Kelly were terse and to the point: "Remain on the alert and attack *anything* I order you to attack!"

CHARLES DI MAIO:
When John Bulkeley came back from Admiral Rockwell's office, he began issuing orders, calmly as though this was just another practice run. He saw to it that we began immediately to put warheads on our torpedoes, at Cavite. It was a good thing, for this was slow and tedious work. It took us from early Monday morning [Sunday, December 7, at Pearl Harbor] to Wednesday morning to put warheads on twenty-four torpedoes and get them ready to be fired.

If Bulkeley hadn't insisted that we rapidly fit out our PT boats, we would have been out of luck—and out of the war—as far as torpedoes went. For when we had put the last armed torpedo on the last boat, all hell broke loose at Cavite.[6]

For two days after Japanese bombers had destroyed major portions of the United States fleet at Pearl Harbor, an ominous stillness settled across the Pacific. In the Manila Bay region, American fighting men waited tensely for the proverbial second shoe to drop. Just before noon on December 10, it fell.

At Cavite, Lieutenant Bulkeley received warning that a force of some 125 Japanese bombers was winging toward Manila Bay. There was no doubt in the skipper's mind where the enemy warplanes were heading—Cavite Navy Yard, the only United States sea base in the Far East, and nearby Nichols Field, the Army Air Corps' major base in the Philippines. Bulkeley led his three PT boats out into Manila Bay, where they would be maneuverable rather than caught at their moorings when bombs began to fall.

Cruising out in the bay, Bulkeley and his men squinted into the bright

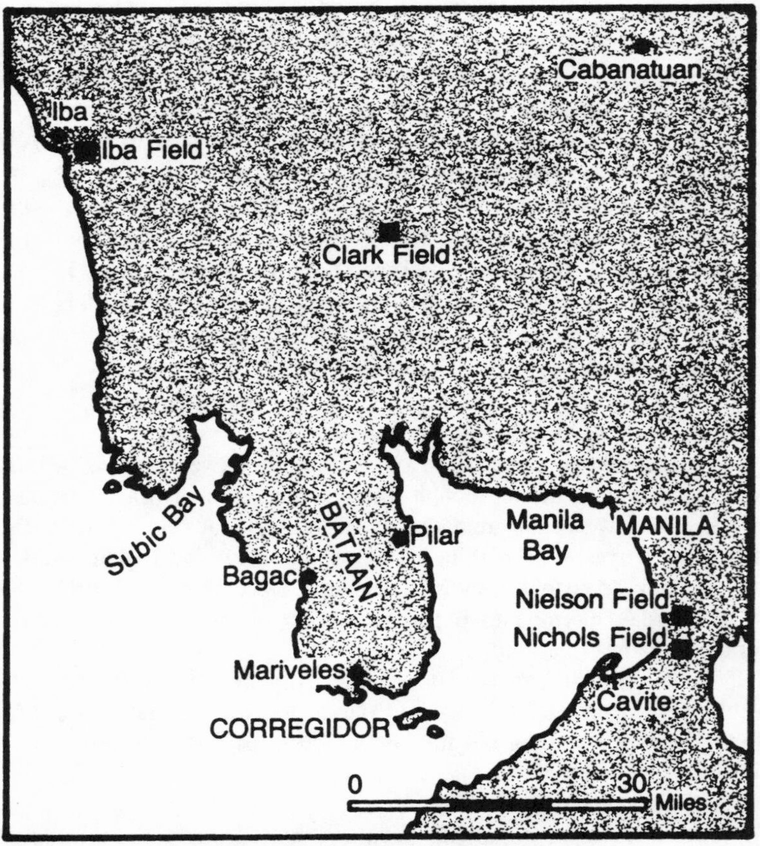

The Manila Bay Region

blue sky at the Japanese bomber stream winging toward them. As though they were passing in review for Emperor Hirohito back over Tokyo, the bombers began circling over Manila Bay, cocksure of themselves, even insolent. Long ago, Nipponese spies in the Philippines had reported that the American antiaircraft guns could reach only 7,000 to 10,000 feet below the bombers, and that the shells were so old that many of them would be duds.

4

Disaster at Manila Bay

High over Nichols Field, the Japanese bomber crews rubbed their eyes in disbelief. Down below, lined up neatly wingtip to wingtip, were scores of United States war planes. The bomber force struck with fury and accuracy. At 12:47 P.M. the first bombs exploded; thirty minutes later Nichols Field was demolished, and the once sleek airplanes were riddled or burning skeletons.

Now the Nipponese bombers turned their attention to Cavite Navy Yard. Cruising in the bay, Lt. John Bulkeley and his three PT-boat crews watched in anger and frustration as the rain of explosives sent great orange balls spiraling skyward and blanketed Cavite with a thick pall of smoke and dust.

Minutes later war became a very personal thing. Five dive-bombers, the ''meat balls'' (rising sun emblems) plainly visible, peeled off and zoomed down on the three PT boats. ''Here come the bastards!'' a voice on Bulkeley's boat shouted. Bulkeley ordered full speed ahead. Like waterbugs scurrying about on a farmer's pond, the PTs dashed around Manila Bay in a pattern of lightning zigzags. When a Zero or Zeke screamed down toward a racing PT boat, the helmsman watched for the bomb to be released, then swerved sharply to one side or the other to avoid the falling explosive. There had been no Annapolis tactics textbook on this survival technique; it was simply common sense, and would become standard PT-boat doctrine for defense against dive-bombers.

Like a swarm of angry bees, the Japanese planes bore in again and again, but each time the little boats darted out from under the bombs. Their explosives expended, the five Zekes and Zeros regrouped in the distance, then roared in again with machine guns blazing. Bulkeley's gunners, under fire for the first time, blasted away, sending a torrent of .50-caliber tracers spewing toward the onrushing planes.

Machinist's Mate Second Class Joseph C. Chalker, a ''good ol' Texas boy'' from Texarkana, fired until his gun barrels were red hot. Jaws clenched tightly, Chalker was *mad,* but as calm as though he had been doing this all his life.[1]

Torpedoman First Class John L. Houlihan, Jr., of Chicopee Falls, Massachusetts, was firing away with the other pair of fifties. He too was cool and angry. Both Chalker and Houlihan concentrated their fire on one Zero, and moments later the men saw the attacker begin to smoke, then wobble, before plunging into Manila Bay about two miles away.[2]

Shouts of triumph rose from the three PTs. The gunners continued to rake the darting Japanese planes, and two were seen to splash into the water. Shooting down three enemy planes hardly avenged Pearl Harbor, Bulkeley and his men agreed. But, one crewman declared, ''It's sure as hell a step in the right direction!''

While John Bulkeley's PT boats had been tangling with the enemy, Cavite Navy Yard had been transformed into a Dantesque inferno. Unopposed, the Japanese bombers had scored direct hits on the powerplant, dispensary, torpedo repair shop, supply building, warehouse (where Bulkeley's spare engines would normally have been stored), signal station, commissary store, barracks, and many ships, tugs, and barges along the waterfront. Cavite had been seriously damaged.

Shortly after 3:00 P.M. the bombers were gone. An eerie hush fell over Manila Bay. Bulkeley took his three boats back into smoking Cavite, and as the squadron skipper and his men picked their way through twisted wreckage, they were sickened by the sight of arms, legs, and other severed parts of bodies. More than 1,000 persons had been killed on the base and in the adjacent town of Cavite.

Bulkeley saw that the quarters where he and the other PT-boat officers lived had been blown into a pile of charred kindling. Far worse, thousands of drums of precious high-octane gasoline, needed desperately by his thirsty boats, had been destroyed.

Amid the shambles, the putrid odor of dead bodies, the clanging of ambulance bells, and the cries of the injured trapped in the twisted wreckage, Bulkeley and his men loaded grievously wounded survivors aboard the PT boats and made repeated runs to the hospital at Cañacao.

Twenty miles to the west across Manila Bay, Lt. Bob Kelly's three PT boats had been cruising off Mariveles. He and his men had seen the Japanese bomber formations fly over on their way to Cavite and Nichols Field. Now the flights were winging home, still in tight patterns—and without a bomber missing. Kelly and his men cursed loudly. Where in the hell was the United States Army Air Corps?

At this point, no American realized the full extent of the disaster. In one fell swoop, the Japanese had bombed, strafed, and wiped out the key American air bases on the main island of Luzon: Nichols Field, Clark Field, Nielson Field, Vigan, Rosales, La Union, and San Fernando. For all practical purposes, United States air power in the Philippines no longer existed.

America had suffered her second Pearl Harbor within seventy-two hours—this one possibly even more catastrophic than the one in Hawaii. The Philippines were wide open to invasion.

John Bulkeley crossed the bay with his three PT boats to Sisiman Bay, a small, secluded cove at the tip of the Bataan Peninsula, where they joined with Bob Kelly's three boats and established an operational base. A shallow dent in the shoreline, Sisiman Bay was hardly a tropical paradise. The men lived in nipa huts—native straw structures on stilts—adjacent to the rickety old fishing dock where the boats made fast. A vacant pig shed was converted with creosote, whitewash, and elbow grease into squadron headquarters. A crudely lettered sign on a plank dubbed the whole complex the "Sisiman Bay Yacht Club."

Hardly had the squadron set up shop than Bob Kelly told Bulkeley that the meager supply of gasoline had been sabotaged. "There's water and rust in it, which could be accidental," Kelly pointed out. "But there's something else in it, too—some kind of waxy substance. When the gasoline sprays out of the carburetor jets, the wax builds up and eventually clogs them."

Bulkeley was furious. First the loss of thousands of fuel drums at Cavite and now this. He and Kelly took a boat out to offshore barges where the gasoline was being kept and guarded by two Filipinos who had been hired for that purpose. The squad dog examined the gasoline, then eyed the pair of Filipinos suspiciously. "Search those men," he snapped.

Four PT crewmen leaped to obey. Trembling from fear, the Filipinos frantically denied any sinister actions. Nothing incriminating was found on the suspects. Then Kelly upended one of the kegs of rice that the two natives had brought aboard for cooking. In the bottom of one keg, concealed under the rice, was a block of paraffin. Each of the other kegs held a similar block.

"Turn these two bastards over to the military police," Bulkeley barked to his sailors. "Recommend that they be shot as spies and saboteurs." Turning to Kelly, Bulkeley said, "I ought to shoot the bastards myself."

From that point onward, the barges with their precious gasoline were guarded by American sailors. But the damage had been done. Squadron 3 would fight constant battles against the wax, for there was no other gasoline available.

Shortly after midnight on December 17, the SS *Corregidor,* an old interisland steamship, was slashing through the black waters of Manila Bay, heading for Cebu, an island of the Philippines to the south. Two hours earlier, some 1,000 men, women, and children, mostly Filipinos, had boarded the *Corregidor* in Manila. They were fleeing from the capital, which would no doubt be the main target of the looming Japanese invasion.

Suddenly, an enormous blast echoed across the black seascape. The *Corregidor* had struck a mine. Lights went out and the old vessel shivered and shook violently. John Bulkeley and his men, who had been asleep in their nipa huts, were awakened by the explosion offshore. They dashed outside and could discern the dim contours of a ship and tiny lights flickering in the water around her. Clearly, a disaster was in the making.

Bulkeley scrambled into a PT boat and, along with two other PTs, raced toward the stricken ship. Hundreds of heads could be seen bobbing in the water. Ladders and lines were pitched out to haul aboard oily survivors. Each time, ten or twelve desperate Filipinos grasped for the line.

Dawn had begun to break over Manila Bay. No more survivors could be found, so Lieutenant Bulkeley ordered his PT boats to head for shore.

Oil-drenched survivors were sitting, lying, crouching, and standing on every inch of the relatively small boats. Not until those rescued had been put ashore could they be counted. Each PT boat had been built to hold two officers and about ten crewmen, but two hundred ninety-six passengers had been plucked from the jaws of death. Among those saved were E. P. J. "Jack" Fee, manager of the Cebu office of Standard-Vacuum Oil Company, and his wife, Dode, who was three months pregnant.[3]

5

A Charge into Subic Bay

At eight o'clock the next morning, January 11, 1942, a flight of white-bodied, twin-engine Mitsubishi bombers was winging through the blue sky toward Fortress Corregidor. With their approach, Jean MacArthur swept up little Arthur and ran to a nearby shelter, an antiquated structure whose iron door stubbornly refused to close.

When the MacArthurs had slipped out of burning Manila on Christmas Eve, the general had moved his family into a cottage on the flat-crowned, 550-foot Topside, instead of into the relative safety of Malinta Tunnel. MacArthur had shrugged off warnings by anxious aides that the exposed cottage would be an inviting target for Nipponese bombers. Jean MacArthur had been apprehensive, especially for Arthur, but she said nothing.[1]

Whistling eerily, clusters of bombs descended on Topside. Near hits shook the shelter where Jean MacArthur and her son were huddled. The long concrete barracks facing Topside's parade ground were shattered, roofs blown off. Huge holes were gouged out of the rock surface, and the thick ties and sturdy rails of the streetcar line were twisted into pretzellike shapes. The din was earsplitting, and the rain of explosives caused the entire island to shudder. Then came the screeching dive-bombers and the seemingly ceaseless chatter of blazing machine guns, the pom-pom-pom of American antiaircraft guns trying futilely to ward off the swarms of Japanese warplanes.

Three miles away, at Sisiman Bay, Lt. John Bulkeley and his PT boaters helplessly watched the frightful pounding of Corregidor, which was now blanketed with a pall of dirty gray smoke and dust. They were angry and anguished. It seemed unlikely that most of those not in Malinta or other tunnels, including the MacArthurs, could survive.

Jean MacArthur and little Arthur shared their flimsy sanctuary with a soldier who had happened by, and each time there was a brief lull between bomber flights, she asked him to dash out and find out what her husband, the man she would forever call My General, was doing. Each time the soldier had the same report. MacArthur was standing by a hedge with his customary, curved-handle walnut walking cane under his arm, puffing on a cigarette in a long, black holder, and counting the Japanese bombers as they came over. There were seventy-two of them to the present, the soldier told Jean on returning from one jaunt.[2]

A 500-pounder exploded in the bedroom of the MacArthurs' cottage, ripping off the roof and shattering the structure. Then a second bomb hit very close to where the general was standing out in the open. Shrapnel hissed over MacArthur's head. His orderly, Sgt. Domingo Adversario, removed his own steel helmet and held it over the general, and fragments from another exploding string of bombs dented the pie plate–shaped steel headgear and ripped open Adversario's hand.

The raid lasted for three hours and fifty-seven minutes. When Jean MacArthur emerged from the shelter, she found her husband glancing at their demolished cottage. "Jeannie, look what they've done to our garden," the general said evenly.[3]

MacArthur refused to be driven underground. Every building on Topside had been demolished or extensively damaged, so the MacArthur family settled into a cottage on Bottomside, the sea-level portion of Corregidor, about 500 yards from the entrance to Malinta Tunnel. Cots were set up in the tunnel for Jean, Arthur, and the boy's Chinese nanny, Ah Cheu, to spend the nights, safer from bombing.

But Jean refused to leave her husband, who insisted on sleeping in the cottage, no doubt as a gesture of defiance. When the air-raid sirens would wail at night, Jean would sweep up Arthur and, along with Ah Cheu, would be driven by a waiting soldier (who slept next to his vehicle in a foxhole) to Malinta Tunnel. There Arthur and Ah Cheu would be left, and Jean would return to the general's side in the cottage.[4]

Early on the morning of January 18, Lt. John Bulkeley reported to Admiral Rockwell's headquarters on Corregidor and was handed a tersely written order by Capt. Harold Ray, Rockwell's chief of staff: "Army reports four enemy ships in or laying off Port Binanga. Force may include one destroyer, one large transport. Send two PT boats, attack between dusk and dawn."

Bulkeley knew that his boats would be poking their noses into a hornets' nest. Port Binanga was located at the top of Subic Bay, and both the port and the bay were infested with Japanese.

It was midnight when PT 31, skippered by Lt. Ed DeLong of Santa Cruz, California, and PT 34, led by Ens. Barron Chandler, reached the mouth of Subic Bay. Chandler was pinch-hitting for Lt. Bob Kelly, who was in the Corregidor hospital with a serious infection. Bulkeley rode with the 34 boat.

A black and eerie stillness blanketed the bay. According to plan, the boats split: Bulkeley and Chandler would prowl up the western shore of Subic Bay, and DeLong would sweep up the eastern side. The two boats would rendezvous outside Port Binanga, but if they failed to link up, each PT was to attack Japanese shipping on its own.

All hands were tense on Bulkeley's and Chandler's boat. Despite the cooling sea breezes, the men began to perspire. No American vessel had ventured into Subic Bay since the enemy had taken control there. Suddenly, the blackness was split by a powerful beam of a searchlight on shore. The PT boat was caught in its unyielding grip. Men froze in place, faces ghostlike in the glare.

Bulkeley turned a hard-right rudder and the 34 sped out into the bay. Now the dreaded boom! boom! boom! was heard. Shore batteries had opened fire. Their aim was errant, and the shells splashed into the dark waters far from the boat. Minutes later a blinking light out in the bay challenged the 34 boat. It made no reply. Then all hell broke loose. Along the shoreline, other searchlights flashed on and big guns began firing.

The men on the 34 boat ducked instinctively as they heard the whistle of incoming shells, but the zigzagging boat sped onward. Bulkeley reached the rendezvous point outside Port Binanga at 1:00 A.M., but when DeLong's boat failed to arrive, the squadron skipper decided to take the 34 boat into Binanga harbor alone and search for targets. Speed was cut to eight knots, and only two engines were running.*

Bulkeley and others on board suddenly tensed. There she was! Less than 500 yards away—the silhouette of a large Japanese ship. While crewmen prepared to fire torpedoes, Bulkeley crept closer to the target. And closer. Then, wham! Like a powerful blow to the face, a searchlight on the enemy vessel erupted in blinding brilliance, bathing the PT boat

* A knot, or nautical mile, is the equivalent of 1.1516 statute (or land) miles per hour.

in its glare. A shout rang out on the 34: ''Fire!'' and two torpedoes were released.

At the wheel, John Bulkeley gave a hard right, and the boat roared off into the night. Glancing behind them, the men on the PT saw an explosion at the targeted ship's waterline, and a fireball shot into the night sky. But there was no time for elation over the first major ''kill'' of the war by a PT boat. Number 34 was in big trouble.

''Port torpedo didn't fire, sir,'' a voice called out in the blackness. ''She's making a hot run.''

It was a chilling situation. The ''fish'' had malfunctioned and failed to clear its tube. It stuck there, half in and half out, propellers whirling madly, compressed air hissing with an earsplitting din. All knew that the torpedo was designed not to fire until its propellers had made a specified number of revolutions. After that, the torpedo was cocked, much like a rifle, and a blow on its nose, such as a slap by a wave, could cause the fish to explode, blasting boat and crew to smithereens. The propeller had to be halted.

Torpedoman First Class John Martino of Waterbury, Connecticut, dashed below to the head, grabbed a handful of toilet tissue, then jumped astride the hissing, quivering torpedo as though it were a bronco. The boat had to be halted for this delicate, life-or-death operation. Frantically, Martino stuffed the tissue into the vanes of the propeller, and with a groan of protest, the blades stopped spinning. Deep sighs of relief came from all hands.

Throttles were thrown forward, and PT 34 roared off toward the mouth of Subic Bay. A bevy of machine guns and a few artillery pieces on shore bid a noisy farewell, but none of the bullets or shells struck the racing boat. Bulkeley waited outside the Corregidor mine field, where he was to rendezvous with Ed DeLong's PT 34. Dawn arrived; DeLong did not.

After the PTs had parted at the mouth of Subic Bay, DeLong's boat had developed engine trouble—from the paraffin put in the gasoline by the pair of Filipino saboteurs. Working by muted lights, the crew got the engine running once more. Then the cooling system conked out. As the frantic crew was making repairs, the boat drifted aimlessly. Then there was a crunching sound; PT 31 had run aground on a reef.

For three hours, DeLong and his men labored feverishly, racing the engines in a desperate effort to back off the reef. Finally the reverse gears burned out. Now a gun far down the shore opened fire, and shells began exploding closer and closer. Lieutenant DeLong gave the order—abandon ship.

Speedily but without panic, the crew wrapped mattresses in a tarpaulin to make a raft, then scrambled onto it. DeLong stayed behind to rip up the gas tanks and blow a hole in the boat's bottom with a hand grenade before setting the marooned craft afire.

Forty-eight hours later, after a harrowing series of hide-and-seek adventures with Nipponese soldiers, Lieutenant DeLong and nine of his men turned up at Sisiman Bay. Ensign William H. Plant, of Long Beach, California, the second officer, had stayed on the raft with two men who could not swim, while DeLong and the remaining nine sailors had eventually made their way to shore where they hid in a thicket until found by American soldiers. Plant, MM1c Rudolph Bullough, and QM3c William R. Dean would never return.[5]

The loss of DeLong's boat meant that Squadron 3 had been whittled down to two-thirds of its strength. On Christmas Eve, another PT had run aground on a reef in the darkness and had to be destroyed.

Eleven thousand miles from the fireworks in Subic Bay, New York was a city gripped by an aura of foreboding, a sense of impending catastrophe for America. Since Pearl Harbor seven weeks earlier, newspaper headlines had been dripping with gloom, disclosing one Allied military debacle after the other.

On the bitterly cold night of January 20, 1942, Alice Bulkeley kissed her sixteen-month-old daughter, Joan, goodnight in the four-room apartment she shared with her mother-in-law, Elizabeth, at 45–42 41st Street, Long Island City, across the East River from Manhattan. Alice switched off the light in the bedroom and glanced at her watch: it was 6:59 P.M.

There was a heavy, urgent pounding on the apartment's front door, and when Alice opened it a swarm of reporters and photographers pushed into the living room. Flashbulbs started popping. Questions were shouted. Alice, taken off guard by the unexpected invasion, began to detect something about a heroic exploit by her husband. In the din, she heard the name Colin Kelly. Fear gripped her heart. Colin Kelly, most Americans knew, had been killed shortly after Pearl Harbor while bombing a Japanese warship.

Slowly the uproar subsided to a degree and Alice learned that the Navy had just released information about the mad charge into Japanese-held Subic Bay and the torpedoing of a 5,000-ton ship by Lieutenant Bulkeley's PT boat. Regaining her composure, Alice began fielding the barrage of questions being hurled at her. No, she was not surprised. "It's just like John to do something like that," she said. Yes, she had been fearful that her husband was dead or a prisoner of the Japanese.[6]

The blonde and petite Alice explained that she had heard nothing from Lieutenant Bulkeley since receiving a letter from him on December 7—the day Pearl Harbor was bombed. At the insistence of the newsmen, she read aloud parts of that letter. Bulkeley said that he was having trouble with infected teeth, and that he didn't want the couple's infant daughter to undergo a similar painful experience when she grew older. "Joan must have lots of milk and calcium in her diet—no candy," wrote the doting father.

Bulkeley asked about Bunky, his small white dog, and Jasper, the family's orange-and-white cat. "Get an extra fifteen cents' worth of liver for Jasper as a Christmas present," he wrote.

The letter closed: "Take care of yourself and Oscar. Loads of love and Merry Christmas."

"Oscar," Mrs. Bulkeley explained, was her husband's pet name for the child the couple expected to arrive in April.

Early the next morning, January 21, Frederick Chauncey Bulkeley, John's half-brother, was following his customary routine, driving from his home in New Baltimore the ten miles to his job in the capitol at Albany, New York. He was the assistant state architect. As had been his habit, he switched on the car radio to pick up the newscasts.

"Good news from the Pacific . . ." the announcer began. Suddenly Frederick felt a surge of exultation. Over the air came the electrifying words: "Lieutenant John D. Bulkeley . . . PT boat . . . heroics . . . Subic Bay . . . torpedoed Japanese ship."

Frederick was choked with emotion. John was alive—and a national hero. By the time he reached the New York capitol, word of the Subic Bay exploit had already flooded the building. The governor, officials at every level, secretaries, and janitors swarmed all over Frederick, pounding him on the back and shouting congratulations. Tears of pride and joy filled the older Bulkeley's eyes.

That day newspapers from coast to coast splashed the Subic Bay action across front pages. Blaring headlines told the story:

U.S. HAMMERS JAP VESSELS

Mosquito Raider Torpedoes Ship; Planes Sink Cruiser

Story on Page 3

DAILY NEWS NEW YORK'S PICTURE NEWSPAPER

BROOKLYN QUEENS LONG ISLAND — FINAL

Vol. 23. No. 180 New York, Wednesday, January 21, 1942 60 Main + 16 Brooklyn Pages 2 Cents

← He Made Them ↑ Proud of Him

The man at the left is Lieut. John D. Bulkeley who commanded a Navy torpedo boat which darted into Jap-controlled Subic Bay in the Philippines and torpedoed a 5,000-ton Nipponese ship. All good Americans are proud of Bulkeley but proudest of all are his wife and their daughter Joan [↑], admiring the hero's foto yesterday in their Long Island City home. —Story on page 4

New York Daily News

HERO DASHES INTO JAPS' MIDST IN SPEEDBOAT
New York World-Telegram
NAVY HERO IN DARING BLOW AT JAPS
San Antonio Light
MOSQUITO RAIDER TORPEDOES JAP SHIP
New York Daily News

Illustrating the newspaper reports were three- and four-column photographs of John Bulkeley, clean-shaven and immaculate in his navy dress uniform, and those of Alice, little Joan, and Mrs. Elizabeth Bulkeley.

> ALICE BULKELEY:
> It was not until the morning after the reporters left our apartment, when I saw some of the New York papers, that I fully realized the extent of the nation's reaction to what John and his men had done in the Philippines. Shortly after dawn the telephone started ringing, and it didn't cease all day. Reporters called from all over the country, and calls of congratulations poured in.
>
> Had John been there he would have shaken his head and said, "What's all this flap about? I was merely doing my duty."

Suddenly emerging as the wife of an acclaimed hero, Alice Bulkeley found that her life had been turned topsy-turvy. She was bombarded with requests for public appearances, but accepted only the ones that she felt might contribute, in a small way, to the war effort.

She was in constant demand for media interviews. Her hectic schedule forced her to give up most personal activities, although she found time to continue her regular rounds as a neighborhood civil defense air raid warden in Sector D, Post 9. Alice wrote to Dean R. C. Samuel at a local college where she had been taking courses:

> It is not often in one's lifetime that one suddenly finds one's self the wife of a national hero. This is my predicament, and the obligations involved are so enormous to one not accustomed to them . . . that I will be unable to continue my studies as before. . . . Although I try to keep my mind on various interesting subjects, the constant fear of my husband's safety cannot help but penetrate my mind.[7]

Back in the Philippines on the night of January 22/23, Lt. Bob Kelly's PT 34 poked its nose into the Subic Bay hotbed. Kelly had been in the

Corregidor hospital for two weeks; his infection had been so serious that he had lost thirty-five pounds from his elongated frame, and surgeons came within a whisker of amputating his arm. But the Annapolis graduate had badgered his doctor so relentlessly to be released to active duty that he finally won out. Typically, John Bulkeley was along on this patrol "just for the hell of it."

The purpose of these patrols was to look for trouble, and that goal was not long in being reached. Lookouts spotted the dim outline of a vessel, and all hands rushed to general quarters (battle stations). Bulkeley warned the men to hold their fire, that Ens. Bill Plant and the other two PT boaters missing in DeLong's misadventure a few nights earlier could have stolen this Japanese craft and be on board.

As Kelly's gunners crouched tensely with itchy fingers on triggers, the 34 boat edged to within seventy-five feet of the other vessel. Bulkeley raised a megaphone and called out: "Boat, ahoy!" In reply, machine guns erupted on the enemy vessel and bullets hissed past Bulkeley's head.

A full-scale shootout raised an enormous din. As the tracers lit up the black seascape, the Americans could see that their foe was a motorized barge, about fifty feet long, crammed with helmeted soldiers. With Ensign Chandler, a South Carolinian and son of a navy officer, at the wheel in the cockpit, PT 34 began circling the barge. The fifties and the two thirties were chattering raucously, and other PT crewmen were raking the barge with rifle and tommy gun fire.

COMDR. BARRON CHANDLER:
There was a hell of a racket going on and bullets were flying everywhere. John Bulkeley was a short distance from me when a burst of Jap machine gun fire seemed to just zip past our heads. I yelled to Bulkeley, "Boy, that was close!" Then I fell to the deck, but really didn't feel anything at the time. However, one of the Jap bullets that I thought had come "real close" had gone through both of my ankles.

Bulkeley and [Bob] Kelly dragged me below. I was bleeding like a butchered hog. Reynolds, the cook, was also acting as the boat's pharmacist [medic] and he tried to do the best he could. He poured almost an entire bottle of iodine on my wounds, and I almost went through the overhead. Bulkeley put tourniquets on both of my legs.

Soon I was hurting like hell, but was aware that our boat was still circling the Jap barge, and that lead was flying around. Throughout the fighting, John Bulkeley would often dash below, call out, "How're you doing, Barron?'' and then bolt back up to the firing deck. I wasn't doing so well, but I didn't tell him that.

The shoot-out ended when the Japanese barge gave one final gurgle of protest and went under, spilling its soldier passengers and crew into the black waters. It was now nearly dawn, so Bulkeley set a course for home. Minutes later, in the growing light, the men on the 34 spotted a flat, low-slung vessel. Bulkeley was eager to go after it, but knew that all hands had had a rough night, and that Barron Chandler was below suffering intensely.

The squadron skipper put the question to his men. ''Let's go get the bastard!'' they chorused, with Chandler joining in.

Racing toward the enemy vessel, the PT boat opened fire with its fifties at 300 yards. But the target was heavily plated, and the bullets ricocheted off her. Now all hands were blazing away. The Japanese vessel kept moving, even as the PT closed to within fifty feet and continued to riddle it with bullets. Then an American bullet hit the vessel's fuel tank, and fire mushroomed upward. Engines halted, and the enemy craft drifted aimlessly.

''Pull up alongside her,'' Lieutenant Bulkeley called out. ''I'm going aboard!''

Bulkeley pitched a few grenades into the vessel, then, clutching a tommy gun in one hand, leapt onto the drifting craft. A number of dead Japanese were sprawled grotesquely on the slimy deck. Three on board were still alive, but wounded. One was a captain. When Bulkeley approached with his tommy gun leveled, the captain fell to his knees and pleaded: ''Me surrender! Me surrender! Don't kill!''

The three surviving Japanese were put aboard the PT boat. Hastily, for the vessel was sinking, Bulkeley began rummaging around in the sludge, filling both arms with papers, briefcases, and documents, all of which might prove of value to intelligence officers. He scrambled aboard the PT boat just as the Nipponese craft went under.

As Lieutenant Kelly began racing back to Sisiman Bay, a sailor with a .45 Colt stood guard over the Japanese captain, who was kneeling with eyes closed, waiting for a bullet through the head. Instead, John Bulkeley, who minutes earlier had been blasting away at him, began gently wiping the oil from the captain's eyes and examining his head wound. Seeing that he was not going to be summarily executed, the Japanese officer became surly.

CAPT. ROBERT B. KELLY, USN (RET.):
One of our prisoners was a dying private of about eighteen and no more than five feet tall. The boy asked feebly for a cigarette, and one of our boys lit one and bent down to hold it in the Nip's mouth while he took a few puffs.

"What a crazy world!" I remarked to John Bulkeley. "A few minutes ago we had been pumping lead, hating every Jap in the world. Now we aren't mad anymore. Now we're sorry for these two Japs—the half-pint guy, even the arrogant bastard captain!"

Bulkeley, Kelly, and the crew watched impassively as the little Japanese private lay on deck. He had five bullet holes in him, but never moaned or even grimaced. The boy would be dead in a few hours. Reaching the dock at Bataan, crewmen carried Ensign Chandler and the wounded Japanese off the boat.

In the crucible of Bataan, MacArthur's emaciated, ragtag army of native troops and civilians and American soldiers, sailors, and marines choked with rage over the means given them to fight. Obsolete rifles refused to fire, old equipment wouldn't function, ammunition was short and aged belts of machine-gun bullets fell apart while being loaded, four out of five grenades failed to explode, and two-thirds of the mortar shells fired were duds.

Now aware that their country had turned her back on them, realizing that they were doomed, MacArthur's foot soldiers painted Vs on their helmets—not the Allied victory sign but for victims—called themselves the Battered Bastards of Bataan, and fought on tenaciously. John Bulkeley and his men fought on with equal determination, for their four decrepit PT boats were now the United States Navy's first line of defense in the Philippines.

6

“General, It’ll Be a Piece of Cake!”

As was his daily custom, on January 24, 1942, Lt. John Bulkeley took a PT boat from the Sisiman Bay Yacht Club on Bataan to Corregidor, heading for Adm. Francis Rockwell’s cubbyhole in Malinta Tunnel to get his orders for the night. Rockwell’s handful of wheezing tugs, antiquated minesweepers, and the four PT boats were still grandiosely designated the Philippines Fleet. Moments after Bulkeley’s PT boat made fast at a rickety pier, a flight of Japanese bombers drew near.

> CHARLES DI MAIO:
> The Jap bombs started whistling down, and those of us in John Bulkeley’s boat looked up and could see them falling. Bulkeley had already gotten off the boat, and was strolling calmly up and down with a cigar in his mouth. He called out to us not to leave the boat, rightly thinking that there was no place for us to take cover. Now the bombs were exploding all around us, but Bulkeley kept pacing leisurely up and down, puffing on his cigar.

That night Lieutenant Bulkeley was on board Ens. George Cox’s PT 41 and steering once more toward Subic Bay. Cox, of Watertown, New York, had volunteered as an ambulance driver for the French army in 1940 and had been awarded the croix de guerre medal for gallantry.

Just before 1:00 A.M. the 41 boat cruised slowly through the entrance of Subic Bay. Engines were muffled. The night was black. Suddenly, off Sampaloc Point, crewmen spotted the shadowy contours of what appeared to be an anchored Japanese transport of perhaps 4,000 to 6,000 tons. All hands leaped to battle station, and PT 41 began creeping toward the target. At 2,500 yards, throttles were thrown forward, and the boat raced toward the transport—and in the direction of a trap that the wily Japanese had designed to snare marauding PT boats as a spiderweb would a fly.

In the nick of time, crewmen glimpsed wires and entanglements floating in the water, and the speeding boat swerved to avoid them. The obstacles had been placed by the Japanese to foul propellers and leave the pesky PT boats dead in the water, helpless targets for shore guns. Bulkeley's boats had become a pain in the neck to the Nipponese.

With George Cox at the wheel, PT 41 closed to within 800 yards and fired one fish. Moments later gunners on the targeted ship opened fire, and shells exploded around the 41 boat. Undaunted, Cox raced his boat alongside the transport as the four fifties raked the enemy ship. The Japanese responded with heavy machine-gun fire. Moments later, the transport was rocked by a blast, lighting up the night: Cox's torpedo had struck home. Geyserlike, bits and pieces of the ship spurted into the sky and fell back all around the speeding 41 boat.

Cox began racing for the mouth of Subic Bay, while shells from shore batteries splashed into the water around the boat; he reached the sea.

John Bulkeley's defiant forays into Japanese-controlled waters, together with his unkempt appearance, had earned him wide renown in the Philippines. He and other squadron officers had lost their shaving gear, clothing, and most personal belongings when Japanese bombers had destroyed Cavite Navy Yard on December 10.

CAPT. MALCOLM M. CHAMPLIN, USNR (RET.):
As aide to Admiral Rockwell, I saw John Bulkeley many times, almost daily. Bulkeley was a wild man. Daring, courageous, and admirable in many ways, but still a wild man. He reminded one, on first glance, of a swashbuckling pirate in modern dress. He wore a long, unruly beard and carried two ominous looking pistols at his side. His eyes were bloodshot and red-rimmed from constant night patrols and lack of sleep, but his nervous energy was tremendous and never seemed to give out. He walked with a cocksure gait, and one could always count on him to raise particular hell with any Jap he met. High-strung, temperamental, brave, and gallant,

John Bulkeley was one of the most colorful figures in the Philippine campaign.

By early February, two months after Pearl Harbor, both the Battered Bastards of Bataan and the men of Motor Torpedo Boat Squadron 3 were fighting not one, but three tenacious enemies: the tough Japanese; a severe shortage of supplies, munitions, and gasoline; and the pangs of extreme hunger. Foot soldiers had a cup or two of boiled rice daily. Bulkeley's men considered themselves fortunate—they had discovered a cache of canned salmon, and for weeks had been eating this seafood morning, noon, and night.

Hungry as they were, the PT boaters eventually grew nauseated over even the thought of salmon. So one sailor took a .45 Colt and plugged a tomcat that had been roaming the premises. Boiled thoroughly, the tomcat was eaten that night. Bulkeley was upbeat—said he thought the cat tasted like duck. The others didn't agree. To them, it tasted like boiled tomcat.

On the night of February 17, a pair of PT boats led by Bulkeley and Bob Kelly again slipped into Subic Bay, riddled shore installations with streams of tracers while racing at high speed, and fired their fish at a large Japanese ship tied up at a pier at Olongapo. Then they hauled out for home.

The next day, Lt. Col. Sidney L. Huff, an aide to General MacArthur, called on Bulkeley at the Sisiman Bay Yacht Club. "Do you think that your boats could take a party on a sea run of a few hundred miles, say, down to Puerto Princess, on Palawan?" Huff asked casually.

Bulkeley hesitated for only a moment. "No question about it," he replied breezily, aware that his four battered boats were deteriorating rapidly. "You have something specific in mind?"

"Maybe," Colonel Huff responded evasively. "I'll be able to tell you more about it later in the month." He added, "If you were to do this job, would you require any special materials?"

Countless "needs" flooded Bulkeley's mind: gaskets, ammunition, food, torpedoes, unadulterated gasoline, spare parts. But he knew that none of these was available. "No, nothing special," the skipper replied.[1]

On February 28, word came to the yacht club that General MacArthur himself wanted to inspect the squadron the following day. So in the morning the battle-scarred PTs, slicked up for the Big Chief's eyes, rumbled across the two miles of Manila Bay to The Rock and tied up at the North Dock. MacArthur and a covey of officers embarked, and for a half hour the general stood on the bridge of the 41, watching Bulkeley put the squadron through its paces on Manila Bay.

Back at the North Dock, MacArthur announced that John Bulkeley was being awarded the Distinguished Service Cross for his actions in the Philippines. Then he invited the squadron leader to supper on Topside, where the general still maintained a small headquarters installation in one of the bomb-damaged buildings.

ADMIRAL BULKELEY:
As soon as General MacArthur and I reached Topside, I became aware that this was more than just a social occasion. MacArthur led me into a bomb-pocked open field, away from prying ears, and while we strolled around side by side, he revealed that President Roosevelt had given him a direct order to leave Corregidor and go to Australia to take command of an army for eventual return to the Philippines. He indicated that he hoped to lead the army back in time to rescue his force on Bataan.

Although alert, the general looked gaunt. He'd lost thirty pounds in two months on skimpy meals of fish, rice, and mule. He ate what his soldiers ate.

All of this he was telling me was top-secret stuff—I wasn't to say a damned word about it to anyone until it was nearly time to shove off.

General MacArthur said he wanted my PT boats to break through the Nip sea and air blockade around Corregidor and carry him and his party some 580 miles south to the Philippine island of Mindanao. There he would hook up with airplanes flown up from Australia for the final leg of the trip.

''But, General MacArthur, sir,'' I said, ''wouldn't it be safer for you to get to Mindanao by submarine or by air?'' But he smiled and said no, that the Nips would expect him to leave like that and would make every effort to intercept him. ''They won't be expecting me to make the breakout by PT boat,'' he added. ''Besides, I've got great faith in you and your boys!'' The general paused briefly, then asked, ''Well, Johnny, do you think you can pull it off?''

Having been young, cocky, and brash, I replied, ''General, it'll be a piece of cake!''

If I were asked today [1987], as a mature individual, if the breakout from Corregidor could have been done, I would have to say, ''No way!'' Those nearly 600 miles of largely uncharted waters, with unseen, jagged coral reefs waiting to rip apart our thin-skinned wooden boats, much of our route covered at night, alone should have warned of impending danger.

And the Japs knew that MacArthur would make an effort to get off The Rock to avoid capture. Seizing him would have been a devastating propaganda victory for the Nips. "Tokyo Rose" had been gleefully bleating for days that General MacArthur would be captured and publicly hanged as a "war criminal" on the Imperial Plaza in Tokyo, in front of Emperor Hirohito's royal palace.[2]

Despite the direct order from President Roosevelt, MacArthur could not bring himself to leave. He was skewered on the horns of a dilemma. If he obeyed, his men on Corregidor and Bataan would accuse him of deserting them. If he refused to leave, he could be court-martialed and charged with gross disobedience.

At a staff conference, MacArthur said he was going to resign from the army—and had in hand his written resignation—then cross over to Bataan and fight to the end as a "volunteer" private. His staff pleaded with him to go to Australia, pointing out that his taking charge of an army there would be the best hope for salvaging the Philippines catastrophe.[3]

A few days later, Roosevelt prodded the reluctant general: "Situation in Australia indicates desirability of your early arrival."

Three more days passed before MacArthur made up his mind to go. On March 9 the general sent for the man he called "that bold buckaroo with the cold green eyes." Until now, no one had even hinted to John Bulkeley about a departure date. Now, in vintage MacArthurese, the general said, "Buck, we sail on the Ides of March"—the fifteenth.[4]

Four motor torpedo boats, all barely gasping after numerous transfusions of cannibalized parts, were to break through the Japanese blockade and carry General MacArthur and a party of twenty from Corregidor to the port of Cagayan on Mindanao, a distance equivalent to that from Chicago, Illinois, to Buffalo, New York.

On returning to the yacht club at Sisiman Bay, Bulkeley sent for his skippers: Bob Kelly, Tony Akers, George Cox, and Vincent Schumacher. The squadron leader outlined the evacuation plan. He stressed that the four boats should keep together, but if one broke down, the others were to continue and let the stalled craft manage for itself.

CAPT. ROBERT KELLY:
John Bulkeley told us that General MacArthur would be riding in his PT 41. We were to avoid the Japs if possible, but if swift enemy vessels

were to spot us and give chase and were overtaking us, I was to lead three boats in an attack on the pursuers. Bulkeley's boat, with General MacArthur on it, would race off and try to get away.

Bulkeley was very uncomfortable when he told us about this. Seeming to be fleeing while his men fought was not to his liking. But we all knew that the objective of the mission was to get General MacArthur to Australia, from where he could lead America back to the Philippines.

General MacArthur's impending departure was something of an open secret, not only on The Rock and Bataan, but also in Tokyo and in Washington, 11,000 miles away. Reporters at President Roosevelt's press conferences were asking: "When is MacArthur going to leave Corregidor? Where is he going?" Roosevelt lied skillfully.

ADM. JOHN BULKELEY:
Almost overnight, I, a lowly navy officer, had become quite popular with some of MacArthur's generals on Bataan, and received lunch and dinner invitations from several of them. I accepted a few of these, for while their rations were meager, the generals had better chow than salmon and tomcat.

Each of my general hosts made virtually the same little speech. Knowing that my four PT boats had some reserve fuel, they hinted that when "doom's day" arrived, that is, when the Japs were about to overrun Bataan, I should pick them up and carry them to the China coast to "fight another day," as they put it. Of course, none of them knew at this time of the planned evacuation of MacArthur. And of course neither General MacArthur nor the other generals knew of their plotting to save their own skins.

On the morning of March 11—four days prior to the Ides of March—MacArthur sent for Lieutenant Bulkeley, leader of what the general now affectionately called "my pirates," due to their unavoidably bedraggled appearances and slashing attacks against the Japanese. "Johnny," MacArthur said evenly, "there has been a change of plans. We're not leaving on the Ides of March—have your boats ready for us to board at nineteen thirty [7:30 P.M.] today."

"Yes, sir," the pirate chief replied crisply. Bulkeley understood why MacArthur had lied to him about the true departure date—security.

Bulkeley had warned the general that he could provide no food for the trek to Mindanao, so for the past few days Jean MacArthur and

Sid Huff had been stealthily collecting what they could, mainly tinned salmon. The foodstuffs were packed into four duffel bags, one for each PT boat.

As the hour to leave approached, ominous danger signals surfaced. There was a sharp increase in Japanese aircraft activities, and surface patrols were reported off Corregidor. A Nipponese destroyer flotilla steaming north at high speed was spotted by coast-watchers in the southern Philippines.[5]

At 6:00 P.M. another chilling report reached Corregidor. Last-minute reconnaissance by one of the four obsolete, patched-up P-40 fighter planes left in the Philippines disclosed that a Japanese destroyer had been sighted in Apo East Pass, just west of Mindoro, and a cruiser southwest of Mindoro, 125 to 175 miles south of Corregidor and directly across the planned course to Mindanao.[6]

That evening, as the sinking sun purpled the sea to the west beyond the mouth of Manila Bay, a messenger brought word to General MacArthur's house that John Bulkeley's boat had departed from Sisiman Bay. MacArthur walked onto the porch, where his wife and young son Arthur were waiting. "It's time to mount up, Jeannie," the general said calmly. The three MacArthurs, along with Ah Cheu, headed for the North Dock.[7]

It was 7:21 P.M. when Lieutenant Bulkeley's 41 boat slipped up to the pier. Over him, looming like a huge bulbous head, was towering, bomb-pocked Topside. As the three 2,750-horsepower Packards idled, the MacArthurs arrived. Jean carried aboard a small case containing a dress and a pantsuit; Ah Cheu's belongings were in a folded handkerchief; and little Arthur clung to Old Friend, a stuffed toy. The general did not have an ounce of personal luggage, not even a razor (he had slipped a toothbrush in his pocket).[8]

MacArthur would be the last to board. Solemnly he shook hands with each of the several generals and colonels who had come to see him off, men who knew that they were being left behind to buy precious time, to die, if need be. Each of them was field-promoted one rank. In a voice choked with emotion, MacArthur bid them good luck. They would need it.

ADMIRAL BULKELEY:

It would have taken an axe to cut the thick emotional atmosphere on the dock. I could sense the fear and abandonment felt by the generals, although most would do their duty and fight to the end. A few of the generals who had tried to con me into saving their hides kept looking at me standing in the 41 boat. They had an added fear, that I had told General MacArthur. I had not.

Before boarding, General MacArthur stood for long moments on the shell-torn pier—a lonely figure, a tragic symbol of America's failure to be militarily prepared. In the gloaming, MacArthur heard a voice ask, "What's his chances of getting through, Sarge?" And the gruff reply: "Dunno. If lucky, maybe one in five!" [9]

It was now nearly dark. Japanese artillery had ceased firing. An eerie hush had fallen over Corregidor, but the putrid smell of filth thickened the night air. MacArthur peered up at Topside and lifted in a final salute his now famous gold-encrusted field marshal's cap. Then he stepped aboard PT 41 and told Bulkeley, "You may cast off when ready, Johnny."

7

". . . Out of the Jaws of Death!"

John Bulkeley rendezvoused with his other three boats at the turning buoy just outside the Corregidor mine field. In order to attract the least possible attention from the Japanese, Bob Kelly, Tony Akers, and Vincent Schumacher had picked up their passengers in obscure coves and inlets on Bataan.[1]

On the PT boats were sixteen military men—fourteen Army and Admiral Rockwell and his chief of staff, Capt. Harold Ray, of the Navy. These were the key men General MacArthur would need when he reached Australia and prepared an offensive back to the Philippines. Selecting those to go had been agonizing: it was a no-win situation. No matter whom MacArthur had chosen, criticism would be heaped on his head. Rank had not been the decisive factor in his selections; one of those aboard was a master sergeant who knew the top-secret radio codes. Left behind on Corregidor and Bataan were some twenty generals.[2]

The crews and passengers aboard the mahogany-hulled plywood boats were perched on powder kegs. The deck of each boat was crowded with twenty steel drums, each holding fifty gallons of high-octane gasoline. An enemy's incendiary bullet could ignite the fuel in a drum and instantly turn the boat into a raging inferno.

As MacArthur's pirates drew away from the dim silhouette of The Rock, all hands had ears finely tuned toward the engines, seeking a telltale clue that all was not well. Engines were meant to be changed every few hundred hours, but after three months of heavy use without adequate maintenance, Squadron 3 had already quadrupled the engines' normal life span. And due to their being clogged with carbon, the once powerful Packards could not gain full speed, so some Japanese vessels might be able to overtake the PT boats.

None of Bulkeley's boats was equipped with a pelorus (a navigational instrument having two sight vanes), so a course would be followed by the use of simple compasses, dead reckoning, and the stars—techniques used by the ancient mariners.

In single file, with Bulkeley's 41 boat in the lead, the tiny flotilla bolted out of Manila Bay. Behind them was the roar of Corregidor's guns, being fired at the Japanese on Bataan to mask the roar of the PT boats. A short time later, the Americans spotted huge bonfires on the shores of the Apo Islands, the historic signal that a night escape through a blockade was in progress.

Clearly, Japanese coast-watchers or Filipino traitors had spotted the tiny convoy and were trying to pass along warnings. If these messages were received on the larger islands of Luzon and Mindoro, it would mean that Nipponese aircraft and speedy destroyers would be scouring the seascape with the arrival of dawn.

On this night the sea was especially violent, causing the boats to pitch about in wild convulsions. Huge waves, fifteen or twenty feet high, thundered over the bows, drenching everyone topside. The boat speed, waves, and wind caused teeth to chatter from the cold, and the salt spray caused eyes to sting and made it almost impossible to see.

CAPT. ROBERT KELLY:

My 34 boat was bringing up the rear. We kept steadily dropping farther behind the others. Finally, Admiral Rockwell blurted out, "Goddamn it, let's close up!" I had not wanted to unduly alarm the admiral, but now I had to tell him the reason for our sluggish performance—our old engines were filled with carbon, and our boat was moving as fast as it could go until the carbon would burn out.

"My God!" Admiral Rockwell gasped.

At 3:00 A.M. the inevitable happened: Kelly's engines went dead, and the 34 boat bobbed about frenziedly and threatened to capsize. While mechanics began frantically cleaning wax and rust from the gasoline strainers, the other three boats charged onward. That was the plan: unless it were General MacArthur's boat, no boat was to halt to aid a disabled companion. In forty minutes, the engines coughed and turned over and Kelly moved ahead.

Bulkeley and his other three skippers had been struggling to remain together, but failed. Each boat steered through the pitch blackness toward Cuyo Islands, halfway point in the trek to Mindanao, where they were to camouflage and hole up until night. Schumacher's boat was the first to reach the rendezvous, and Kelly's arrived at midmorning. A short time later, Bulkeley's 41 with MacArthur glided into the small cove.

Bulkeley and the others waited anxiously for Tony Akers and his PT 35 to arrive, but they never appeared. Only later would the squadron skipper learn that Akers's boat had been beset by repeated engine breakdowns, but would make its way alone to Mindanao.

It was a long, hot day. Nerves were taut. But General MacArthur, who had been ill during the night from the pitching of his boat, sat calmly on deck in a wicker chair and puffed on a corncob pipe. Next to him was his wife, smiling and chatting, outwardly unconcerned. Four-year-old Arthur was happily chasing General Tojo, a pet monkey belonging to the 41's cook, and John Bulkeley had to remind the boy to be careful not to fall overboard.

Shortly after a lunch of salmon and orangeade, MacArthur, Admiral Rockwell, and Lieutenant Bulkeley held a council of war to decide a crucial question. The convoy was already at least two hours behind schedule due to the heavy seas and rash of breakdowns, so in order to reach Mindanao on schedule at dawn the following morning, should the tiny flotilla continue the voyage in daylight, thereby risking detection by searching Japanese warships and aircraft?

ADMIRAL BULKELEY:

If we failed to arrive on time at the port of Cagayan on Mindanao, the fly-boys coming up from Australia might be struck by anxiety fits—there were a lot of Japs on Mindanao—and bug out, marooning General MacArthur and his party. The submarine *Permit* had been ordered to meet us at our Cove Islands assembly point, to give the general an option to continue the trip underwater. This was a tempting course of action, for there had been all kinds of indications that the Nips knew that our boats were heading south.

But Admiral Rockwell pointed out that the *Permit* might never arrive. "I think we should get the hell out of here—now!" he said. So the submarine was discarded. Now the question was: should we leave now, in broad daylight, or wait until darkness? If we waited, we sure as hell would miss our arrival time at Mindanao.

General MacArthur turned to me and said calmly, "Well, Johnny, you're the skipper. The decision is yours."

I cautioned him that the sea was going to be rough as hell again, but that we should shove off as soon as possible. He replied, "Okay, Johnny, let's go!"

Schumacher's boat had lost its deckload of gasoline, and only one engine was functioning properly. So Bulkeley ordered Schumacher to get his boat to Panay island as best he could, and there he could refuel, work on the engines, and continue to Mindanao. The four brigadier generals on Schumacher's boat were taken aboard the remaining craft, and Bulkeley's and Kelly's boats cast off. This time Kelly was in the lead and Bulkeley followed in the other's wake to give the sixty-two-year-old MacArthur a smoother ride. Perhaps twenty minutes after pulling away, a crewman called out: "Sail-ho! Looks like a Jap cruiser!" Bulkeley grabbed his high-power binoculars and peered at the enemy warship, then shouted for the engines to be cut. Those aboard the PTs waited, hardly daring to breathe, for the first burst of shell that would summon the American craft to identify themselves. The seconds ticked past . . . thirty seconds . . . sixty seconds . . . ten minutes. After what seemed to be an eternity, the cruiser steamed steadily westward across the path of the PT boats. Apparently the high, froth-whitened waves had masked the low-slung torpedo boats.

Later in the day a Japanese destroyer was spotted dead ahead, and again the PT boats escaped detection by cutting engines and playing possum.

The black cloak of night fell over the Philippines, and shortly afterward a Japanese coastal battery on Negros Island suddenly switched on its searchlight and sent a long finger of white stabbing into the sky. No doubt the enemy gunners, only a few hundred yards away, had heard the roar of the PT boats' powerful engines and thought that American warplanes were overhead. The little craft bore onward, almost under the muzzles of the enemy guns on shore.

ADMIRAL BULKELEY:
Throughout most of the trek from Corregidor to Mindanao, General MacArthur was violently seasick from the constant shaking of the boat and the way the big waves were pitching it about. He spent most of the time lying on a bunk in the lower cockpit. Mrs. MacArthur was also ill, and had vomited several times, but she sat on the deck beside her husband, held his hand, and mopped his brow.

One time she came up on deck and saw a Nip warship in the distance,

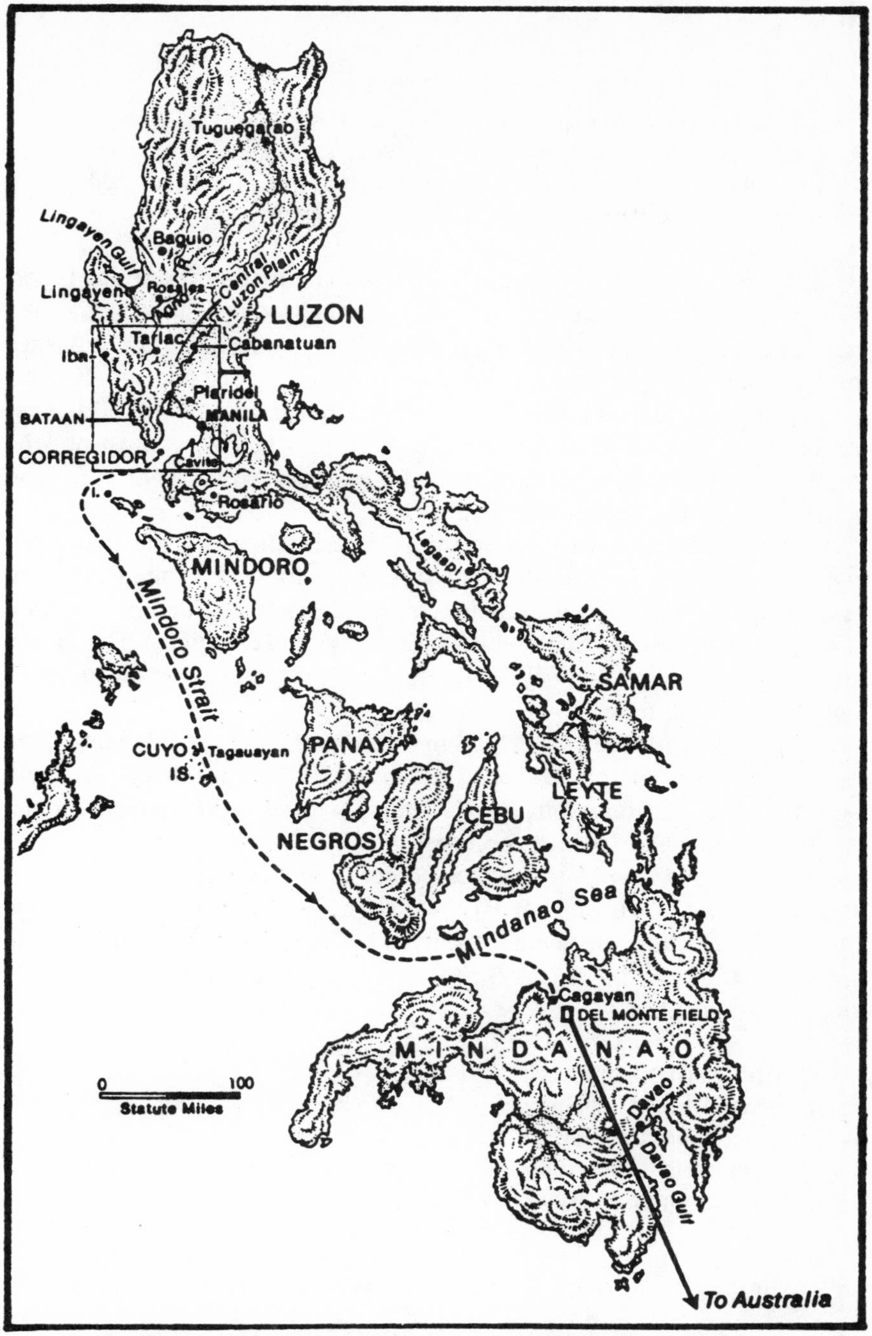

MacArthur's Escape from Corregidor (U.S. Navy)

> then went below without showing any sign of fear or concern. What stands out in my mind about the breakout even today [1987] is Jean MacArthur's courage. She knew as well as any of us the heavy odds we faced in ever getting to our destination.

As John Bulkeley had predicted, the storm demons shrieked that night. Heavy, angry waves deluged the boats, tossing around those below like peas in a pod and nearly washing overboard those topside. Jagged flashes of lightning ripped open the black sky. Landlubbers on Bob Kelly's boat were also deathly ill. One general, draped over a torpedo tube, refused the offer of a young sailor to help him below, away from the torrential deluges of water and incessant blasts of wind. "No, no," the general moaned, "let me die here!"

In the gathering dawn, the storm subsided. Those on the two boats were electrified when, at about 6:30 A.M., a lookout spotted the light on Cagayan Point—the destination. After thirty-five grueling hours on the often-angry sea, without sleep for three days and two nights, navigating by primitive means, John Bulkeley had hit the target right on the nose and precisely on time.

At the dock, MacArthur helped his wife step from the PT boat. Then he walked over to the bearded, exhausted Bulkeley, shook his hand warmly, and said emotionally, "Johnny, you've taken me out of the jaws of death—and I won't forget it!"

The commander of United States Forces in the Far East called together the officers and men of both PTs. "You have performed in true naval style," MacArthur told them. "It gives me great pleasure and honor to award each of you the Silver Star for gallantry and fortitude in the face of heavy odds." [3]

> ADMIRAL BULKELEY:
> As General MacArthur turned to leave, I caught up with him and said, "Sir, one more thing. What are my orders?" He pondered the question a few moments, then replied: "You will conduct offensive operations against the empire of Japan in waters north of Mindanao."
>
> So I, a lowly lieutenant, had in effect been named commander of the United States Fleet in the Philippines. A thought struck me: "That's a hell of a lot of water for my 'fleet' of two beat-up PT boats to cover!"

General MacArthur and his party were driven inland for several miles to the Del Monte plantation where the guest lodge and clubhouse had been set aside for them to await the B-17s from Australia. That afternoon, MacArthur, through confidential sources, received a shocking report. Feisty, diminutive Manuel Quezon, MacArthur's former boss and president of the Philippine Commonwealth, was wavering in his loyalty to the United States and on the verge of defecting to the Japanese.[4]

8

A Mission for MacArthur

At this critical time, President Manuel Quezon was on the island of Negros, about 100 miles northwest of the Del Monte plantation across the Mindanao Sea. Quezon had slipped out of Corregidor on the night of February 20 aboard the submarine *Swordfish.* Leaving with him were his vice president, Sergio Osmeña, and Quezon's wife, son, two daughters, and a covey of government officials. Before departing, Aurora Quezon, the Philippines' first lady, proposed to Jean MacArthur that she and her young son leave on the *Swordfish.* "No," replied the general's wife, "we three have drunk from the same cup. We shall stay together." [1]

When told of his wife's decision, MacArthur remarked to an aide, "Jeannie is my finest soldier." [2]

Since the Japanese invaded his country three months earlier, Manuel Quezon had altered drastically his viewpoint toward the United States. In the early days, Quezon had been convinced that President Roosevelt, whom he considered to be an old and trusted friend, would rush massive reinforcements to the embattled islands and that MacArthur would soon drive the invaders back into the sea. When not a single soldier, airplane, or warship arrived, the commonwealth president suspected the truth: "old friend" Roosevelt and his military brain trust had abandoned the Philippines and would concentrate first on defeating Adolf Hitler's legions.

President Quezon grew bitter. When he had been a virtual prisoner on surrounded Corregidor, Quezon was shocked to hear on Japanese-controlled Radio Manila the voice of longtime comrade, old Gen. Emilio Aguinaldo, urging Douglas MacArthur to surrender. Then a Japanese functionary came on the air to announce that the Nipponese strongman, Gen. Hideki Tojo, had decided to grant independence to the Philippines in the near future.[3]

Quezon was thunderstruck. The Tojo "promise" made a deep impression on the bewildered man many considered to be first and foremost a Philippine patriot. His bitterness grew. His loyalty to America wavered. In his cubbyhole office in Malinta Tunnel, he heatedly exclaimed to Carlos P. Romulo, a trusted aide: "We must try to save ourselves, and to hell with America. The Philippines is being destroyed. . . . The fight between the United States and Japan is not our fight."[4]

Now, weeks later on Mindanao, General MacArthur dispatched an officer to locate Lt. John Bulkeley, his troubleshooter. The aide had no trouble finding his quarry. Even though Bulkeley had been without sleep or rest for forty hours during the trek from Corregidor with MacArthur's party, the skipper was at the Cagayan Pier patching up his boat.

At Del Monte, Bulkeley found nearly everyone but Douglas and Jean MacArthur in a state of acute jitters. Word that the famed American general had arrived on Mindanao had reached the ears of the Japanese, and they were moving forces northward from Davao, in southern Mindanao, to kill or seize MacArthur.

ADMIRAL BULKELEY:
General MacArthur took me out on the porch of the old clubhouse. I was shocked over the general's appearance. His shirt and trousers, usually immaculate, were soiled and wrinkled, and he had a heavy beard stubble. His eyes were bloodshot from lack of sleep and illness from the long trek.

I'd never seen the usually calm general so agitated. His jaws were clenched and his face was flushed red. He said he had another crucial job for me to do, wanted me to hop over to Negros, find Quezon, and bring him and his whole tribe back to Del Monte. "I don't care how you get them here, just do it!" he said, almost snarling. The general even was swearing on occasion, and I'd never heard him swear.

MacArthur added that "we're sending Quezon to Australia to form a Philippine government in exile, whether he likes it or not." I hadn't been aware of all the high-level machinations, so I was quite puzzled by it all. But if General MacArthur wanted Quezon back there, then I intended to bring the son of a bitch back—one way or the other.

His briefing concluded, MacArthur introduced Lieutenant Bulkeley to Don Andres Soriano, a Filipino who was said to be an aide to President

Quezon. ''He will serve as your guide in the rescue operation,'' the general said. *Rescue operation?* To Bulkeley, it looked like a kidnapping.

Bulkeley, by gut reaction, took a dislike to Soriano and was uncertain of his loyalty. He made a mental note to keep a watchful eye on his guide during the mission. If Bulkeley failed to survive due to Soriano's treachery, then he'd make certain that Soriano didn't come back, either.

MacArthur shook hands with both men, then reminded his Chief Pirate: ''Don't forget, Johnny, bring him back—by whatever means is necessary!''

Back at the Cagayan piers, Bulkeley's adrenaline was pumping hard once again. Shortly after dark, he cast off in PT 41, with George Cox as the skipper, along with Tony Akers's 35 boat and plunged into the blackest of nights. An hour later lookouts spotted the dim outline of a Japanese ship, and the two boats hid behind a small island until the destroyer had disappeared.

The little port of Dumaguete on Negros was deathly still when Bulkeley's boats edged into it on muffled engines. No one had charts, but when the water was found to be extremely shallow, Bulkeley decided to lie to offshore and wade in, rather than to risk getting the boats shot up in an ambush. President Quezon was supposed to be at a house in Dumaguete.

Clutching a tommy gun in one hand, Bulkeley began striding through the surf. With him were Soriano and two heavily armed crewmen. Before departing the boat, the skipper had taken the two sailors aside and told them to shoot Soriano and ask questions later if it looked as though they had run into an ambush.

Reaching the pier, Bulkeley and his men headed rapidly for Quezon's house, but ran into a constable who said the president had left earlier that day for an undisclosed locale. The Filipino added that Quezon had instructed him to tell any Americans who might appear that he was not interested in leaving Negros.

''Where did President Quezon go?'' Bulkeley asked.

''I'm not supposed to tell you that,'' the constable replied.

Cocking his tommy gun and putting the muzzle to the Filipino's head, Bulkeley roared, ''The hell you can't—now start talking!''

Badly shaken, the constable blurted out that Quezon had gone to Bais, a village about twenty-five miles up the coast. Bulkeley and the others returned to their boats and raced to Bais. There Tony Akers was directed to patrol the shoreline in his 35 boat while the squadron skipper searched for the elusive president of the Philippines.

A local informed Bulkeley that Quezon was in a house a few miles inland, so the lieutenant "borrowed" a pair of ancient automobiles and he and Soriano roared off into the night. At the designated nipa hut, perched on the side of a low hill, Soriano called to Quezon. Two minutes ticked past. The house remained dark. The guide shouted again. Moments later a light glowed inside, and the president of the Philippines appeared in the doorway, a small, lonely figure clad in nightclothes.

Quezon, coughing spasmodically from the tuberculosis that racked him, was ill at ease. Bulkeley noticed that the president's hands were trembling. Part of Quezon's uneasiness may have resulted from his first good look at John Bulkeley, who resembled a reincarnated pirate. The skipper wore no uniform, only an old oilskin. His boots were mud-caked, and his unruly black beard and longish hair tied around his head with a bandana gave him a menacing appearance. Embellishing that sinister look, Bulkeley clutched a tommy gun, wore a pair of pistols, and had a nasty-looking trench knife in his belt.

ADMIRAL BULKELEY:
It was now about oh-two-thirty [2:30 A.M.] so I had no time to waste on idle chitchat. If we were to get Quezon, his family, and assorted strap-hangers across the hundred miles of open sea before daylight, to avoid Nip warships and planes, we had no time to lose.

As soon as I told Quezon that we had come to take him to MacArthur, he dug in his heels. Said he wasn't going. I stared hard at the bastard, and minced no words, reminding him of repeated Japanese treachery in the Far East, but not letting on that I knew he intended to go over to the enemy.

By now, fifteen minutes had gone by. I said to him sternly, "Well, Mr. President, are you ready to come with us?"

Quezon was caught between a rock and a hard place. Whatever may have been his plans, he was now confronted by someone who claimed to be a United States Navy officer but who looked—and acted—like a pirate. He was shaking even harder. Finally, in a soft voice, he replied, "I am ready to go."

Quezon's family and officials in an adjoining hut were rapidly rousted out of bed and herded into the pair of borrowed automobiles. Crammed into them were Bulkeley, Soriano, Quezon and his wife, son, and two daughters, Vice President Sergio Osmeña, a general, and two cabinet officials. With a raucous revving of motors and thick clouds of exhaust smoke, the old cars leaped forward for another wild dash across the dark countryside.

Reaching the rickety Bais pier, Bulkeley learned that Akers's patrolling boat had struck a submerged object, gouging a gaping hole in her bow, and had to be beached. Hopefully it could be salvaged later.

Now, as if by magic, seven more of Quezon's cabinet appeared at the pier. So too did huge amounts of baggage. Among the cargo were seven bulging mail sacks filled with United States currency. Depending upon the denomination of the bills, there was perhaps twelve to fifteen million dollars.

Bulkeley glanced at his watch: it was 3:05 A.M. The pier was in utter chaos. The Filipinos were jabbering excitedly, arguing over who would sit where on the boat and which pieces of luggage would get favored positions. "All right," Bulkeley shouted over the hubbub, "everyone get aboard—and leave those goddamned suitcases on the dock!"

There would be no room for baggage. The PT boat would be crammed with its own crew, along with Quezon's good-sized entourage and Ensign Akers and his men from the beached 35 boat.

The Filipinos began scrambling on board. All but Manuel Quezon. He came up to John Bulkeley and said matter of factly, "I've changed my mind. I'm not going to go." The skipper, already exhausted from three days without sleep, was nearly apoplectic. A shouting match erupted, after which the reluctant president of the Philippines got onto the boat.

PT 41 cast off. Some forty minutes out to sea, a violent squall erupted, pitching the craft about as though it were a canoe. Within minutes nearly all of the passengers were ill and vomiting. But Bulkeley had more pressing concerns: he was keeping a sharp eye open for the seven Japanese destroyers that reportedly were prowling between Negros and Cagayan on Mindanao.

Now a chilling new specter reared its head. A heavy wave had snapped the shear pins of two torpedoes, causing the engine of one fish to start while still in the tube with its nose in the water. This activated the firing mechanism, so that a sharp slap by a wave could detonate the torpedo, blowing boat and passengers to smithereens.

Lieutenant Bulkeley and torpedomen John Houlihan and James Light began working feverishly at the delicate task of forcing the armed torpedo out of the tube and into the water. The bucking of the boat threatened to wash the three men overboard, but they finally succeeded in dislodging the ticking time bomb.[5]

As if Mother Nature were rewarding the three men for their intrepidity, the winds ceased howling and the sea calmed. PT 41 and its cargo of humanity, packed sardinelike, were halfway to Mindanao.

> ADMIRAL BULKELEY:
> With the storm and the armed torpedo stuck in the tube, at the time I didn't give two cents for our chances for survival. But now President Quezon came up to me and said that he wanted to go back to Negros. I was fed up with him and told him he'd sure as hell have to walk on water to get there.

At 6:00 A.M. the 41 boat tied up at the Mindanao pier. Notified by radio that Bulkeley was bringing in the ''rescued'' president of the Philippine Commonwealth, Brig. Gen. William F. Sharp, commander of the ill-equipped United States troops on Mindanao, had an honor guard on hand to greet America's staunch ally.[6]

9

Shoot-out Off Cebu Island

On St. Patrick's Day 1942, America and large portions of the free world were electrified when, in a press conference in the Oval Office of the White House, President Roosevelt announced that General MacArthur had escaped from Corregidor and was now in Australia. "I'm sure every American admires, with me, General MacArthur's determination to fight to the finish with his men in the Philippines," the president declared. However, MacArthur would be far more valuable as supreme commander of the entire Southwest Pacific than if he had stayed on Corregidor, Roosevelt added.[1]

That evening the radio airwaves of America were saturated with stories of MacArthur's bold breakout from The Rock, although one crucial factor was not mentioned: how the startling feat had been achieved. For the present, wraps were being kept on the role played by John Bulkeley and his PT-boat warriors. The following day, March 18, screaming headlines were splashed across the nation. Trumpeted the *New York Times:*

MACARTHUR IN AUSTRALIA
AS ALLIED COMMANDER

A subhead reflected the almost total ignorance of America's painful military weakness: "Move Hailed as Foreshadowing Turn of the Tide."

Far from the "tide" being nearly turned, America was in big trouble in the Pacific and facing even more devastating defeats. Hardly had

MacArthur landed at an airstrip fifty miles from Darwin, in northern Australia, than he was jolted by the most shocking news of his military career: the "army" that he was to lead in a swift return to the Philippines to rescue the Battered Bastards of Bataan did not exist. Counting Australians, there were only 32,000 Allied troops in the entire land, and nearly all of them were noncombat types. There were less than a hundred serviceable airplanes, most of them obsolete and timeworn, and not a single tank existed in all of Australia.

For one of the few times in his life, Douglas MacArthur was plunged into despair. When given this scandalous news by Brig. Gen. Richard J. Marshall, his deputy chief of staff, MacArthur's jaw clenched and he whispered hoarsely: "God have mercy on us!" [2]

Traveling by rail from Alice Springs to Melbourne, a trek of 1,000 miles, General MacArthur paced the aisle of the decrepit, dusty, stiflingly hot and fly-infested wood coach and reflected on the breakout from Corregidor. He knew that Dame Fortune had smiled on him and his party, while at the same time recognizing the skills of John Bulkeley and his pirates who had brought them through. "It was a close thing," MacArthur admitted privately to Gen. Dick Sutherland, possibly his most trusted confidant, "but that's the way it is in war. You win or lose, live or die—and the difference is just an eyelash." [3]

MacArthur's mounting fury was directed at "Washington," meaning President Roosevelt, who, the general was convinced, had betrayed him by implying in a series of messages that significant help was on the way to the Philippines. This had led MacArthur, in turn, to unknowingly deceive his besieged men on Bataan and Corregidor by urging them to hold on, that reinforcements were coming. Never again would MacArthur trust Roosevelt.[4]

Arriving at Melbourne, a cheering crowd of thousands buoyed MacArthur's spirits. In a wrinkled, ribbonless, khaki bush jacket, he made a stirring and emotional speech to the throng, coining a phrase that would become the rallying battle cry in the Philippines, throughout the South Pacific, and on the American home front: "I came through, and *I shall return!*"

Meanwhile, a couple of thousand miles north of Melbourne on Japanese-encircled Corregidor, Ens. Barron Chandler, the South Carolinian, was lying in pain on a cot in the crowded hospital bay in Malinta Tunnel. He had been a patient since being shot through both ankles while on a

PT-boat raid in the hotbed of Subic Bay with John Bulkeley and Bob Kelly, late in January.

> COMDR. BARRON CHANDLER:
> After I had been wounded, Bulkeley came to see me in the tunnel almost every day—or night. We lost track of the time in that dugout, didn't know if it were night or day. Wounded guys were moaning and screaming. The air was putrid. On March 10, Bulkeley came once more. It was always just small talk. He told me what he could about our PT-boat operations and the situation in general.
>
> Of course, I looked forward to his visits. Suddenly, he failed to come. The days went by and no Bulkeley. I was convinced that he had been killed—or worse, perhaps, taken prisoner, for he had become a pain in the neck to the Nips.
>
> About ten days later, an excited navy enlisted man bolted up to my cot and blurted out: "Lieutenant Bulkeley and his boys were the ones who got General MacArthur out!" Now I knew why Bulkeley had ceased coming to see me.[5]

All around the world, the fallout spread from General MacArthur's daring dash through the enemy blockade of The Rock. In the United States, the general, who had figuratively thumbed his nose at Hirohito and Tojo as a parting gesture, was praised by hundreds of newspapers as one of history's greatest commanders. In the hallowed halls of Congress, senators and representatives fell all over each other in a mad scramble to gain the floor in order to eulogize MacArthur. The Blackfoot Indians of Montana adopted him into their tribe. Schools, streets, bridges, and libraries were renamed after the general, and scores of christened babies were given the middle name MacArthur. Strident demands echoed across the land for the Hero of Bataan—as the media called him—to be brought to Washington and given command of American military operations worldwide.

General MacArthur's escape from Corregidor when the Japanese were trying desperately to capture him gave hope to the captive people of the Philippines, and provided a prodigious boost to an American home front still shocked and reeling from a series of military debacles in the Pacific and elsewhere. Of equal importance, President Roosevelt's order, as intended, had saved MacArthur to lead the Allies back to the Philippines and on to Tokyo.

In Berlin, Adolf Hitler's propaganda genius, Paul Joseph Goebbels, held a different view. ''MacArthur,'' Goebbels bellowed in the Nazi press, was a ''fleeing general.'' In Rome, the Fuehrer's crony, Italian dictator Benito Mussolini, labeled MacArthur a ''coward.'' And in Tokyo, Tojo's printed mouthpiece, the *Japan Times,* howled that the general was ''a deserter'' who had ''fled his post.''[6]

In Washington, Gen. George Marshall, the army chief of staff, was worried about the harmful effects of this drumfire of Axis propaganda, concluding that the best counterstroke would be to award MacArthur the nation's highest decoration, the Congressional Medal of Honor. Marshall bounced the proposal off of Dwight Eisenhower, who had gained his general's star only a few months earlier. Eisenhower, who had never seen combat but once served as MacArthur's aide, frowned on it. He was not a dues-paying member of the MacArthur fan club. But Marshall forwarded the Medal of Honor recommendation to President Roosevelt, who quickly approved. MacArthur received the decoration on March 26 at a dinner given for him by John Curtin, the Australian prime minister.[7]

In Manila, Mrs. Dorothy Janson, the American wife of Swedish consul Helge, was one of the countless civilians whom the Japanese tried to mislead about John Bulkeley's rescue of Douglas MacArthur. Due to the fact that Sweden was neutral, Helge Janson's wife was not interned.

> MRS. DOROTHY JANSON:
> My husband and I were more shocked than electrified by General MacArthur's escape. That's because we had no way of knowing the truth, for we lived on rice, rum, and rumor. The Japanese-controlled *Manila Tribune* headlined that General MacArthur had cowardly deserted his post.[8]

Not long after the MacArthur party had reached Australia, the submarine USS *Permit* tied up at a pier in Albany, a port in the same country. Scrambling out of the hatch were Lt. Vincent Schumacher, skipper of PT 32, and his crew. When the 32 boat had been left behind in the Cuyo Islands on March 13, and John Bulkeley's and Bob Kelly's boats continued toward Mindanao with General MacArthur, Schumacher had concluded that his boat was unseaworthy. So when the *Permit* had arrived as planned, everyone climbed into the submarine and PT 32 was scuttled by gunfire.[9]

Halfway around the globe on March 23, Alice Bulkeley answered the telephone in the suburban New York City apartment she shared with her mother-in-law, Elizabeth. The caller identified himself as a reporter for the *Long Island Star.* Alice felt a twinge of fear. Was this the call she had long dreaded, a newsman bringing word that husband John had been killed?

"How do you feel about Lieutenant Bulkeley's latest heroics?" the scribe asked.

A surge of relief swept through Alice, but she was puzzled. "What heroics?" she asked.

"You mean you haven't heard about it?"

Told that she had not, the reporter excitedly exclaimed, "The Navy just released the whole story—your husband led the PT boats that carried General MacArthur through the Jap blockade of Corregidor!"

Filled with pride, relieved to know that John was still alive, Alice was virtually speechless. Finally she said, "Oh."

Suddenly it was the Subic Bay caper aftermath all over again: pounding on Alice's door by a large covey of reporters and photographers, the incessant phone calls from media all over the country—most of them seeking a new angle—the Niagara of congratulatory telegrams and letters by the mailbag, a renewed deluge of requests for public appearances, Paramount Newsreel wanting to do a documentary on her, radio bulletins, blaring headlines. Finally the Navy sent a public-relations officer to work full time with Alice, who was now eight and one-half months pregnant.

Back in the Philippines, before taking off from Del Monte for Australia, MacArthur had General Sutherland write up special orders for John Bulkeley, making the skipper independent of all commanders in the islands. The orders stated that he was operating directly under General MacArthur, and commanders were directed to "assist Lieutenant Bulkeley in every possible way in the furtherance of his mission." It was a command setup that may have been unique in United States history: a navy combat lieutenant directly responsible to a four-star general.[10]

With the Japanese closing in on the Del Monte plantation locale in a continuing futile effort to capture General MacArthur, John Bulkeley took his remaining three PT boats northward across the Mindanao Sea to Cebu, a long, slender island that lies snugly in a northeast-southwest direction off the east coast of Negros. The squadron set up a base at Cebu City, where there were commercial repair facilities. Momentarily

Long Island Star

Bulkeley Commanded Navy Boats That Took MacArthur From Batan

The man who piloted the leading boat of the flotilla of four which carried General Douglas MacArthur and his staff from the Philippines to a rendezvous with planes that took them to Australia was none other than Lieutenant John Duncan Bulkeley of Thomson Hill, it was revealed today by the official story from MacArthur's headquarters in Australia.

Bulkeley was one of the first American heroes of World War II. It was he who piloted another motor torpedo boat into Binango Bay, on the west coast of Luzon, running a gamut of Japanese gunfire to sink a 5,000-ton Japanese vessel.

Bulkeley's wife, mother and 16-month-old daughter live at 45-42 41st street.

Hazardous Trip

The official version of the dramatic dash from Batan Peninsula, which emphasizes the fact that it was not an "escape," tells how General MacArthur was nearly fired upon by members of his own party. Although the official story doesn't say so, it appears that the gunfire nearly came from the boat commanded by Bulkeley.

This is how it happened:

The four speedboats carrying the party, behind schedule, dashed individually by daylight along the Philippine Islands, in danger every moment of attack by sea or air, and stopping occasionally in hope of gaining contact with each other.

JOHN D. BULKELEY

General MacArthur's boat approached one island. Another speedboat was there already. It thought that MacArthur's boat was a Japanese one. The deck was cleared for action and the machine guns were manned. It was a lucky chance that MacArthur's boat was identified, at the last moment, before the .50 calibre guns went into action.

It was revealed also that a United States submarine had been ordered to "back-stop" the Flying Fortresses detailed to pick up the party. The submarine was ordered to make for a secret rendezvous along the way toward the place where the planes were due.

One Boat Disabled

When one of the four PT-type speedboats was disabled, it was debated whether the entire party should wait at the intermediate rendezvous for the submarine, to make sure that none of the party was marooned.

It was decided to redistribute the 19 Army men and the general's wife and 4-year-old son, in three boats. The fourth boat was repaired and continued later.

Two instead of an expected three Flying Fortresses arrived at the final rendexvous, and the entire party abandoned baggage, arms and equipment so that all might get aboard.

The four patrol torpedo boats in

(Continued on Next Page)

free of pressing duties, Bulkeley allowed his men an evening ashore, their first liberty in many weeks.

Shortly after sundown on April 8, John Bulkeley in George Cox's PT 41, followed by Bob Kelly in the 34 boat, which had just undergone extensive repair work in Cebu City, raced off to intercept two Japanese destroyers and a cruiser carrying four seaplanes. Spotters had reported the enemy warships steaming toward the southern tip of Cebu.

Two hours later QM1C DeWitt L. Glover, of Stockton, California, called out from the PT-41 deck: "There she is!" He had discerned the dim silhouette of a ship. Moments later, Glover shouted: "Jumping Jesus! There she *is!*" [11]

What Glover had seen some 5,000 yards ahead was a Nipponese cruiser, heavily steel-plated and bristling with guns and automatic weapons. It would be yet another David-and-Goliath encounter to the death, as the enemy warship was perhaps 100 times larger than the plywood and mahogany PT boats, which would rely on speed and maneuverability—and the guts of their skippers and crewmen.

Undaunted by the heavy odds, Bulkeley gave orders to attack. Like a giant jungle cat stalking its prey in the blackness, PT 41 crept toward the shadowy hulk of the warship. Before the cat could spring—that is, fire its torpedoes—it had to get in close . . . closer . . . still closer. Only the sounds of the muffled engines marred the seascape silence. Apparently the Japanese lookouts had not spotted the 41 boat.

Now, at 500 yards' distance from the cruiser, the shout "Fire!" rang out in the night, and Ensign Cox sent two torpedoes knifing through the water. The fish missed, straddling the cruiser. On the other side of the enemy vessel, Bob Kelly had sneaked his 34 boat in close, and now he also fired a pair of fish. Both missed. Despite the flurry of activity, the prey gave no sign that she knew she was under attack.

The 41 boat made a wide circle, then moved back in close to fire its last two torpedoes. Crew members felt a surge of exultation: the fish appeared to have slammed into the warship. But there was no explosion, no fiery flash, only a plume of water gushing upward.

Suddenly, the blacked-out cruiser came angrily to life. All hell broke loose. Japanese gunners began sending torrents of tracers racing over the water, seeking out the pesky tormenters. A powerful searchlight beam grasped PT 34. "Shoot out that goddamned light!" Lieutenant Kelly shouted. Now shells began splashing around the little boats. One projectile clipped off the 34's mast. Commissary Steward Willard J. Reynolds, of Brooklyn, was blasting away at the searchlight with a pair of .50-caliber machine guns when he suddenly felt an agonizing bolt of pain, as though white-hot pokers had been jabbed into his neck and shoulders. Shrapnel had ripped into him, and he collapsed to the deck. Another man leapt to the machine guns and resumed firing.

Still bathed in the searchlight beam, Kelly's 34 continued to bore in on the cruiser, and, at 300 yards, fired its last two fish. Kelly gave a hard rudder to race away, but now a destroyer some 2,000 yards to starboard sent shells whistling toward the speeding little craft. Shrapnel tore into 34's topside, already riddled with bullets.

As the torrent of lead hissed past and into the 34, TM John Martino quickly looked back over his shoulder and could see two water spouts shoot skyward at the cruiser's waterline. Through binoculars, Kelly saw the geysers too. Apparently PT 34's final two torpedoes had scored bull's-eyes, for the cruiser's searchlight began to fade, then flickered off.

Meanwhile, Bulkeley's boat, out of torpedoes, had pulled astern of the cruiser to draw her fire so that Kelly could get in for his second attack. The 41 boat's gunners were blasting away when crewmen saw that the warship was enveloped in a thick cloud of smoke.

Now Kelly and Bulkeley realized that they had stumbled into a hornets' nest—there were other enemy ships around them. Its fish and machine-gun ammunition expended, Kelly's 34, zigzagging violently, raced away. Suddenly, from out of the darkness dead ahead loomed the outline of a Japanese destroyer, charging toward the 34 boat at high speed, clearly bent on ramming. Kelly avoided the mad rush by swerving to port.

Bulkeley's boat was catching hell, and was caught in the brilliance of a warship's searchlight beam. Shells splashed into the water around the 41 boat. In an effort to get out of the trap, Bulkeley sped east, bumped into a destroyer, altered course to the north and was confronted by another warship, then darted east once more and came upon a pair of destroyers. There was only one escape route, if any—to the south—so Bulkeley roared off in that direction, running a gauntlet of fire. All night destroyers gave chase to the 41 boat, and just before dawn Bulkeley edged his craft into an inlet where the water was too shallow for destroyers.

At the same time Bulkeley was holing up under foliage, Kelly's shrapnel- and bullet-riddled PT 34 was limping into the narrow (400-foot-wide) Cebu City channel. It was now daylight, a dangerous time for a PT boat to be out on the water.

CAPT. ROBERT KELLY:

We were chugging up the channel at fifteen knots. Reynolds, our wounded gunner, was feeling better and sitting on deck. We had only three guns, the others having been shot away in the night fight. Suddenly, out of the sun, four Jap planes jumped us, loosing bombs and strafing. For thirty minutes they hit us. Our quartermaster [Albert P.] Ross, having shot down one of the attacking planes, was himself shot by the next diving plane. Our torpedoman [Donald W.] Harris was killed at his battle station in the starboard machine-gun turret—a bullet through his throat. A machinist's mate took his place, but then our guns were disabled.

The Nips were coming lower and lower, to within a hundred feet of us. Our boat was riddled with holes. We couldn't return the fire, had only two engines and could only try to dodge in the narrow channel. Then our engineer yelled that the engine room was full of water. We were sinking, so I had to beach the boat on a tiny island if we were to save our wounded men. I went below to the engine room. Our engineer [Velt F.] Hunter was a ghastly sight, covered with blood and his arm practically blown off. But he remained at his post.

Reynolds had been hit again, and as our radioman [John] Martino and I lugged him ashore over sharp coral that cut our feet, Reynolds's guts kept falling out of the hole in his belly. He had pleaded with us not to carry him off, saying we should tend to the other wounded men. Reynolds died a short time later.

At 12:30 P.M. another flight of Japanese planes came over to finish off what remained of the beached PT 34. They set the boat afire, and for more than an hour the war-torn bantam burned and finally exploded.[12]

Motor Torpedo Boat Squadron 3 now had two craft left. On April 12, with Japanese troops pouring into Cebu City, the skipper of PT-boat 35, Lt. Hank Brantingham, burned his vessel at the dock to keep it out of enemy hands.

Then there was only one.

10

Summons to Australia

Two days after Lt. Bob Kelly's boat had met disaster in the Cebu City channel, John Bulkeley called on the Mindanao army commander, Gen. Bill Sharp, at Cagayan. He was there to beg for torpedoes, and told Sharp that he intended to go back into action with the lone remaining boat in the Philippine ''fleet.''

Too late, Sharp replied. There were no more torpedoes. Besides, the army planned to take PT 41 to Lake Lanao, fifteen miles inland, and use it to prevent Nipponese floatplanes from landing on the water there.

A strenuous effort was subsequently made to haul the 41 over a steep, twisting mountain road to Lake Lanao. But up in the heights the boat was detected by a Japanese force and had to be destroyed.

Now there were none.

Before lifting off from Mindanao for Australia, Gen. Douglas MacArthur had asked Lieutenant Bulkeley to ''take a hard look at the beaches'' where the Cotabato River flows into the sea on Mindanao. Holding the belief that an army awaited him Down Under, the general had anticipated a rapid return to the Philippines, and an initial landing might be made around the mouth of the Cotabato.

Bulkeley went to the targeted region and in a short period of time organized a network of native guerrillas, dressed them like fishermen, and had them paddle about the Cotabato region in *bancas* (small boats). The ''fishermen'' took soundings in bays and inlets by the primitive means of lowering strings with rocks tied to the ends of them; they recorded their findings on crude maps.

Bulkeley collected this information and sent it on to General MacArthur in Australia along with a terse note: "Cotabato River beaches no goddamned good for large-scale landings."

By early April, the final curtain was being lowered on the epic drama of Bataan. Each day the survivors had become weaker in body and spirit, and their power to resist had dwindled. They were wracked by disease—malaria, dysentery, scurvy, and beriberi—and for several weeks had existed by eating mule, dog, cat, lizard, monkey, and iguana, and by gnawing on tree bark and eating leaves.

On April 9, word that Bataan had fallen reached Melbourne, and a pall of gloom was cast over Douglas MacArthur's headquarters. An aide slipped into the general's office to confer with his boss and saw MacArthur, seated at his desk, grim-faced and cheeks streaked with tears.[1]

ADMIRAL BULKELEY:
General MacArthur was not only a military genius and absolutely fearless, but a man of great compassion—despite the nonsensical tripe that some historians have written about him. Strong-willed? Certainly he was. A large ego? Certainly. That's what great men are all about. War's not a game.

On April 13, General Sharp sent for Bulkeley. He had a shocker for the navy skipper. General MacArthur had personally ordered Bulkeley to leave the Philippines, and he was to fly to Australia on a B-17 bomber that would take off from the Del Monte airstrip that same night.

The Wild Man of the Philippines was plunged into emotional turmoil. Although he had no boats in which to fight, if he left for Australia it would look as though he were running out on his men. But he reflected on what MacArthur had told him a month earlier at the Del Monte plantation: "Johnny, I'm going to get out your officers and key men. I'm not going to let you die in a foxhole with a rifle."

That thought resolved Bulkeley's dilemma. What good would a bunch of dead or imprisoned PT-boat skippers be to the war effort? MacArthur believed strongly that new PT boats would play a crucial role in the bloody Pacific battles yet to come, he had told the squadron leader, so the general must have had something specific in mind for him and his officers.

Bulkeley sent word to the others that he would push hard in Australia to get them out as soon as possible, then got aboard the departing bomber. As it prepared to take off, the Japanese dive-bombed the field, knocking out one of the B-17's engines. But the flight proceeded to its destination in routine fashion—minus one engine.

Had Australian authorities hewed to the technical line, John Bulkeley would probably have been barred from entering that country due to having no visible means of support. Nearly all of his few personal belongings had to be left behind. He wore sneakers, pants, and a jacket; he had no shirt. He didn't have a dime, and was exhausted.[2]

A young member of the Australian Women's Auxiliary Service met the plane and took Bulkeley to her home, where she lived with her family, and they put him to bed. He slept for thirty-six straight hours, and when he awoke they provided a uniform, shoes, socks, and underwear for him. The tidy sum of $150 in cash was in a pocket of the uniform. Later, when Bulkeley wanted to pay it back, the family refused the offer.[3]

As American forces in the Philippines disintegrated, the eighty-three officers and men of Squadron 3 became widely dispersed. Many grabbed rifles and joined the guerrillas. Thirty-eight of Bulkeley's men, including most of those in the Manila Bay region, were taken prisoner. True to his word, General MacArthur had Lieutenant Kelly and Ensigns Cox and Akers evacuated by air, and they joined Bulkeley in Melbourne. Lieutenant Hank Brantingham, who had had to burn the next-to-last squadron boat in Cebu City, eventually made his way to Australia also.[4]

Not long after John Bulkeley reached Melbourne, and unbeknownst to him at the time, the PT-boat skipper had become the center of a high-level squabble. General MacArthur had recommended Bulkeley to receive the army Medal of Honor for his heroics in the Philippines. Hearing of MacArthur's recommendation, Adm. Ernest King, the chief of naval operations in Washington, was furious. The Big Bear (as Roosevelt called King for both his size and sometimes gruff disposition) fumed to aides, "No way is MacArthur going to dictate a Medal of Honor for one of my officers. *I* will make the recommendation for the Navy."

Meanwhile, Lieutenant Bulkeley was invited by MacArthur to a small luncheon honoring President Quezon. The head of the Philippines Commonwealth would leave soon on the liner *President Coolidge* for the United States, where he agreed to organize a government in exile. Bulkeley briefly pondered how he would be received by Quezon, for he was the skipper who had, in essence, kidnapped the president from Negros.

Bulkeley's appearance had changed drastically since his weeks as the Wild Man of the Philippines. He was clean shaven, his hair was trimmed to regulation length, and he wore an official navy uniform. He would be in for a monumental surprise.

During the meal, President Quezon was in an expansive mood. The atmosphere was friendly, as though Quezon had not ever been kidnapped to the Allied side at the direction of MacArthur. Rather Quezon related in appreciative detail how he had been rescued from Negros by "an old American sea wolf." Bulkeley was puzzled. Who in the hell was this "old sea wolf" Quezon was talking about?

Nearly finished with his tale, the president turned to the youthful looking Bulkeley and said, "I want to express my sincere appreciation to your father, the sea wolf, and commend him on his great courage and seamanship!"

Customarily imperturbable, Bulkeley was taken aback. *"My father?"* he finally blurted out.

MacArthur and the other Americans broke out in a gale of laughter. Quezon had been confused, mistaking the clean-shaven, immaculately dressed Bulkeley for the son of the grizzled, menacing, old sea wolf who had suddenly appeared at Quezon's house on Negros that black and stormy night a few weeks earlier. When Quezon realized his error, he joined in the laughter.

Meanwhile, John Bulkeley had been concealing a deep-rooted personal concern. "Oscar," as he had referred to the child he and Alice had been expecting, should have been born on the due date of April 5. The child had indeed been born, at the expected time, but Alice had no way of informing her husband of the blessed event. She named the boy John D. Bulkeley, Jr., for mother and relatives did not expect the father to survive the war.

On April 26, Alice Bulkeley was the featured guest on the popular radio show, "We the People," on WABC in New York. Even though the program was beamed overseas, Bulkeley did not hear it. Had he been listening, the skipper would have received glad tidings, for Alice had received the Navy Department's blessing to announce the arrival of John Junior. However, an Australian tailor, who was making a uniform for Lieutenant Bulkeley, saw the story in a newspaper, clipped out the item, and stuck it in a uniform pocket so that it was barely protruding. When the skipper picked up the uniform, he learned of the birth of his namesake, and that all was shipshape with mother and son.[5]

Back in the States, there was a growing clamor by an insatiable public

(Revised 1941)

REPORT ON THE FITNESS OF OFFICERS

(To be submitted in accordance with Section 5 of Chapter 2, U. S. Navy Regulations, 1920, and Bureau of Navigation Manual, Article C–1007)

(Before making out this report read latest Bureau of Navigation circular letter on the subject of fitness s)

The following four questions to be made out by the officer reported on:

BULKELEY, John D. (Surname first), Rank Lieutenant U. S. N.

Ship or Station Motor Torpedo Boat Squadron THREE (Ship aviation units enter ship to which attached) Period from 16 March 1942 to 29 Apr 1942

1. Regular duties Squadron Commander

Additional duties None

(State watch duties, both deck and engineering. After each duty insert in parenthesis number of months, this reporting period)

2. Present address of
   - wife (if married) Alice Bulkeley, 4542 41st, Long Island City, NewYo
   - next of kin (if unmarried)

(Indicate above the best address at which the Bureau of Navigation may communicate with the wife or next of kin in an emergency. The above address does not relate to the usual residence (home) which is maintained in the Bureau. See Art. 135(2), U. S. N. R., 1920.)

3. Proficiency in foreign languages, stating which ones, and ability therein

French 3.5

4. My preference for next duty is—

(a) Sea Flotilla Commander, Motor torpedo boats. Fleet Southwest Pacific

ore Location 12th Naval District

John D. Bulkeley (Signature)

..g to be made out by Reporting Officer:

5. Reporting Officer: Name DOUGLAS MacARTHUR, Rank General, U. S. Army

6. Reporting officer's official status relative to officer reported on Commanding Gener l, U.S. Forces in the Far East.

REMARKS

14. Is this officer professionally qualified to perform ALL the duties of his grade? Yes X No – If deficient in any particular, comment is required. Give in this space a clear, concise estimate of this officer's personal and military character, his fitness for promotion, and duty performed worthy of special mention, and any information which might be of value to the Department in making assignments to duty. A check opposite "No," except for inexperienced Ensigns, or a statement that performance of duty is clearly unsatisfactory constitutes an unsatisfactory report. A statement of minor deficiencies either in character or performance of duties constitutes an unfavorable report. (THIS SPACE IS NOT TO BE LEFT BLANK.)

Lieutenant Bulkeley is an outstanding officer who has exhibited the highest qualities of courage, leadership and initiative. His operations in command of Motor Torpedo Boat Squadron Three during the Philippine Campaign were brilliant. He has demonstrated in action his fitness for promotion. I especially desire to have this officer assigned to this command.

5. An *unsatisfactory report* must have statement of officer reported on attached; an *unfavorable report* requires that officer reported on has been informed of his deficiencies either verbally or in writing. Has this been done? What improvement, if any, has been noted?

Douglas MacArthur (Signature) 16—22799

(Do not write in unruled portion of this space)

(Author's collection)

This is a composite reproduction of two pages in the original Fitness Report.

for information on John Bulkeley and his PT-boat warriors. So on April 30, navy public-relations officers in Washington trotted out forty-year-old John T. McCabe of Grosse Point, Michigan, before a mob of reporters and a battery of photographers.

McCabe was a civilian engineer for the Navy who had helped keep Bulkeley's boats running in the Philippines; just before the curtain started to lower there, he had made his way to Australia and then to the United States. Despite navy regulations forbidding such practices, McCabe had gone on a number of patrols with the Sea Wolf.

Describing Bulkeley as "looking like a pirate with a big black beard," McCabe said he had asked the skipper why he didn't shave. "Bulkeley said he didn't intend to—that his beard brought him good luck," McCabe related. He added, "John Bulkeley is either a fearless man without a nerve in his body, or he's crazy—maybe a little of each." [6]

The reporters were unaware that Bulkeley, Bob Kelly, Tony Akers, and George Cox had been ordered back to the States, where they would form new PT-boat squadrons for eventual return to the South Pacific. Bulkeley would leave carrying a secret: back home he was to receive the Medal of Honor from President Roosevelt himself.

A short time before the PT-boat skippers were to depart, General MacArthur sent for Lieutenant Bulkeley. Less than two weeks earlier, MacArthur had been appointed Allied Supreme Commander in the Southwest Pacific, but it was still a paper command with few trained men or adequate weapons and aircraft with which to launch an offensive.

Drawing on his corncob, MacArthur told the navy skipper less than half his age, "When you get to Washington, I want you to stress to the president and to the secretary of war the crucial need to retake the Philippines at the earliest possible time." The supreme commander cautioned Bulkeley to put nothing on paper, not even to make notes of their discussion.

For nearly an hour, MacArthur briefed Bulkeley on precisely what to say. No punches would be pulled. The young Sea Wolf was instructed to explain to the Washington bigwigs how stunned MacArthur and all fighting men had been on learning that the Philippines was being sacrificed on the altar of global strategy. Knowing the aggressive Bulkeley as he did, the general grinned and said, "And Johnny, don't add or subtract anything!"

MacArthur had another vital message he wanted delivered to Roosevelt:

> I want a hundred or more motor torpedo boats here . . . two hundred boats, if possible, within eight months. . . . With enough of this type of craft, hostile Japanese shipping could be kept from invading an island or a continent [Australia].[7]

Allied military disasters continued to pile up in the Pacific. On May 6, white flags flew from every staff still standing on embattled Corregidor. The Japanese shuttled the 11,000-man American force on The Rock to Bataan. In Melbourne, Douglas MacArthur, straining to conceal his inner torment, told reporters: "Corregidor needs no comment from me. It has sounded its own story at the mouth of its guns. It has scrolled its own epitaph on enemy tablets. But through the bloody haze of its last reverberating shot, I shall always seem to see a vision of grim, gaunt, ghastly men, still unafraid." [8]

At the same time that a solemn yet defiant Douglas MacArthur was reciting that eulogy in Melbourne, far away over the vast expanses of the Pacific a flying boat was winging toward San Francisco. Among its passengers were Lieutenant Bulkeley and his three skippers—Kelly, Akers, and Cox. None had a clue that a national acclamation was awaiting them; they considered themselves to be just average junior navy officers looking forward to going home.

When the big aircraft splashed down off San Francisco, Bulkeley and Kelly went ashore and immediately dashed to a nearby hamburger joint, where they gorged themselves with a total of perhaps a dozen hamburgers and six milkshakes. In the midst of devouring his third or fourth burger, Bulkeley told his companion, "Sure beats the hell out of boiled tomcat."

That same afternoon, Alice Bulkeley answered the telephone at her apartment in Long Island City. The caller identified himself as a navy officer in Washington, and he had a message that caused the new mother's heart to thump with joy: her husband and two other MacArthur Pirates would land at New York's LaGuardia Field at 9:00 A.M. the next day, May 8.

It would be a bittersweet homecoming for John Bulkeley and his three comrades. Their joy over anticipated reunions with loved ones was tempered by the specter of the debacle in the Pacific. By spring 1942, Japan's mighty war machine had conducted a blitzkrieg that dwarfed

Adolf Hitler's vaunted conquests in Europe. Under Gen. Hideki Tojo, the military mastermind in Tokyo, the Japanese had conquered the Philippines, Singapore, Hong Kong, Dutch East Indies, Malaya, Borneo, the Bismarck Islands, Siam, Sumatra, the Gilberts, the Celebes, Timor, Wake Island, Guam, most of the Solomon Islands, and northern New Guinea.

Emperor Hirohito, whom most Japanese revered as a god, now reigned over one-seventh of the globe. His empire radiated for 5,000 miles in several directions.

Banzai!

11

A Tumultuous Homecoming

Early on the morning of May 8, 1942, Alice Bulkeley drove to LaGuardia with her father-in-law, Frederick. She had hoped to have a private reunion with her husband, but on approaching the airport, Alice's hopes were dashed: awaiting the arrival of the PT-boat skippers was a throng of many hundreds, including a reinforced platoon of reporters, photographers, and camera teams from Paramount and Movietone News.

ALICE BULKELEY:
My mind was in a turmoil. Naturally I was extremely happy to be able to welcome my husband home, and thankful that he was alive and in one piece. But the thought of him meeting his one-month-old son for the first time kept preying on my mind, knowing the tragic misfortune of his birth with cerebral palsy and other physical defects.

I had kept this from my husband. John was always a very sensitive, proud and private person, and he wanted a son to follow in his footsteps in the Navy. How would he take the news? Here he was, loved and admired by the whole nation as our first World War II hero. Why did this have to happen now, to take all the joy out of our lives at this moment?

I wondered if my husband could take this added blow. He had been through disaster. It was not fair. I felt I had failed him.[1]

At 10:22 A.M. a United Airlines plane rolled to a stop, and the Wild Man of the Philippines, Bob Kelly, and Tony Akers alighted. (George Cox had gone directly to his home.) An enormous roar from the crowd echoed across LaGuardia and into adjacent locales. Bulkeley, smiling and immaculately tailored and groomed, showed no sign of the ordeal he had endured in the Pacific. Eagerly seeking out Alice in the multitude that clawed and pulled at him, Bulkeley displayed great patience as jostling photographers delayed him from reaching her side.[2]

While cameras clicked furiously, the lieutenant watched Alice fondly, then the two hugged as Frederick Bulkeley stood to one side, awaiting a turn to grasp his famous son's hand. Alice noticed that her husband looked thin—he had lost thirty pounds since Pearl Harbor.

> ALICE BULKELEY:
> The newsmen were all around, snapping pictures. No privacy whatsoever. John is not a demonstrative man in public, and newspapers later reported that he was shy. They were calling for a picture of us embracing, so I took this opportunity to whisper in John's ear that all was not well with his new son.
>
> He took the news without change of expression, and outwardly remained in this happy, jubilant mood for the world to see. John's mother and I had kept the tragic news of our son's birth from the media, so they knew nothing about it.
>
> It was a wonderful homecoming, but a sad one too.

Lieutenant Bulkeley was almost literally dragooned (as he later would describe it) before the newsreel cameras and bombarded with questions. His keen competitive spirit was still intact. Praising the Japanese as "tough, courageous fighters," Bulkeley added, "but one of our boys can lick five of them."

Speaking with the candor that would become his trademark, the Sea Wolf said that "weapons and supplies are badly needed over there," but that once these items arrive, "we'll steamroller the Japs!"[3]

A squad of hard-pressed New York policemen escorted the three Bulkeleys through the milling throng to their private automobile. On the drive home, the navy skipper remarked that he was looking forward to "a few days of peace and quiet." Tranquility would have to wait. When the Bulkeleys arrived at their apartment, several hundred people had gathered in the street, and their cheers rocked the neighborhood when the Sea Wolf alighted. Scores of frantic hands nearly ripped off the smiling Bulkeley's uniform.

In the next forty-eight hours, the skipper was flooded with requests for public appearances, but he accepted only those directly related to

Everybody Wants to See War Hero No. 1; Bulkeley Begs 'Quiet Leave' With Family

It was the month-old namesake he hadn't seen until his triumphant arrival home—and not the sneaky Japs—that was the greatest interest today in the life of Lieutenant John D. Bulkeley Sr., fearless Thomson Hill torpedo boat commander.

Bulkeley, showered with requests for public appearances in his honor, romped on the floor of the Bulkeley apartment with 19-months-old Joan Isabelle Bulkeley, his overjoyed daughter. He beamed proudly over the son he thought he might never see.

John Duncan Bulkeley Jr., born April 3 in Brooklyn Naval Hospital while his daddy was making things miserable for the Nipponese, cooed.

The lieutenant ,arriving home yesterday by plane from General Douglas MacArthur's headquarters in Australia, vowed then at LaGuardia Field that he was going to spend his leave "quietly with Mrs. Alice Bulkeley and their children.

Much in Demand

But the naval lieutenant was finding this more difficult than his celebrated dash into warship-infested Subic Bay.

Requests to appear at meetings in his honor were pouring in at a terrific clip. In response to most of them, Hero Bulkeley begged off, pointing to little time he will have to spend with his family.

He tentatively accepted, however, an invitation of Borough President Burke to appear today at Borough Hall in Kew Gardens for a reception and a dinner later with the borough president and his wife. He will also speak at the Thomson Hill Mother's Day rally tomorrow.

The Bulkeleys live at 45-42 41st street, where Mrs. Bulkeley and the lieutenant's mother, Mrs. Fred S. Bulkeley, had been waiting anxiously prior to Thursday for some word that their fighting hero might soon return.

Flowers from Neighbors

That was the day he landed by plane in San Francisco from Melbourne with three fellow-officers from the far-off war zone. Bulkeley first went to Washington.

He and two of his buddies arrived at LaGuardia Field at 10:22 A. M.

(Continued on Page Three)

"He's grand. He gets a Navy 'E' for excellence." That's what Lieutenant John D. Bulkeley of Thomson Hill, hero of the torpedo boat attack on the Jap fleet in the Pacific, exclaimed when he saw his son for the first time. Lieutenant Bulkeley is shown outside his home with his wife, Alice, and John D. Bulkeley Jr., born April 3.

First to greet Lieutenant Bulkeley as he stepped from an airliner at LaGuardia Field were his wife, Alice, and father, Fred S. Bulkeley, above. Then came the press and the cheers of the crowd and the Navy's scourge of the Japs in the Philippines became the nation's hero.

HOME TOWN LIONIZES BULKELEY

(Continued from Page One)

yesterday. He was greeted by his wife and father and a roaring crowd of admirers.

At 11 o'clock he was whisked out of the reach of clamoring photographers and reporters and taken to his home, where a large committee of neighbors gave him a rousing reception in the street.

When the party was finally able to break through and reach the apartment, Bulkeley found a huge bouquet on the living room table.

A tag bore the words: "From your neighbors."

Sees Son First Time

Of more interest to the returning hero, however, was John D. Jr.

"He's grand!" he exclaimed as the elder Mrs. Bulkeley brought the infant from the nursery. Bulkeley took him in his arms as little Joan stood shyly nearby.

Bulkeley shooed reporters, whom he told earlier of his views on the war with the Japs.

"If we'd have had 200 more torpedo boats we could have swept the Japs from the seas," he said, "remarking on the shortage of men and supplies in the Philippines.

He told of his exploits—in which he escorted MacArthur from the Philippines and sank a Jap cruiser, two transports and four other craft—before asking politely to be left alone with his family.

—*New York Journal-American*

the war effort. At Bayonne, New Jersey, Alice christened a new PT boat, and John gave a rock-'em, sock-'em talk to the thousand-plus shipyard employees. Waving his fist for emphasis, Bulkeley stressed that "construction of these boats will have to be stepped up if we are going to whip the Japs and Nazis. Our PT crews are ready to fight to the last man, but you must build these boats faster, faster, ever faster!"

Now the crowd had reached a high pitch of excitement, and when Bulkeley bellowed over the loudspeaker, "Are you going to let 'em lick us?" a thousand voices screamed, "No! No! No!" [4]

Two days after reaching home, Lieutenant Bulkeley was honored by a parade in the New York borough of Queens. The skipper, whom a Long Island daily had labeled, "The First Father of Queens," and Alice rode in a closed car at the head of 3,000 marchers, scores of floats, and a string of vehicles carrying celebrities.

Before the parade began, there had been a hitch to the proceedings. FBI agents, charged with Bulkeley's security, had refused to allow the couple to ride in a convertible with the top down, so parade officials had to rapidly dig up a closed car.

Despite a sudden drenching rain, 2,000 persons stood outside the Queens Borough Hall to cheer the man who the *New York Journal American* would report "made the little PT boat the terror of the Jap fleet." Borough President James A. Burke presented Bulkeley with a scroll of honor in recognition of his deeds in the Pacific.[5]

Large as it was, the Queens celebration was dwarfed on May 13 when New York City gave one of its traditional rousing welcomes to John Bulkeley and his comrades, Bob Kelly and Tony Akers. With ticker tape, confetti, and shredded telephone books streaming down from windows in towering office buildings, John and Alice Bulkeley rode up Seventh Avenue in a convertible, trailed by Kelly and Akers in other open cars.

An estimated 250,000 cheering men and women, ten rows deep, lined both sides of Seventh Avenue, and tens of thousands more leaned out of building windows to watch and applaud. Army, navy, and marine units; a score of military bands; and 1,000 members of the Women's Voluntary Service and the Red Cross marched along the fourteen-block route. A huge white sign held high read: "All New York Welcomes John D. Bulkeley." [6]

From 31st Street, where the parade formed, to 35th Street, comparative order was maintained despite the huge crowds. From that point on to

41st Street there was wild disorder. The police apparently had underestimated the enormous outpouring of workers from the buildings in the garment district, and frenzied throngs battled their way out into Seventh Avenue, threatening to engulf Lieutenant and Alice Bulkeley. Only the efforts of the six mounted New York policemen who surrounded the convertible kept the crowd from climbing on running boards and reaching the Bulkeleys.[7]

Forced to bore their way through the sea of humanity, the lead automobiles reached the reviewing stand at Duffy Square, near 41st Street, where 25,000 persons had congregated. Bulkeley was again nearly mobbed when he, Alice, Kelly, and Akers climbed from their cars and joined Mayor Fiorello La Guardia on the reviewing stand.

At the conclusion of the parade, a semblance of order had returned, and over a loudspeaker Mayor La Guardia introduced the three navy officers individually. The din was earsplitting. "Haven't seen anything like it since the Lone Eagle [Charles A. Lindbergh] was given the same treatment in 1927," a veteran New York policeman declared.

Since his return from Australia, Bulkeley had been concerned with the widespread complacency he had found among Americans, who didn't seem to grasp the nature of the brutal war into which the nation had been plunged. "Think of those men on Bataan," he told the mass of people. "How badly they needed your help!"[8]

Riding at her husband's side in the parade, Alice Bulkeley's beaming face concealed an agonizing burden that she carried. Her father, Capt. Cecil Wood, was interned at Shanghai by the Japanese, and her mother, Emily, sisters Leilah and Edith, and Edith's husband, Arthur Hanson, and their two children all were interned in Hong Kong. Alice's brother, Eric, a civil engineer and a corporal in the Hong Kong volunteers, fought with the British at Hong Kong and was captured and sent to a prison camp at Osaka, Japan. Alice had not heard a word from them or knew of their whereabouts—or even if they were alive.[9]

Four days later, May 17, was another blockbuster event for Lieutenant Bulkeley, Bob Kelly, and Tony Akers. Some 1,250,000 men, women, and children (by police estimate) stood shoulder to shoulder in New York's Central Park Mall, overflowing into the Meadow, into Fifth Avenue, and into Central Park West and far down the side streets. Public officials said it was the greatest crowd ever assembled in one place in the nation's history.[10]

This Clipping From
NEW YORK, N.Y.
TIMES

MAY 15 1942

BROADWAY HAILS PT-BOAT HERO

(*Story on Page 5*)

(Mirror Photo)

Waving to the New York throng which turned out to pay homage yesterday, Lt. John Bulkeley rides up Broadway with his proudly smiling wife. Two torpedo boat co-heroes, Lt. Robert Kelly and Ensign Anthony Akers, were also in parade.

The Army and Navy Emergency Relief parade for Lieutenant John D. Bulkeley headed north on Sevent Avenue on the way to Times Square.

The sea of humanity had come from far and near to observe I Am an American Day. Along with the three PT-boat skippers, the speakers' platform was loaded with celebrities—heavyweight champion Joe Louis; composer Irving Berlin; Supreme Court Justice Hugo Black; operatic stars Lily Pons, Marion Anderson, and James Melton; orchestra leaders Fred Waring and Andre Kostelanetz; and a host of Hollywood stars and other notables.

As each celebrity was introduced, the crowd applauded vigorously. But a thunderous roar went up for John Bulkeley. For nearly five minutes, rousing cheers rocked mid-Manhattan.[11]

When the uproar subsided, Lieutenant Bulkeley spoke briefly: "Our fighting men need to know that the people at home are behind them. This gathering today is stirring proof that your pride in being an American places you very much behind our servicemen. On the next I Am an American Day, I hope our flag waves over a world of peace and freedom."

Paul Muni, one of the great names of stage and screen, recited an anonymous poem dedicated to the dead of Bataan, which read in part: "They are what the war is about / Do not ask them why they died / They wouldn't know how to tell you, were they alive / They were just plain fighting men—who died for you."

In dealings with reporters—they trailed him everywhere—Bulkeley needed the patience of Job and the wisdom of Solomon. One night in the Stork Club, a reporter asked the navy officer if he thought that Berlin or Tokyo should be bombed first. "Berlin!" Bulkeley fired back. "Why is that, Lieutenant?" The skipper replied, "Business before pleasure!"

Lieutenant Bulkeley was given the full, five-star celebrity treatment in the widely read New York newspaper gossip columns—those penned by Ed Sullivan, Walter Winchell, Leonard Lyons, and Louis Sobel. Writing in the *New York Journal American,* Sobel disclosed that Bulkeley had a notorious addiction—ice cream. The skipper was at the posh 21 Club, as guest of Hollywood stars James Cagney and Robert Montgomery, and finished off four heaping portions of chocolate ice cream, Sobel breathlessly informed his readers. And then, as Cagney and Montgomery grinned, Bulkeley sheepishly canceled a fifth order.[12]

Lieutenant Bulkeley was fond of Chinese cuisine. While enjoying a leisurely meal at a popular restaurant, Ruby Foo's, he was approached by a "ten percenter," as the Broadway stage crowd called a theatrical agent who earned a ten-percent commission. Would Bulkeley be interested in making stage appearances? Big money in it, the agent assured his target.

Bulkeley smiled but made no reply. "I could easily get you two weeks at Loew's State," the ten percenter insisted. "No, thanks," the skipper replied. "The only theater I'd be interested in playing is Loew's Tokyo!" [13]

Since a month after Pearl Harbor, Dave Elman, a popular WABC-radio personality in New York, had been conducting a victory auction at 9:00 A.M. each weekday. Elman solicited items to be auctioned over the air, and a winning bidder paid by buying war bonds in the amount bid. At the request of Elman, John Bulkeley contributed his PT-boat tie clasp and his collar rank insignia. The bidding was hectic, and the two items were bought by Arthur J. White, a New York restaurant owner, for the equivalent of $16,000 in war bonds, a hefty sum at the time.

On the morning of May 19, wiry Manuel Quezon, the Philippine Commonwealth president in exile, was holding forth before the Washington press corps at the resident commissioner's quarters on Massachusetts Avenue. Fifty or more journalists were present—columnists, straight reporters, newsroom prima donnas, photographers—for Quezon's first press conference since reaching the United States.

Punctuating his remarks with the gesticulations and fractured English oratory for which he was noted, President Quezon explained how he had escaped by submarine from Corregidor—"where I had expected to leave my bones"—to a number of Philippine islands and finally to Negros.

"I am all ready to leave Negros [for Australia] when here comes a message from General Wainwright for me to cancel my trip and remain right there," said Quezon, eyes gleaming and arms waving. " 'The sea around you is filled with Japanese destroyers,' it says. It was stormy night. Suddenly my aide, Colonel Soriano, appears out of darkness and introduces me to man who looks like a fierce Spanish pirate, a sea wolf, with a formidable black beard and a cloth tied around his head like turban." [14]

Seated in a chair behind a handsome desk, Manuel Quezon, a master showman, looked around to satisfy himself that he was generating the proper amount of curiosity over the identity of the black-bearded mystery pirate. Sensing that his audience was responding, the Filipino disclosed the "pirate's" name in a conspiratorial tone: Lt. John Bulkeley.

After a suitable pause for effect, Quezon continued: " 'I most certainly urge you, sir, to take my boat to Mindanao,' the pirate told to myself. 'By gosh,' I said to self, 'this is the right man!' So I ignored General Wainwright's order and got into the [PT] boat."

Now the commonwealth president was in high gear. "A month later," he continued, "a young naval officer was presented to me in Australia. It was Lieutenant Bulkeley. Only this time he had no beard. He was no pirate. In fact he looked like a young boy. 'Goddamn,' I told him, 'if I had seen your face I would not have gone with you!' "[15]

The journalists broke out in gales of laughter.

12

Lecturing President Roosevelt

In early August 1942, wartime Washington was hot, sticky, and seething with office seekers and entrepreneurs. Every huckster with a tool kit or a machine shop was trying to land a government contract. The capital's society lionesses were euphoric over the touch of excitement the wartime atmosphere lent to their parties. Hotel rooms were at a premium, apartments out of the question.

Late in the morning of August 4, recently promoted Lt. Comdr. John Bulkeley walked alone to the gate at 1600 Pennsylvania Avenue and told the guard that he had an appointment with President Roosevelt. When the guard asked to see his invitation, Bulkeley said he had not brought the papers with him.

The security man was suspicious. It was not likely that the president of the United States would be conferring with a navy officer of modest rank. A flurry of phone calls from the guard booth to inside the White House resulted in word for the visitor to be admitted. Two officials came outside to escort the Sea Wolf into the Oval Office.

ADMIRAL BULKELEY:

Just outside the president's office door were several Nervous Nellies, Mr. Roosevelt's assistants. They hemmed and hawed, but I grabbed the gist of what they were telling me—I was not to upset the president by telling him the unvarnished truth about America's disaster in the Philippines.

When I entered the Oval Office, Mr. Roosevelt was seated behind his big desk. He had been crippled by polio at age thirty-nine, I knew, and had to wear a heavy metal cast on each leg. The president flashed that famous big smile at me as though he didn't have a worry in the world. "Hello, Commander Bulkeley," he said in real friendly fashion.

I moved over beside him, leaned down and he placed the Medal of Honor around my neck. It was for my actions during the Philippines, not for the evacuation of General MacArthur, as many people have thought over the years. When he was putting on the medal, Mr. Roosevelt whispered into my ear, "Come back tonight for a chat, Commander."

At the time I thought it was sort of strange, the commander-in-chief of the armed forces having to whisper orders to me. But after I had left the White House, it struck me that some of his assistants had been trying to protect the president, that they wanted me to keep mum on the fact that we had taken a licking in the Philippines, that General MacArthur and every man on Corregidor and Bataan had thought big help was on the way.

But I decided to hell with those namby-pamby people around Mr. Roosevelt. We weren't going to win the war by hiding the facts of life from the president of the United States. I have never believed in pussyfooting with facts. General MacArthur had ordered me to tell President Roosevelt the whole damned sordid story, and, by God, that's what I would do.

When Commander Bulkeley walked into the Oval Office that night, a glittering galaxy of high army and navy brass was seated solemnly around the room. Neither the presence of the president of the United States nor the sea of gold braid and silver stars intimidated the thirty-one-year-old Bulkeley. In respectful tones and without even a subtle hint of bitterness or rancor, the Sea Wolf told of the Philippines disaster, how stunned the fighting men had been to learn that no aid was on the way, how shocked General MacArthur had been on reaching Australia and finding that there was no army for him to command.

On behalf of General MacArthur, Bulkeley pleaded for troops, weapons, airplanes, ammunition, and ships to be rushed to Australia in order to launch an offensive to recapture the Philippines. Chapter and verse, he relayed MacArthur's urgent request for two hundred PT boats within eight months. Despite MacArthur's warning to him, Commander Bulkeley could not resist the temptation to throw in some of his own views on how the war in the Pacific should be conducted.

Bulkeley Gets Congressional Medal of Honor

Roosevelt Presents Award for Services 'Believed To Be Without Precedent'

From the Herald Tribune Bureau

WASHINGTON, Aug. 4.—Lieutenant Commander John D. Bulkeley, of New York, the Navy torpedo boat leader whose mosquito fleet sank several Japanese warships in Philippine waters, received today the Congressional Medal of Honor, the nation's highest award for valor, from the hands of President Roosevelt for services "believed to be without precedent."

President Roosevelt read the citation in a brief ceremony in the White House and then placed the beribboned medal around the hero's neck.

"Thank you, sir," Lieutenant Commander Bulkeley said simply.

Rear Admiral Randall Jacobs, chief of the Bureau of Navigation, witnessed the presentation.

The citation, which did not mention the hazardous trip in which Commander Buckeley took General Douglas MacArthur out of the Philippines, read:

"For extraordinary heroism, distinguished service and conspicuous gallantry above and beyond the call of duty, as commander of Motor Torpedo Boat Squadron 3, in Philippine waters during the period, Dec. 7, 1941, to April 10, 1942.

"The remarkable achievement of Lieutenant Buckeley's command in damaging or destroying a notable number of Japanese enemy planes, surface combatant and merchant ships, and in dispersing landing parties and land-based enemy forces during the four months and eight days of operation, without benefit of repairs, overhaul or maintenance facilities for his squadron, is believed to be without precedent in this type of warfare.

"His dynamic forcefulness and daring in offensive action, his brilliantly planned and skillfully executed attacks, supplemented by a unique resourcefulness and ingenuity characterized him as an outstanding leader of men and a gallant and intrepid seaman. These qualities, coupled with a complete disregard for his own personal safety, reflect great credit upon him and the naval service."

As Bulkeley Received Nation's Highest Award for Valor

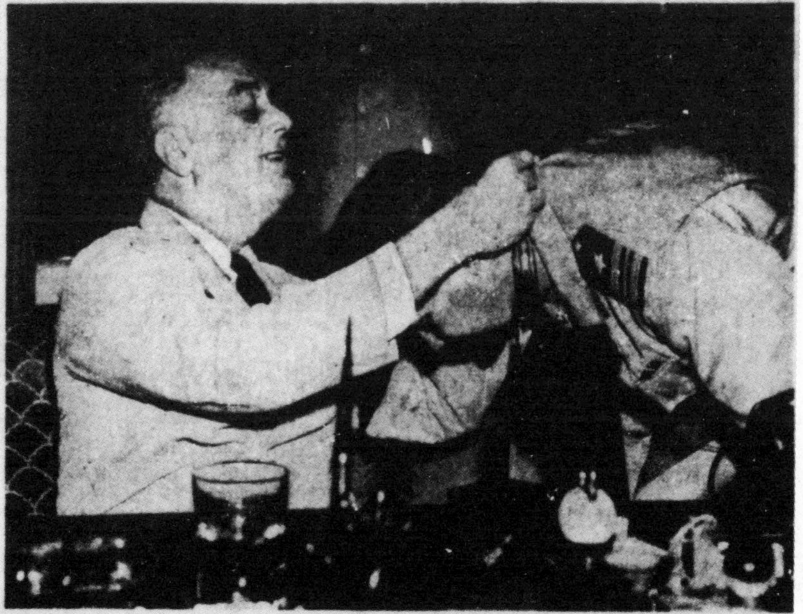

Herald Tribune—Acme

"Thank you, sir," was Lieutenant Commander John D. Bulkeley's brief and modest acknowledgment when President Roosevelt, as shown here, placed the beribboned Congressional Medal of Honor about his neck yesterday for his exploits against Japanese ships, planes and land forces in the Philippines

—*New York Herald Tribune*

When the Sea Wolf concluded what, in essence, had been a lecture to President Roosevelt and his military brain trust, a pin could have been heard dropping on the thick carpet. President Roosevelt said calmly, "Thank you, John." Bulkeley strolled from the Oval Office and past the sober-faced assistants, who were glaring at him.

Now that John Bulkeley had been awarded the Medal of Honor, he became America's most-decorated fighting man. The skipper had already received the Navy Cross, two army Distinguished Service Crosses, the army Silver Star medal, the army Distinguished Unit Badge, and the Philippines Distinguished Conduct Star.

By early August, Commander Bulkeley had been back in the United States for more than three months and was itching to get back into action. "You don't know you're in a war when you're here," he told a reporter for *New York PM*. "There's no sense of immediate danger. That's the thing I miss most. The sense of being on the alert." [1]

The skipper paused briefly and drew on his pipe. "When I came home in May," he told the scribe, "I'd as soon kill a man as look at him. Here the bombs don't fall and the planes don't machine-gun the streets. That's what's happened to me. Now I'm different. There's something in safety that dulls that edge." [2]

Bulkeley's growing anger over a complacent home front edged to the surface. "Look," he told the *PM* reporter. "I'm no soapbox orator. All I know is that there are 60,000 of our boys in Jap hands, those who fought for every minute, every hour, every day in a delaying action to buy time. Here not many people seem to give a damn. There are thousands of dead men [in the Philippines]. They fought for time. What are we doing with it? All I know is that we're losing time, losing it here where we can sleep peacefully at night." [3]

At least one publication, the *New Republic,* frowned on the torrent of publicity and adulation being heaped upon John Bulkeley. In an editorial headed, "It's War, Not a Circus," the magazine declared:

> We are fighting all over the western Pacific, and in general, we have been doing far from well there. Lieutenant Commander Bulkeley's place is in the front line. Somebody has sold the navy a Hollywood idea that American morale needs to be whipped up by these circus stunts, by playing up our heroes. . . . What we need to boost our morale is a few thumping good victories.[4]

While the Electric Boat Company in New Jersey and Higgins Industries in Louisiana were working around the clock to build PT boats, John Bulkeley was dashing around America, going wherever the Navy sent him. He was the magnet at countless rallies to sell war bonds, but was not comfortable in the role of pitchman. An Atlanta newspaper headlined a front-page story: "I Feel Like Darned Fool Asking Folks to Buy War Bonds!" [5]

During one of his infrequent breathing spells at his suburban New York apartment, Bulkeley received a telephone call from an anxious young woman who identified herself as the fiancée of one of Squadron 3's skippers, Lt. Hank Brantingham, who had been stranded on Japanese-invaded Cebu Island in mid-May after burning PT 35 to keep it out of enemy hands.

COMDR. HENRY BRANTINGHAM:
Bulkeley told my future wife Elaine that I was on my way to the United States. A month later I escaped from Cebu to Australia and did return home. I asked Bulkeley, "How come you told Elaine I was on the way back to the States when you didn't even know if I was dead or alive or where I was?" His reply: "Oh, I knew you would make it, Hank, boy!"

Along with his war bond huckster duties, Commander Bulkeley was assigned by the Navy to recruit PT-boat skippers at universities. Speedy motor torpedo boats were just so much hardware unless manned by skilled and dedicated officers and crews. A crash program to train these seagoing cavalrymen had been launched at the Motor Torpedo Boat Squadrons Training Center at Melville, Rhode Island.

In his search for new skippers, Bulkeley concentrated on Ivy League universities, because a basic requirement was that the candidate have extensive experience in handling small boats. And most Ivy Leaguers had owned their own boats or had grown up around yacht clubs and raced in someone else's craft.

REAR ADM. JOHN HARLLEE, USN (RET.):
I had been a PT-boat skipper at Pearl Harbor when it was bombed, so I went along with John Bulkeley on some of his college recruiting tours. He gave highly effective talks before the students. He told them, "Only one in ten of you will return from the war if you are selected to be a PT-boat skipper." Then the entire group would rush forward to volunteer.[6]

On September 4, Commander Bulkeley was in Chicago to speak before the 1,024 midshipmen at the navy's officer training center at Northwestern University. The assembly hall was packed with young men eager to hear what he had to say.

RUSSELL E. HAMACHEK:
Naturally, John Bulkeley's fame and his reputation as a hard-nosed fighting man was well known to us midshipmen at Northwestern University. We were deeply moved by his and Squadron 3's actions in the Philippines, so there was a great deal of anticipation among us when we heard of his arrival—complete with Congressional Medal of Honor. None of us was disappointed.

The Sea Wolf gave his customary rip-roaring speech, warning his listeners that "those of you who want to come back after the war and raise families need not apply—PT-boat skippers are not coming back!" He stressed that he was seeking fifty men who "want to get in the scrap without delay . . . who are straining at the leash, who demand action." [7]

At the conclusion of his fire-eating oration, Bulkeley was nearly stampeded. Almost every listener swept forward to sign up. The commander, along with his staff, then settled down to try to pick out fifty of the "fightingest, most eager SOBs in the house." (Many midshipmen were quickly eliminated because they had no small-boat background.)

WILLIAM F. LIEBENOW:
I went into the interview with a fellow midshipman, Clinton "Red" McClain. Both of us were scared to death. We'd heard what a tough officer Bulkeley was, and we held him in awe.

Bulkeley was seated at a desk looking at some papers. Even though all of us were uncovered [not wearing headgear], Red and I tried to salute. That was our first mistake. Bulkeley ignored all this arm-waving. Those were McClain's and my records spread out before him. I can still recall the verbal exchange.

"You both have a few problems," he said. "Can you explain these low marks?"

"We both want to kill Japs, sir," McClain blurted out.

"Yeah, Commander," I chimed in. "We want to get where the action is!"

"But I want to know about these marks," Bulkeley insisted.

"Well, Commander," says Red, pointing to his head, "we may not

Bulkeley Asks 50 ---1,024 Volunteer

CHICAGO, Sept. 4 (INS).—Lieut. Commander John Duncan Bulkeley, of New York City, mosquito boat hero of the Philippines, was in Chicago today on one of his toughest assignments.

He wanted 50 young men of "surpassing courage" to enter the dangerous service in which he distinguished himself, and when he issued his invitation at the Naval Officers School here, he practically was swept off his feet as 1,024 young Ensigns, virtually every one in the battalion, stepped forth and asked for the job.

He then settled down with his staff to interview volunteers, trying by his own judgment to pick the 50 "fightingest," most aggressive, most eager men—which was not easy. His selections will train for torpedo boat commanders at the Navy's new mosquito boat school at Melville, R. I.

PRAISES PT BOATS.

The man whose torpedo boat interspersed its career of sinking Jap warships, with carrying Gen. MacArthur, and then President Quezon to safety from the Phillippines, said he was looking for commissioned officers between 22 and 30 who "want to get into the scrap without delay and who have plenty of guts."

Then he dilated with pride on his deadly little ship, saying:

"The PT boat is a great weapon. The enemy has not yet won a brush with one. Our little half squadron sank one Jap cruiser one plane tender and one loaded transport, badly damaged another cruiser, set a tanker on fire and shot down four planes.

A GREAT GAMBLE.

"It's a great gamble, if you leave the thought of human life out of it—risking a $200,000 PT boat that capable built in a few days for a chance, to sink a $15,000,000 cruiser to sink $15,000,000 cruiser or battleships that couldn't

"The PT boat is so good the Japs haven't been able to touch one in battle, but no weapon is better than its commander and personnel.

"In short, what we want is officers who are straining at the leash, who demand action—we'll give it to them."

Bulkeley said 500 PT boats could give the United States mastery over all the Pacific, and that a sufficient force could stop any kind of land invasion.

New York Journal American

have too much up here, but'' . . . he laid his hand over his heart . . . ''we've got it right here!''

''You're both accepted!'' Bulkeley snapped.[8]

Back at his apartment in New York the following week, John Bulkeley received a telegram that invited him to lunch the next day at the Plaza Hotel. It was signed Joseph P. Kennedy, Sr.

The elder Kennedy, Bulkeley knew, was a self-made multimillionaire who had been highly influential in the Democratic party since strongly supporting Franklin Roosevelt in 1932. Roosevelt had rewarded Kennedy's loyalty by appointing him the first head of the Securities and Exchange Commission and later ambassador to Great Britain.

Joseph Kennedy's oldest son, Joe, Jr., and next eldest, Jack, were both handsome, driving, poised, and gregarious. They had been ticketed by their father to become world-famous political figures—possibly even president of the United States, one or the other.[9]

Daddy Joe may have been a little disappointed over Jack's political potential, for the personable youth had failed to survive even the primaries in an effort to become freshman class president at Harvard.

At the appointed hour—1:00 P.M.—John and Alice Bulkeley arrived at Joe Kennedy's ornate suite at the Plaza.

ADMIRAL BULKELEY:

Joe Kennedy had been fired as ambassador to England by his old friend Roosevelt, and he had a lot of bitter things to say about the president. Kennedy said that his son John Fitzgerald Kennedy was a midshipman at Northwestern, and that he thought Jack had the potential to be the president of the United States. Joe said he wanted Jack to get into PT boats for the publicity and so forth, to get the veterans' vote after the war.

Joe wanted to know if I had the clout to get Jack into PT boats, and I said that I did and would interview his son the next time I was at Northwestern. If I thought Jack could measure up, I would recommend his acceptance, I told Joe.

Mr. Kennedy seemed quite pleased and said he hoped Jack could be sent someplace that wasn't too deadly, as he put it.

That was the longest lunch I ever had—the conversation continued until eight o'clock that night.

Twenty-five-year-old Jack Kennedy passed muster with flying colors. In his interview, the handsome young man appeared to be fearless and eager, and he had sailed his own sloop in Cape Cod since he was fifteen years old. These assets would seem to make him an ideal PT-boat skipper.

At about the same time that Ensign Kennedy was reporting to Melville, John Bulkeley received the orders he had been seeking. He was to take command of the new Motor Torpedo Boat Squadron 7 for eventual return to the Southwest Pacific—and revenge against the Japanese.

13

Back to the Pacific

"We're going out to the Pacific to kill Japs, and I can promise you that this boat is not coming back to the States!"

So exclaimed Lt. Comdr. John Bulkeley on a gray morning in early October 1942 as he spoke on the foredeck of PT 131 at the commissioning of his new Squadron 7 at the Brooklyn Navy Yard.

Ensign Joseph R. Ellicott and other boat skippers cast furtive glances at each other. What did Bulkeley mean by this fire-eating promise, that the boat itself would not survive or the boat *and* its personnel would never return home?

Bulkeley had chosen the 131 to be his flagboat because it was the one-hundredth PT boat manufactured by Elco and because his father, Frederick, had hidden a lucky penny someplace in the hull during construction.

Squadron 7 trekked to the Panama Canal under its own power, and there the six PT boats were loaded aboard the Esso tanker *White Plains*. On Christmas Eve, the ship edged out of Balboa harbor and, unescorted, set a course for Brisbane, Australia. She traveled at a painfully slow pace and would require twenty-four days to reach her destination.

About halfway in the crossing, on a clear night, the PT boaters spotted the ghostly silhouette of a blacked-out, good-sized ship slipping past in the opposite direction. John Bulkeley ordered his six crews to man their weapons, which were sitting in cradles on the main deck of the PT boats, then he requested permission from the elderly civilian captain of the *White Plains* for permission to challenge the mystery ship to make known her identity. If the other vessel failed to respond with the proper recognition signal, it was Bulkeley's intention to open fire with all the PT-boat guns that could be brought to bear.

The request made the old skipper nervous, and he denied permission to challenge the mystery ship. Bulkeley was outraged, and for more than an hour he stomped about the deck, chomping furiously on a cigar and loudly damning the "gutless captain" who may have been allowing a Japanese vessel to escape unmolested.

Nearly three weeks after departing the Panama Canal Zone, the *White Plains* sailed into the harbor at Nouméa, New Caledonia, an island some 750 miles east of Australia that the Navy utilized as a major anchorage. Bulkeley went ashore to navy headquarters and promptly got embroiled in a hassle with a two-star admiral who wanted to divert Squadron 7 to the South Pacific theater of operations, commanded by Adm. Chester W. Nimitz in Hawaii.[1]

The Sea Wolf insisted that General MacArthur had specifically requested that Bulkeley's new squadron be sent to his Southwest Pacific theater. As a clincher to his argument, Bulkeley displayed two chamois undershirts that MacArthur had asked Bulkeley to bring with him from the States. These garments would retain the wearer's body warmth when his skin was soaking wet, researchers had confirmed, and one undershirt was to go to MacArthur and the other to his chief of staff, Gen. Dick Sutherland. Apparently having no desire to butt heads with four-star General MacArthur, the two-star admiral gave in: Squadron 7 could continue to Australia.

Actually, John Bulkeley had scrounged thirty of the chamois undershirts in New York, and the remaining twenty-eight went to his men to wear while standing watch.

On arrival at Brisbane in late January 1943, Commander Bulkeley received orders to take his squadron to a PT-boat base at Kana Kopa, at the southeastern tail of New Guinea, the world's second largest island. Shaped like a huge rooster, New Guinea was a land that God had forgotten, a throwback to the Stone Age, a roadless, largely trackless fastness of green mountains, thick jungles, swamps, crocodiles, and cannibals.

In the eight months since John Bulkeley had left Australia for the United States, Douglas MacArthur had been hacking a jungle trail toward the Philippines, skillfully deploying the limited forces that had been sent to him under Washington's Hitler-first policy. From an advanced headquarters at Port Moresby, New Guinea, 300 miles across the Coral

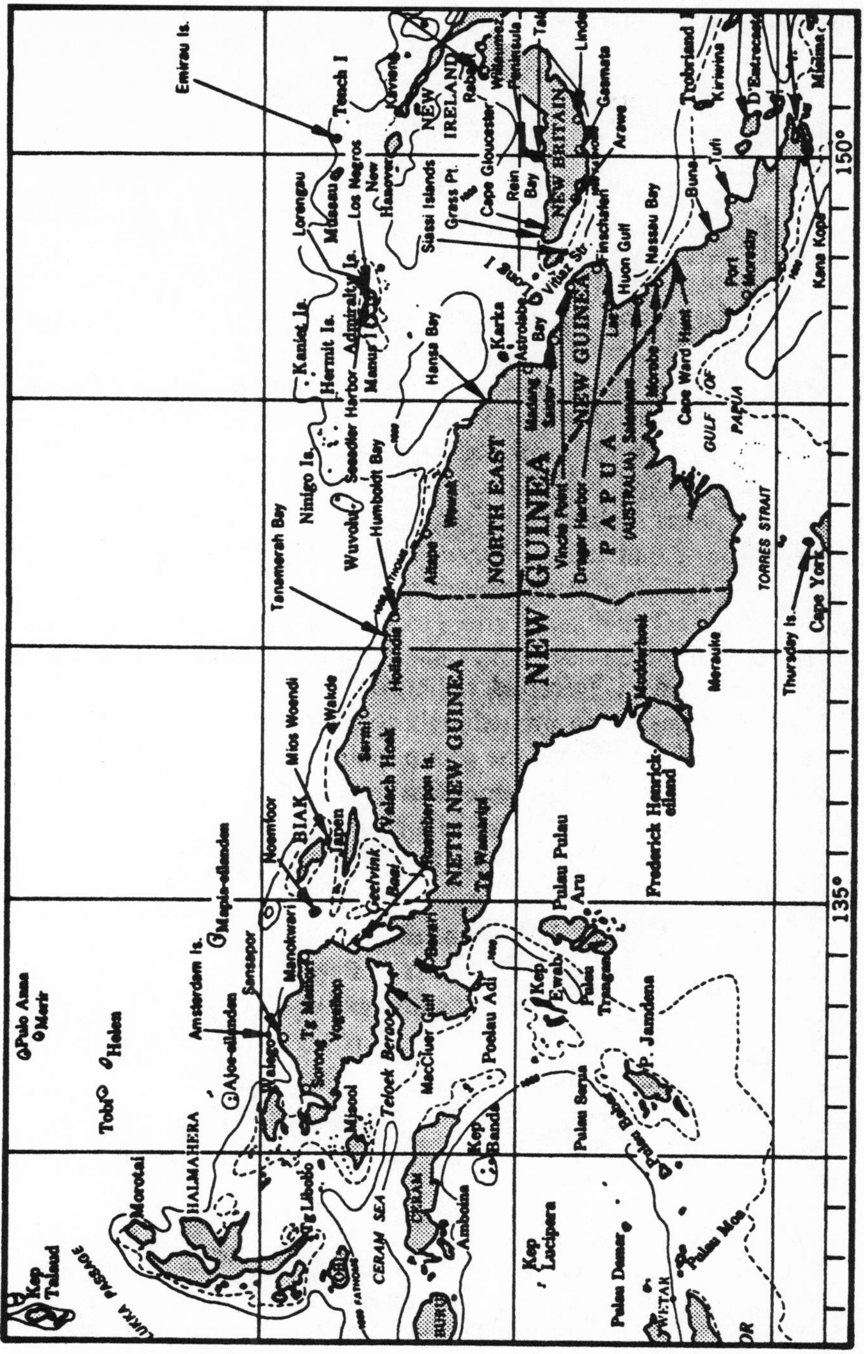
Emirau Is.
Tench I
New Ireland
New Britain
Rabaul
Cape Gloucester
Rein Bay
Gasmata
Arawe
Los Negros
New Hanover
Lorengau
Mussau
Admiralty Is.
Manus I.
Kaniet Is.
Hermit Is.
Seeadler Harbor
Ninigo Is.
Wuvulu
Humboldt Bay
Tanamerah Bay
Hansa Bay
Karkar
Astrolabe Bay
Vitiaz Str.
Siassi Islands
Gasser Pt.
Finschhafen
Huon Gulf
Nassau Bay
Buna
Trobriand Is.
Kiriwina
D'Entrecasteaux
Misima
Port Moresby
Kana Kopa
Cape Ward Hunt
Gulf of Papua
Papua
(Australia)
North East
New Guinea
Neth New Guinea
Hollandia
Wakde
Sarmi
Mios Woendi
Biak
Japen
Noemfoor
Geelvink Baai
Manokwari
Sansapor
Amsterdam Is.
Mapia-eilanden
Ajoe-eilanden
Sorong
Vogelkop
Mc Cluer Golf
Teloek Beraoe
Poelau Adi
Kep Ewab
Pulau Pulau Aru
Pulau Trangan
P. Jamdena
Frederick Hendrik eiland
Merauke
Thursday Is.
Cape York
Torres Strait
Pulau Serua
Kep Banda
Amboina
Ceram
Ceram Sea
Buru
Halmahera
Morotai
Kep Talaud
Pulo Anna
Merir
Helen
Tobi
Mijsool
Kep Lucipara
Pulau Damar
Pulau Moa
Wetar
135°
150°

New Guinea

Sea from northern Australia, MacArthur was leapfrogging along the rugged, 1,500-mile spine of New Guinea.

Once a star baseball player at West Point, MacArthur used diamond terminology to describe his tactics: "I'll hit 'em where they ain't!"

In Tokyo, Gen. Hideki Tojo planned to invade Australia through New Guinea, so he began pouring men and supplies—mainly at night—into his strongholds of Lae and Salamana in an all-out effort to halt the American push up New Guinea's spine.

MacArthur had no intention of getting a bloody nose at these enemy strongholds, but rather bypassed them and left them to "wither on the vine." His PT boats, warplanes, and destroyers were given the task of strangling the Nipponese supply lines.

Late in February 1943, MacArthur learned, through Magic, code name for the supersecret interception and deciphering of Japanese electronic messages, that an armada of eight enemy transports, crammed with 6,912 troops and escorted by eight destroyers, was bound for Lae and Salamana. On March 2, American scout planes spotted the convoy in the Bismarck Sea and approaching New Guinea.

General MacArthur sent every airplane that could fly, American and Australian—207 bombers and 129 fighters—to pound the enemy ships. It was a great slaughter. Seven of the eight transports were sunk, as were seven of the eight destroyers. Many hundreds of Japanese soldiers and sailors were adrift in rubber rafts, in life preservers, and clinging to debris.

Now for the knockout punch. At dusk that day, March 3, a swarm of PT boats, among them ones from John Bulkeley's squadron, rushed to the massacre site in Huron Gulf with orders to mop up anything that might have survived. For the next two days, the PT boats blasted rafts out of the water and machine-gunned Japanese soldiers and sailors. In the Pacific savagery, it was dog eat dog, no holds barred, no quarter asked, none given. These were the ground rules that had been set by the Japanese armed forces many months earlier.

CAPT. STANLEY BARNES:

While I was at the Naval War College shortly after the war, Bill McGovern was a professor of political science on sabbatical from Northwestern University. He spoke Japanese fluently, and had served as a commander in Joint Intelligence during World War II. Once he was ordered to the Western Pacific to see if something could be done to get more intelligence from

Japanese prisoners, the few who might be persuaded to surrender. Hardly any of the Japs ever did. The best place to pick up a few Japs, he was told when he got out in Westpac, was during operations against enemy coastal barges by John Bulkeley's PT-boat squadron.

McGovern went on a patrol with Bulkeley in high hopes of getting at least one live Jap. Sure enough they did shoot up and board a barge loaded with troops. The professor jumped in the resulting carnage and threw himself across a man he thought might survive. Bulkeley came running up, yelled, "The son of a bitch is still alive!" pulled McGovern away, and proceeded to finish off the Jap.

In Tokyo on March 7, General Tojo and his brain trust had been shaken by the Bismarck Sea wipeout. For the first time since the Rising Sun had launched its powerful offensive toward Australia fifteen months earlier, a major disaster had been inflicted on the Japanese juggernaut. Never again would the Imperial Navy risk its transports in New Guinea waters under the menacing shadow of American and Australian air power and the impudent little PT boats with the potent stings. In the future, only coastal barges—low-slung craft 50 to 100 feet long—would attempt to sneak troops and supplies into New Guinea strongholds.

Consequently, almost nightly, the coastal waters of New Guinea were ablaze with gunfire as the Green Dragons (as the Japanese called the PT boats) clashed with the *diahatsu* (barges).

On the night of August 28/29, John Bulkeley was prowling the New Guinea coast in PT 142 (*Flying Shamrock*), skippered by Lt. John L. Carey. Trailing was Ens. Herbert B. Knight's PT 152. Bulkeley was disappointed. It was nearly dawn and there had been no sign of enemy barges. Suddenly lookouts spotted three barges, and the two PT boats charged, blasting away with all machine guns. One barge sank, but bullets ricocheted off the other pair of barges. Ensign Knight's 152 made a wide circle, raced in, and dropped a depth charge next to each barge, but the explosives failed to destroy the targets, which apparently were steel-plated.

Now John Carey's boat rushed forward, let two depth charges drop, and one barge gurgled and went under. The third barge refused to go down.

"Pull up alongside the bastard!" Bulkeley shouted to Carey. When next to the barge, Bulkeley, Lt. Oliver B. Crager, and Lt. Joseph L. Broderick pulled out their .45 Colts and leaped onto the dark Japanese vessel. They spotted the dim outline of a helmeted figure slipping around the wheelhouse, and Bulkeley squeezed off a shot. The figure collapsed in a heap, a bullet hole in the forehead.

Cautiously, the three Americans inspected the barge and found twelve armed Japanese soldiers sprawled grotesquely in death. No doubt the pistol shot and the earlier fireworks had alerted the garrison in nearby Finschafen, so Bulkeley and the others scrambled back onto Carey's boat. A round from the 37mm deck gun sent the barge to the bottom, and the pair of Devil Boats raced for home.[2]

RUSSELL HAMACHEK:
I was a skipper in Squadron 8 under Lt. Comdr. Barry Atkins, and we had been operating from a base at Tufi on Cape Gloucester. In midsummer 1943, my PT 150 was at the rear base for overhaul when we were alerted that John Bulkeley was coming and interest was high. I wondered if he would remember that he had recruited me at Northwestern University's midshipmen's school a year earlier.

Bulkeley came bouncing up the gangway of the PT-boat tender *Hilo,* saluted the colors and was greeted by the ranking officers. He finally worked his way down to us lower ranking officers, and indeed he did recognize me. He put out his meaty hand, smiled broadly and said, "Hello, sucker!"

Since his return to the Pacific, John Bulkeley had been a demon possessed, one imbued with a fierce resolution to wreak vengeance on the Japanese for Bataan and Corregidor. To the Sea Wolf, it was no longer simply fighting, it was a holy war. Consequently, he refused to relax, to take even brief respites from the tension-packed patrols.

L. RUMSEY EWING:
Those of us who were around John Bulkeley on occasion were amazed over how he could bear up under such constant strain—physical and mental. He would go out hunting Japs with one or two PT boats—maybe from eight to twelve hours of incessant tension and often a shootout or two. Then when this patrol returned to base, its exhausted men would hit the sack. Not Bulkeley. He'd leap aboard another boat that was heading out to look for trouble and be gone another ten or twelve hours.

I was skipper of PT 191 and wasn't even in Bulkeley's squadron. But when my boat went on its first patrols in August 1943, Bulkeley came along—three times. Of course, being new to combat, we were all scared to death, and having John Bulkeley along certainly made us breathe easier. Bulkeley was indestructible—or so we thought at the time.

In late summer, Commander Bulkeley found himself confronted by an unyielding foe that he could not overpower—jungle malaria. Thirty pounds had melted from his frame, so in September 1943, he received orders to return to the States for treatment of his debilitating disease. Protests availed him nothing. Going home with him was Penny, a large bitch of widely diversified ancestry.

Several weeks earlier Bulkeley had found Penny (the name he had given her) along the New Guinea shoreline. She had been badly injured, possibly by shell fragments, and had curled up under a bush to die. The skipper took Penny aboard his boat and nursed her back to health. So the big canine became deeply devoted to Bulkeley, and refused to leave his side. She viewed with suspicion any stranger who approached her master—an emotion the stranger would reciprocate.

On reaching San Francisco, Bulkeley made arrangements for Penny to be sheltered, then checked in to Oak Knoll Hospital, across the bay in Oakland. While a patient, the skipper was wracked by frustration as well as malaria: America was fighting around the world, and he was lying in bed.

14

Spy Running for the OSS

In November 1943, John Bulkeley, still weak from malaria, received secret orders to report immediately to Washington for a new assignment. Reaching the capital, he was taken in tow by a navy captain and led to the roof of the main navy building, away from prying ears. The day was bitterly cold, and an icy gale was blasting the two men on the rooftop.

Speaking in a conspiratorial tone, the captain explained that Bulkeley was to form and lead to England a squadron of PT boats for the task of slipping Allied spies, saboteurs, and certain secret items into German-occupied France. His boats would bring out other agents and "mail"—that is, intelligence that had been gathered by spies and the underground in France.

Commander Bulkeley was unaware that his secret mission had resulted from a high-level, behind-the-scenes dispute between the fledgling Office of Strategic Services (OSS) and its counterparts, the various divisions of the British secret service. Steeped in a tradition of centuries of clandestine operations, the English spy masters looked on OSS officers as fresh and innocent inductees from highbrow finishing schools into a business whose principal assets were fraud, deceit, stealth, skulduggery, and periodic mayhem.

There was considerable merit to the British viewpoint. Chief of the OSS London branch, under whom John Bulkeley and his spy runners would operate, was tall, handsome Col. David K. E. Bruce, the multimillionaire son of a United States senator. The forty-four-year-old Bruce had been selected for the key London post by Maj. Gen. William J. "Wild Bill" Donovan, head of OSS and a legendary World War I figure. Although bright and energetic, Bruce was still groping his way through the shadowy world of cloak-and-dagger machinations.[1]

Allies to the world, the American and British spy masters ran competing operations. At the close of 1943, the mighty cross-Channel invasion of Hitler's Fortress Europe (Operation Overlord) was being mounted in the British Isles. Wild Bill Donovan fretted over his inability to get arms and agents to the French underground at a time when the British were launching ten sea and air sorties to France for every one mission launched by the OSS.[2]

This disproportion had become so great that General Charles de Gaulle, leader of the Free French in London, was reported to believe that the cross-Channel espionage sorties were entirely British. To remedy this situation, General Donovan had gone to Adm. Ernest King, the U.S. chief of naval operations, with an urgent plea for PT boats to smuggle agents into France for the OSS.[3]

Fired up by the prospect of perilous action, John Bulkeley began recruiting volunteers for what he told them would be "suicide missions." Despite that chilling description, ranks were rapidly filled, mainly by battle-tested PT-boat veterans who had been rotated home from the Pacific. His new Squadron 2 was commissioned at Fyfe's Shipyard, Glenwood Landing, Long Island. Unlike the customary twelve boats in a PT squadron, Bulkeley's unit would have but three craft, all of which had been battered by heavy service as training boats at Melville and needed overhauling.[4]

In mid-April, Bulkeley's three spy-running boats were hoisted onto the deck of the tanker *Fisher's Hill* in New York harbor. Forty-eight hours later, the ship joined a large convoy and set sail for Europe. Halfway across the Atlantic, the convoy was pounded by a fierce gale, and the tanker became separated from the convoy.

JOSEPH ELLICOTT:
After serving under Bulkeley in the Pacific, I was now skipper of his PT 72. Prior to the storm, Bulkeley had us loosen the turnbuckles on the mainstays of our PTs, so in the event our tanker was torpedoed by U-boats and settled gradually, it might be possible to float our PTs clear of their deck cradles. Should one or all of the PTs survive a torpedoing, Bulkeley said, we might be able to save our own men and the tanker's

crew—and even attack the submarines. Most persons, if torpedoed, would be thinking of survival, but Bulkeley was thinking of attacking U-boats.

Huge, angry waves threatened the heaving, pitching tanker. Bulkeley and his men, armed with crowbars, had to continually tighten the turnbuckles to keep the PT boats from breaking loose, careening about, and causing the *Fisher's Hill* to sink. Each time a wave thundered over the deck, the working men had to grab a piping or railing to keep from being washed overboard. But the tanker rode out the storm. The PT boaters had suffered cuts, bruises, and intense fatigue, but the only casualty was John Bulkeley's prized scrambled egg–visored commander's cap. It had been swept away by a wave.

During the remainder of the voyage, the main topic of conversation among the men of Squadron 2 was the nature of their secret mission.

JOSEPH ELLICOTT:
Fearless as he was, Bulkeley had a penchant to scare the hell out of his fellow man. One evening in the *Fisher's Hill* wardroom, our brand-new ensign in charge of base force stores [supplies, munitions, and equipment] brought up the subject of our mission. Bulkeley pulled on his pipe, looked sly, and said that he had to keep mum until receiving official orders. However, in discussions in Washington, he said he had been led to believe that the PT boats would be towed from England to their base of operations to save wear on the engines, and that the ensign and his base force and their equipment would be parachuted into the new base.

The young ensign turned a ghostly white.

Even the Pacific veterans' imaginations ran wild. They concluded that their three boats were going on a suicide mission to sink the mammoth German battleship *Tirpitz,* which was holed up in a Norwegian fjord and had defied efforts by the British air force to destroy her by bombings.

On April 24, Squadron 2 reached its main base at Dartmouth, a secluded port on the English Channel. There the PT boats were fitted with special navigational equipment that would give them pinpoint accuracy in locating a beach, even on black nights. Bulkeley then took the squadron to Frenchman's Creek in Cornwall, where officers and men practiced unloading from the PT boats lightweight dories, which were pulled by four cupped oars and constructed with padded sides and muffled oarlocks. All of this was done under a cloak of intense secrecy, for Nazi agents had been planted among the population of southern England, Bulkeley had been told by British intelligence.

Less than a week after the spy-running squadron had reached Dartmouth, Bulkeley was summoned to a headquarters, where a Royal Navy captain gave him orders for a bizarre operation. Bulkeley was to cross the Channel at night in a PT boat and, together with a couple of his men, sneak onto what was code-named Utah Beach and bring back bucketfuls of sand scooped up at precise intervals of fifty yards. At the time, the skipper was not privy to the fact that Utah would be one of the American assault beaches on D day.

ADMIRAL BULKELEY:
That was the most ridiculous order I had ever received during my navy career. A suicide mission if there ever was one, for the Germans knew that the Big Invasion was going to hit soon, and they'd be alert.

I found it astonishing that Allied brass would risk a PT boat and the lives of its crew to bring back some damned French sand. So I contented myself by roundly cursing the harebrained twits who were sending us on this stupid mission.

In the eerie stillness at 2:10 A.M., Bulkeley's PT boat dropped anchor over the Bay of the Seine some 500 yards off the Normandy beach. Slipping noiselessly into a rubber dinghy, the Sea Wolf and two men began rowing. Their faces and hands were smeared with black grease. Reaching the beach, they paused and listened; the only sound was the gentle lapping of the surf.

None of the invaders carried a weapon, for their cover was that they were on a rescue mission searching for downed pilots. But Bulkeley and his men knew that, if captured, they would probably be turned over to the Gestapo, charged with being spies for aiding the French underground, and possibly shot.

ADMIRAL BULKELEY:
I was a hundred yards or so down the beach from where we had left the dinghy, and had just scooped up a final bucket of sand. It was dark as hell. Suddenly a Kraut, wearing a steel helmet and armed with a rifle, leaped in front of me and shined a flashlight beam into my face. He was a stupid bastard—came right up to within three feet of me.

I knew that I would have to dispose of this gentleman properly, or my goose was cooked. So I pitched the sand in the bucket I was holding

> into his face, pounced on him, and threw him over on his back. Then I leaped astride him and began strangling him with my hands. When the Kraut went limp, I ran like a jackrabbit back to the dinghy and, after quickly checking to make certain that the sand samples were aboard, we got the hell out of there—in a hurry.

It would be years before Bulkeley learned the reason for the bizarre mission from which he thought he would never return. Long after the landing beaches had been selected, a scientist who had escaped from France and claimed to have knowledge of the region dropped a blockbuster on invasion planners: the shoreline known as Utah Beach consisted largely of peat, with only a thin covering of sand. If that shocking revelation were true, it would mean that tanks and vehicles would bog down while crossing the beach on D day. The Sea Wolf's sand relieved worried minds.

On the morning of May 19, Lt. Comdr. Ray Guest paid a visit to Squadron 2 at Dartmouth. Prior to the war, he and his brother Winston were widely known as two of the high-goal polo players representing the Meadowbrook Club polo team on the north shore of Long Island, New York. Ray Guest was one of Col. David Bruce's bluebloods who had a zest for action, and he had been serving as liaison between Bulkeley and OSS headquarters in London, where he worked with the British to organize spy-running sorties into France.[5]

Commander Guest brought orders for Squadron 2: it would launch its first mission that very night, landing a spy on the closely guarded coast of Normandy, more than 100 miles across the English Channel.

> EDWARD SLATER:
> The British had a gift for picking landing sites [on the French coast] for us that only madmen would go into. On my first spy run, the point chosen was a small beach, a cliff with long-range guns on it, guards and searchlights—the works. Maybe the Brits figured that the Germans would think no one would be crazy enough to land there.

John Bulkeley chose PT 71, skippered by Lt. William M. Snelling, to make the first cross-Channel run. When anchored off the French rendezvous point, Snelling was to exchange recognition signals with the resistance men hidden on shore. If the Frenchmen had been apprehended and were being forced to give the recognition signal, a predesignated word would be inserted to tip off the PT boaters that they were running into an ambush.

Speed would be crucial. England was on double-daylight time, which, coupled with her high degree of latitude, meant that there would be a mere six to seven hours of darkness for a mission. When not carrying torpedoes, the spy boats were capable of speeds up to forty-five knots, so it was calculated that a cruising speed of thirty to thirty-five knots would permit completing the mission while it was dark. Night was also needed to avoid detection by the Luftwaffe and the *Schnellboote,* speedy, heavily armed craft similar to PT boats and known to the Americans as E-boats.[6]

Just before dusk on the nineteenth, the spy to be carried to France arrived at the Dartmouth dock and slipped below on Lt. Bill Snelling's PT 71. Dressed in the clothing of a French peasant, complete with beret, the agent was from the stable of the Special Operations Executive (SOE), the British clandestine agency that Winston Churchill had created on the outbreak of war with the stirring directive: ''Set Europe ablaze!''

Before handing the spy over to the American PT-boat men, members of The Firm (as SOE men called their organization) gave him a painstaking final search. A forgotten London bus or theater ticket stub, a grocery receipt, a handwritten note could doom him to a Gestapo gallows. Earlier the spy had been given his cover story and forced to repeat it endlessly while shouting members of The Firm, acting as Gestapo agents, browbeat and threatened him.

The ''Joe,'' as the British called secret agents being smuggled into German-held Europe, kept out of sight below. He never made his true name or the nature of his mission known to his American chauffeurs. Without a word, the Joe had handed his orders to Snelling, who noted the rendezvous point on the French coast. Snelling then determined the map coordinates by transferring the information on the spy's orders to a specially designed chart.

At dusk, PT 71 cast off. Due to the painstaking planning of Commander Bulkeley, Ray Guest, and the British Navy, the mission was completed without a hitch. The spy was rowed to shore; a large, canvas bag filled with bits and pieces of intelligence gathered by the French underground was taken aboard; notes were recorded about the obstacles that the Germans had planted by the thousands along the waterline; and the spy runners raced for Dartmouth. Exhausted but elated over the success of the first mission, Bill Snelling and his boys received a conquering hero's welcome from Squadron 2 mates.

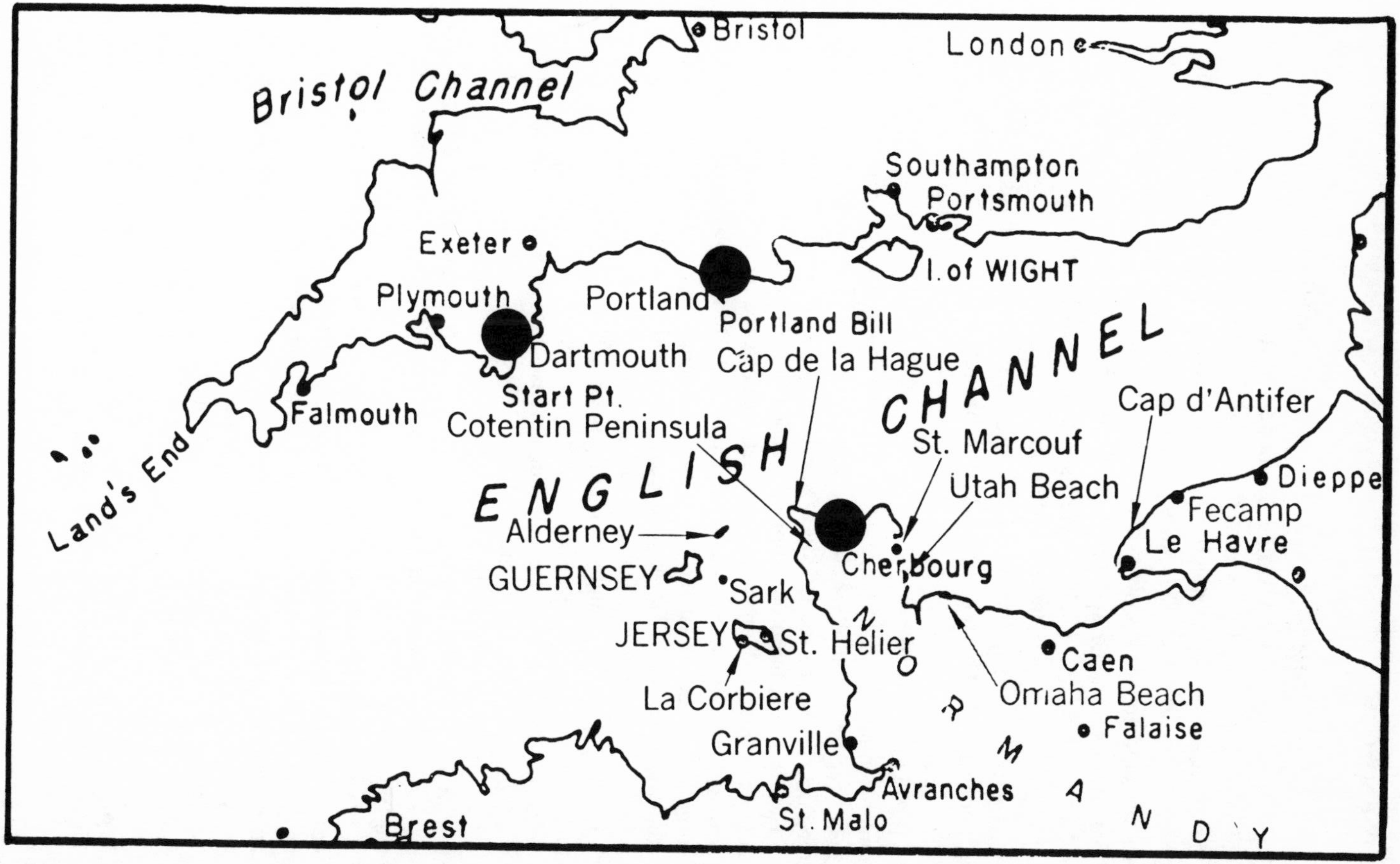

Lt. Comdr. John Bulkeley's spy boats crossed the Channel from their base at Dartmouth. Later, for D day, the main PT-boat base was at Portland. The main German E-boat base was at Cherbourg. (PT Boats, Inc.)

Two nights later, John Bulkeley made his first run to France, and a Royal Navy officer, who knew the coast intimately, went along. The PT boat reached its destination, a small cove, without incident, and anchored just offshore. Suddenly the shadowy contours of four vessels were detected moving slowly across the entrance to the cove—German E-boats. Those on the spy boats held their breaths. After what seemed to be an eternity, the E-boats were swallowed up by the night.

"Blimey," the Englishman called out in a hoarse stage whisper, "what a bloody rotten formation the Huns are keeping these days!" Muffled laughter erupted. The tension had been broken.

WILLIAM LIEBENOW:
One black night, John Bulkeley took a boat to the French coast to deliver two "bodies" (our name for the agents). I was in command of two dinghies and we rowed quietly ashore to drop off the bodies.

Everything in these operations depended on timing. We had a precise number of minutes to row to the beach, deposit the bodies, pick up info or whatever from French underground men, and return to the PTs. Bulkeley himself had laid down the rules: if the dinghies were not back at the specified time, the PTs were to depart promptly for England, leaving the dinghy men behind. There would be no exceptions.

On this night, my dinghy ran into problems. The Channel was rough, the tide against us—and a German with a dog was patrolling the beach. Dogs we dreaded, because they could sense and track us a lot easier than could the German soldiers.

Our dinghy crept in, lying to about fifty yards offshore. It was a nervous few minutes. We all held our breaths until the German and the dog had passed. And we knew that every second lost was delaying our return to the PTs.

We would be four minutes and thirty seconds late in getting back (a crime in such an operation). We knew that would be far too late, that the PTs would have left. We contemplated our options: (1) go ashore and have the underground hide us, (2) row to England—a hundred miles away over choppy waters, or (3) surrender.

We remembered that the British had told us, "If you fall into German hands, you will probably be shot as spies!" We chose Option 2.

But the PTs were still waiting. John Bulkeley had always lived by the book, and violated his own edict for one reason—he would not desert his men. He would never let one of his own down. And all of us knew it.

Allied cloak-and-dagger agencies, mindful of the close call that John Bulkeley had had when he was detected by the German sentry on Utah Beach, now sent the spy-boat skipper a "secret weapon"—several boatswain mates whose military designation was simply "X." These men were crack archers and had worked for the movies in Hollywood, even though their faces had never been seen on the silver screen.

The archers' specialty had been Western movies. When audiences saw a man getting hit in the back with an arrow, the target for these off-camera archers had a steel plate next to his back, then a cover of cork on top of that. The archer let fly, and when he hit his cork target, it would give the illusion that the victim had an arrow sticking out of his back—after which he would fall off his horse.

The idea was for an archer to accompany each spy boat and go ashore in the dory. If a German guard were encountered, the archer would nail him—silently and with no fuss. There would be no rifle shot to spread the alarm that intruders were on the beach.

The "X" boys gave an eye-popping demonstration of their skills for Bulkeley and his men. Without fail, the archers sent arrows through man-sized straw dummies fifty yards away. After that the archers went on occasional spy runs, but were disappointed that they never had the chance to draw a bow against a German.

In late May, John Bulkeley jeeped to London to confer with British naval officers planning the spy missions. He had some free time, and had a few drinks with a good friend, Lt. Comdr. Mark Armistead, a Hollywood executive in peacetime. Armistead was chief of the London branch of Field Photographic, whose function would be to provide moving-picture coverage of Operation Overlord. Meanwhile, the unit had been conducting air reconnaissance of the French shoreline and its German defenses.

Back in 1940, when Europe was a raging battleground and war clouds were drifting toward the United States, famed Hollywood director John "Pappy" Ford, a lieutenant commander in the Naval Reserve, had formed Field Photographic, a sort of ad hoc unit without official status. Ford had signed up some of the biggest names in Hollywood: cameramen, sound men, special effects wizards, editors, and writers. One of his recruits was Mark Armistead.

Pappy Ford formed his talented cinema civilians into a military type of unit, taught them the basics of military discipline, then tried tenaciously to get Washington navy brass to absorb Field Photographic into the official reserves. For more than a year, Ford pleaded his case, but he was given the cold shoulder by the navy hierarchy.

Shortly before Pearl Harbor, lightning struck from an unexpected source. Field Photographic was swept up intact, not by the admirals in Washington but by the dynamic Bill Donovan, who was convinced that Pappy Ford's combat-film unit would be a valuable OSS tool for propaganda purposes and for the gathering of intelligence.

Since January 1944, Mark Armistead and his camera crews had flown countless missions in B-25s to photograph nearly the entire shoreline of northern France. But he was not satisfied with just his miles of film footage, so he picked the brains of anyone who might know the Far Shore. One of the experts Armistead interrogated was John Bulkeley, who had gained a knowledge of the beaches, coves, bays, inlets, and adjacent terrain and defenses while he and his men were sneaking spies into and out of France.

Now, after drinks in the London pub, Commander Armistead decided that his boss, the hard-driving, hard-drinking, and profane film genius Pappy Ford, should meet the famed Pacific war figure. He took Bulkeley to Claridge's, the elegant hotel where the director was staying.

John Bulkeley had long been a movie buff, and he knew that the forty-nine-year-old Ford had been acclaimed with three Academy Awards for directing such blockbusters as *The Grapes of Wrath, Stagecoach, Young Mr. Lincoln,* and *How Green Was My Valley*. Nevertheless, Pappy had turned his back on the glamor and fabulous financial rewards of Hollywood to do his bit for the war effort.

ADMIRAL BULKELEY:

We went up to Pappy Ford's room in Claridge's, and Mark Armistead beat on his door so damned long and hard that I thought he was going to knock it off the hinges. After a few minutes of ham-fisted pounding, a gruff voice inside bellowed, "Well, come on in, goddamn it!"

Pappy was still in bed, and he propped open one eye. No doubt he had a king-sized hangover and was mad as hell over being so rudely disturbed. But when Mark introduced me, Ford leaped out of bed, stood at strict attention, saluted me, and said: "I'm proud to salute the man who rescued General MacArthur!"

I didn't know quite how to react. Pappy had just been promoted to captain and outranked me, and he was standing at attention—stark naked.

Wide awake now, Ford threw on a tattered old robe—he was never fussy about his garments—and began bombarding Bulkeley for details of the MacArthur rescue. Bulkeley deflected the conversation to Hollywood and the superstars—Clark Gable, Lana Turner, Tyrone Power, Gary Cooper, Rita Hayworth. Pappy, a stubborn cuss, kept returning to Bulkeley's feats as the Wild Man of the Philippines.

"The whole thing happened at a time when the country was looking for heroes," Bulkeley said of the early days in the Philippines. "Frankly, I've already had too much publicity. I'm a professional navy man. Nothing more, nothing less." [7]

Pappy grinned widely, delighted with his new friend's candor and modesty. In Ford's mind they were the true marks of Bulkeley's greatness.[8]

15

Tip of the Invasion Spearhead

Late in May 1944, invasion fever saturated the British Isles when the gargantuan Allied operation known as Overlord was activated. All over southern England the dusty roads and the narrow-gauge rail lines groaned under the weight of the mighty army edging southward to the Channel ports. Seaborne assault troops, grim and tight-lipped, marched into assembly areas called sausages because of their oval shapes on high-level military maps.

Almost nightly, E-boats based in Cherbourg and Le Havre had been prowling the English Channel to raid Allied shipping and to watch for indications that the *Grossinvasion* was imminent. The specter of these speedy, heavily armed E-boats, manned by veterans, dashing out from France under cover of darkness and wreaking havoc on the approaching invasion fleet had caused sleepless nights at Supreme Headquarters, Allied Expeditionary Force (SHAEF) in London.

SHAEF had been shaken after a disaster that had taken place shortly after midnight on April 27, with D day only six weeks away. Nine E-boats from Cherbourg had stumbled onto a target—a large convoy of Allied transports and warships, many loaded with troops of the U.S. 4th Infantry Division, bound from Plymouth to Slapton Sands, a wide beach in southern England, for Exercise Tiger, a full-scale dress rehearsal for the Utah Beach assault. Also on board were a number of secret weapons to be sprung on the Nazis on D day, including "swimming tanks," which had been modified with inflated canvas skirts that would allow them to reach shore under their own power.[1]

Eleven miles off Slapton Sands, the E-boats stole in among the Allied ships, then struck with lightning speed. An LST (landing ship tank), loaded with assault troops, was torpedoed and blew up; within moments 151 of the 282 army men and 94 of the 165 sailors on board were killed or drowned. Another LST was hit amidships and exploded. The blast killed 310 of the 354 soldiers and 114 of the 142 navy men. Then there was a third enormous explosion; an LST was blasted out of the black water, killing 12 men and wounding 22.[2]

SHAEF nervousness over the Slapton Sands catastrophe intensified a few days later when evidence was uncovered that the E-boat crews, before racing back to Cherbourg, had fished the bodies of dead American officers—and a few live ones—out of the water. An unknown number of these Americans were ''bigots,'' the code name that SHAEF gave to officers privy to D day secrets, including the location of the landing beaches.

General Eisenhower and his brain trust had given serious consideration to altering the Utah Beach assault, or even changing it to another locale. But such a rash proposal had to be discarded; there simply was not enough time to draw up and implement an entire new operation.

Meanwhile, PT boats and their crews had steadily been arriving in England, and on May 21 Bulkeley was given command of all PT boats for Operation Overlord. He was replaced by Lt. Robert R. Read as skipper of the spy-running squadron. Bulkeley's command was designated Task Group 122.4.4. and was based in the Portland-Dartmouth-Weymouth region of the Channel coast.[3]

ADMIRAL BULKELEY:

The Slapton Sands disaster scared the hell out of the Allied high command, and Admiral [Alan G.] Kirk, commander of U.S. invasion naval forces, went all out to get as many PT boats as possible to counteract the E-boat threat and to guard the minesweepers that would spearhead the assault landings. Kirk directed me to find parking places for them along the Channel—a hell of a job as all harbors and bays were already crammed.

Among other places, I went to Portland Bill [Royal Navy shipyard] and made known my needs to the commanding officer, Captain Farquahrson—a bloody Scotchman. He was busy as hell, of course, and said no way—there was no room. Besides, he had no time for a navy officer from the Colonies two ranks his junior.

Well, I had to put those damned PTs somewhere. So I reminded Farquahrson that my mother's maiden name was MacCuaig, a good Scotch lass, and that she belonged to the same clan as his. And didn't he think he owed it to me and my mother and to clan loyalty to find some parking places for my boats? That did the job. My Scotch pal found us the parking spots.

As June neared, John Bulkeley was invited to a dinner given by a wealthy American who lived on a sprawling estate outside London. No doubt the Sea Wolf's fame had triggered the invitation, for he was the lowest-ranking person—by far—among the guests, who included King George VI and Winston Churchill. The British monarch, a polite, reticent man, had little to say, but the rotund, sixty-nine-year-old Churchill asked Bulkeley, "What is your job, Commander?" Like Franklin Roosevelt, The Prime (as American leaders called him) had always been fascinated by intrigue, and he listened avidly while Bulkeley spun tales of his squadron's spy runs to France.

A week after the London dinner, Churchill and King George, who had traveled to Portland to inspect elements of the invasion fleet, climbed aboard PT 504, Commander Bulkeley's flagboat. Seldom, perhaps, had such a small craft been invaded by so much gold braid: the king in the uniform of a five-star admiral of the fleet, U.S. Rear Admirals Kirk and Arthur D. Struble, and a squad of Royal Navy brass.[4]

As soon as the VIPs were on board, each was approached by the boat's young quartermaster first class, whose task was to record the names and ranks of visitors. Pen and pad at the ready, the sailor passed from one admiral to the other, asking for names. When he reached the king, whom he did not recognize, he asked, "Sir, may I please have your first name?" Without change of expression, the monarch replied, "George." The sailor scrawled "George" on his pad. "And your last name, sir?" The king responded, "Windsor."

Again the hasty scribbling. The youth read out: "Fleet Admiral George Windsor, Royal Navy. Thank you very much, sir."

Churchill, puffing on a long, black cigar, and King George poked into each nook and cranny of the 504 boat, The Prime bombarding Bulkeley with questions about the craft and combat operations. Seated on a bunk in a compartment below, Churchill insisted that the Sea Wolf relate details of his dash through the Japanese blockade of Corregidor to carry out General MacArthur.[5]

Then Churchill and the king and their entourage were taken on a high-speed tour of Portland harbor on another PT boat that darted among the assembled warships, transports, and landing craft. While the torpedo boat was returning to its dock, the chart-room door popped open, and the beaming face of the cook appeared.

"Would yer Majesty like a cuppa jamoke?" he asked. Eyebrows were raised. King George looked puzzled. When the question was explained, the monarch went down the ladder to the wardroom, where he drank two cupfuls and complimented the cook for the "most excellent coffee."

Few complaints would be heard again about the quality of this particular cook's chow. "If it's good enough for the King of England," he would tell the complaining crewmen, "it's sure as hell good enough for youse guys!"[6]

Neptune, the assault phase of Overlord, was unmatched in scope and complexity in the annals of warfare. The printed plan was five inches thick, and even the typed list of American units—1,400 of them—required thirty-one pages. On D day alone the equivalent of 500 trainloads of troops—57,506 American and 75,215 British and Canadian—along with their weapons, vehicles, ammunition, and supplies would be put ashore in Normandy. Thousands of Allied paratroopers and glidermen would jump and land behind the beaches.[7]

There would be landings by five great naval task forces in the Bay of the Seine, which was divided into the American assault area on the west (Utah and Omaha beaches) and the British and Canadian assault area on the east (Gold, Sword, and Juno beaches). Commander John Bulkeley's PT-boat task group would be part of the Western Naval Task Force, led by Admiral Kirk.

Bulkeley was called in by a two-star admiral and given his final invasion orders. All available PT boats were to escort four groups of minesweepers toward Utah Beach in advance of the main fleet. The ugly duckling minesweepers and the PT boats would be the tip of the Utah invasion spearhead, and the chilling wording on John Bulkeley's orders indicated the official view of the perils expected: "You will proceed with the utmost determination regardless of losses."

General Eisenhower, after lengthy deliberations with SHAEF's chief meteorologist, Group Capt. John Stagg of the Royal Air Force, and top commanders had chosen June 5 for D day. The minesweeping flotilla was to be off Utah Beach at midnight on June 4, finish its work by

5:15 A.M., and clear out to make way for the bombardment and assault landings. Bulkeley's principal function was to prevent the fifteen or more E-boats known to be in Cherbourg from interfering with the minesweeping.

After six channels to the beach had been swept, the PT boats were to return to Portland, refuel and rearm, and by 5:00 P.M. on D day be back at the invasion scene. There Bulkeley's boats would form a picket line extending at right angles from north of Utah Beach out into the Bay of the Seine for five and a quarter miles, linking up with the twelve-mile-long Mason line of destroyers and British motor torpedo boats to seal off the entire invasion area. Specifically, the PT task group was charged with intercepting E-boats that might come down from Cherbourg and charge toward the landing beaches and the vulnerable, thin-skinned troop transports lying offshore.

By the morning of June 3, the ports of southern England and those stretching through Wales and all the way up to the Firth of Clyde in Scotland were jammed with vessels of every type, size, and shape.

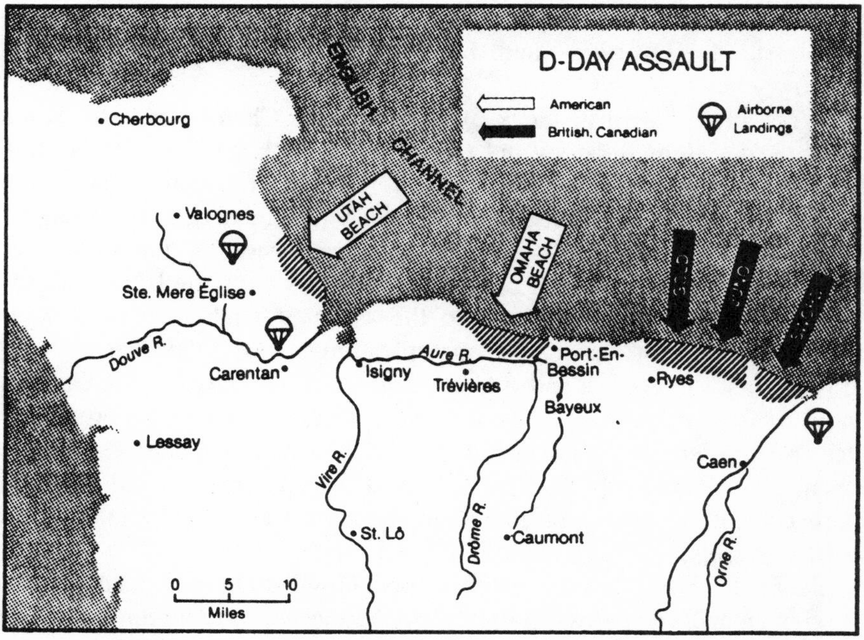

Assault troops, burdened with heavy battle gear, were filing grimly into the suffocating holds of transports. At noon that day, three plodding groups of minesweepers began chugging toward the Far Shore.

Early on the morning of June 4—D day minus one—three of Bulkeley's PT boats, under Lt. Herbert J. Sheretz, rendezvoused with one of the minesweeper groups off the Isle of Wight and proceeded through the choppy Channel toward the Bay of the Seine. In the meantime, Group Capt. John Stagg had alarming news for General Eisenhower and his commanders, who were convening at Southwick House, a mansion overlooking Portsmouth.

Stagg forecast heavy waves and strong winds in the Channel for D day, conditions that could capsize vessels and blow far off course the Allied airborne armada. Reluctantly a glum Eisenhower postponed D day for twenty-four hours, until June 6. But Commander Bulkeley at Portland received belated notice of the postponement, and frantic efforts to radio Sheretz's three PT boats were unsuccessful. When the little flotilla, whose detection would have tipped off the Germans that the invasion was at hand, was halfway to France, Providence intervened. A patrolling British destroyer spotted Sheretz's boats and the minesweepers and turned them back to Portland.

Disaster for Overlord—and the PT boats–minesweeper flotilla—had narrowly been averted.

When night pulled its cloak over the English Channel on June 5, the eve of D day, John Bulkeley and a swarm of his PT boats were shepherding a flock of nearly 100 minesweepers toward Utah Beach. This flotilla was the vanguard of Neptune. The slow, ugly duckling minesweepers, the unsung heroes of many earlier American invasions around the globe, had to sweep channels clear of mines all the way from the Isle of Wight, off southern England, right up to the sands of Utah Beach. (Similar operations were taking place at the other four invasion beaches.)

Thousands of contact and antenna mines had been sewn by the German navy in recent weeks along the central English Channel. Fortunately for the invaders, these mines had been rigged with "flooders" to cause them to sink by early June, when the Germans felt that the invasion threat would be over. But countless stragglers were waiting to blow up Allied vessels.[8]

As his PT boats and the minesweepers crawled closer to Utah Beach, Commander Bulkeley was puzzled by the fact that the fifteen to twenty E-boats known to be in Cherbourg had not charged out to challenge the minesweepers. And like everyone else, he was astonished that the powerful lighthouse beam at Pointe Barfleuer was burning brightly. Bulkeley was amazed that the Germans had shown no awareness of what was unfolding offshore.

Gunners on the PT boats joined in the minesweeping by using deck guns to blow up eight floating mines. Lt. Comdr. Mark Armistead was with Bulkeley and noticed that he had a camera strapped around his neck. Each time a mine was exploded in the blackness, the Sea Wolf snapped a picture of the brilliant orange flash.[9]

All night long Bulkeley's PT boats crept up and down the nine-mile length of Utah Beach while the minesweepers did their work. Not as many mines were exploded as had been expected, because most of them were the delayed-action type, which came to life only after several sweeps. These mines would keep popping off for many days, resulting in more American casualties than from all other causes.

Curiously, shore batteries had not opened fire on the PT boats and minesweepers, sitting ducks perched virtually under the Germans' noses.

Meanwhile at Cherbourg, some twenty-five miles northwest of Utah Beach as the crow flies, Rear Adm. Walther Hennecke, commander of German naval forces in Normandy, on this night had failed to send his E-boats prowling the English Channel. He concluded that the weather was too foul for the Allies to launch the *Grossinvasion,* a view shared by German leaders all the way up the totem pole of command. But at 3:09 A.M. radar picked up unidentified blips in the Bay of the Seine, and Admiral Hennecke sent fifteen E-boats dashing out of Cherbourg to investigate.

By now, the Bay of the Seine was crawling with hundreds of Allied vessels, but at dawn the E-boat flotilla returned to Cherbourg and its *Kapitaen* reported that he had seen nothing unusual and had to give up his search because the weather was so bad.[10]

At Le Havre on the invasion's east flank, lanky Lt. Comdr. Heinrich Hoffmann, a legendary figure in the Third Reich due to previous E-boat exploits, had been alerted that something was going on in the Bay of the Seine. The thirty-four-year-old leader of the 5th Flotilla quickly rounded up three E-boats and raced out of Le Havre and into the menacing blackness of the bay. Sixty minutes later Hoffmann was jolted by the shock of his life: he had come face to face with what surely must have been the entire Allied fleet.

Moments later shells began exploding around the three E-boats, but

Hoffmann gave the order to attack. The Schnellboote charged the armada, loosed several torpedoes, and one fish slammed into the boiler room of the destroyer *Svenner*. There was an enormous explosion. The *Svenner* seemed to lift out of the water, then broke in two as though she were a matchstick. There were thirty dead, wounded, and injured.

Commander Hoffmann sped back to Le Havre and raised the alarm.[11]

Some ninety miles west of Le Havre, U.S. Lt. Comdr. George E. Hoffman, thirty-three-year-old skipper of the destroyer *Corry,* was moving into position to fire on Utah Beach. Hoffman had waited a lifetime for this moment, having ''fleeted up'' on the *Corry* from lieutenant to skipper in less than three years. He was enormously proud of his ship and his men.

Suddenly, at 5:04 A.M. the Germans broke their silence at Utah Beach, and shore batteries began pounding the sitting-duck minesweepers and the *Corry*. Skipper Hoffman's gunners fired back as the *Corry* took violent evasive action, but in her throes struck a mine amidships. The explosion almost tore the *Corry* in half.

Commander Hoffman tried to head for the open sea by hand steering, but in five minutes all power was lost. Nearly all the men in the number two boiler room were dead—scalded when the boiler had blown up. Hoffman had been stunned by the blast, but was aware that some of his guns were still firing; without power, his gunners had continued to load shells and fire manually.

Corry tilted crazily and began to go under. At 6:41 A.M. the order was given to abandon ship. Thirteen men had been killed, thirty-three were wounded, and scores of crewmen were floundering around in the water with shells crashing around them.

A short distance away one of Bulkeley's skippers, Lt. Bill Liebenow, who was riding PT 199, and his comrades had been watching the *Corry* disaster unfold. The 199 boat had been running spies to France, but on D day its task was patrolling around the USS *Bayfield,* command ship for the Utah Beach assault, to guard against darting attacks by E-boats.

WILLIAM LIEBENOW:

For the next couple of hours, our entire PT-boat crew was fishing *Corry* men out of the water—those dead, half-dead, alive. This was the first time that I had ever given artificial respiration. We checked them over as best we could and pumped air into them by the old back-pressure method. A few we saved by doing this, others we did not.

I'm not sure how many we rescued, but I heard later that it was 61 survivors. But I do know that PT 199 was loaded, and we took in tow a lifeboat of people. We deposited the entire lot on a hospital ship and returned to our station. We stayed on station at the landing beach for five days and nights. I don't think I went to sleep during this whole period for more than a few minutes at a time.

At dawn the first Allied broadside was hurled shoreward to jar open the front door of Hitler's Fortress Europe. In minutes Utah Beach was seared and aflame, and a thick cloud of dust, gunsmoke, and the smoke of exploding shells stretched for miles along the shoreline. When the bombardment was a half-hour old, the sun timidly broke through the clouds and a majestic rainbow arched over the incredible scene of death and destruction.

On a PT boat named *Stratus,* the skipper, Lt. R. C. Burleston, called out exuberantly: "That's good luck for us!" [12]

Indeed it may have been good luck at Utah Beach. Contrary to the predicted bloodbath, American infantrymen stormed ashore with moderate casualties.

But at the other American beach, Omaha, assault troops charged into a buzz saw and were pinned down on the shore.

16

Rescues from Two Sinking Warships

Offshore on the heavy cruiser USS *Augusta,* flagship for the Western Naval Task Force (Utah and Omaha beaches), fifty-two-year-old, bespectacled Lt. Gen. Omar N. Bradley was undergoing the torments of the damned. A soft-spoken but tough-minded Missourian, Bradley was leader of American ground forces for Neptune. It had been six and a half hours since the initial assault at Omaha, and all that Bradley knew was that a savage struggle was raging on the beach.

Finally, at 1:30 P.M., a junior officer dashed up to Bradley with a message from shore: "Troops formerly pinned down on beaches . . . advancing up heights beyond the beaches." There were sighs of relief on the *Augie*. The crisis was over.

Exhausted, hungry, his head spinning from the deep emotions of one of history's monumental days, Omar Bradley, without removing his boots, at midnight flopped onto a cot and in moments was deep in fitful sleep. Hitler's "impregnable" Atlantic wall had been breached and nearly 150,000 Allied soldiers were ashore in Normandy.

At the same time that Omar Bradley was stealing a few winks, Comdr. John Bulkeley and his PT boats were in position along the Mason line, the floating barrier stretching for more than six miles from shore out into the Bay of the Seine. Not all of Bulkeley's PT boats would be manning the picket line at one time, but would rotate between the Mason line and Portland. An average of twenty PTs would be along the barrier at any given time to intercept and destroy or drive off E-boats charging southward from Cherbourg toward the vulnerable unloading areas at Utah Beach.

If John Bulkeley was hoping to tangle with E-boats that night, he was disappointed. For whatever his reason, Adm. Walther Hennecke in Cherbourg kept his E-boats in port, so the hours of darkness passed routinely on the Mason line.

However, on the evening of June 7—D day plus one—a lookout on Lt. William C. Godfrey's PT 505 (*Diana*) called out: "Periscope! Periscope!" *Diana* was patrolling the Mason line near two tiny islands called Saint-Marcouf, four miles offshore. Godfrey gave chase, but the U-boat periscope disappeared when his boat came within seventy-five yards of it. He was about to give the order to release depth charges when *Diana* was jolted by a blast: it had hit a submerged mine.

PT 505 went down quickly by the stern, but remained afloat. Godfrey jettisoned his torpedoes and depth charges, then transferred his forward guns, radar, and radio equipment to PT 507 (*Hemingway Hotel*), which had pulled alongside to help despite the clear danger that it, too, might be blown to bits by a mine. A towline was attached to the crippled 505 boat, and it was towed to calmer waters in the lee of Saint-Marcouf. Bill Godfrey's 505 had the dubious honor of being the first of Bulkeley's boats to be put out of action during Operation Neptune.[3]

That same night, a flotilla of five E-boats slipped out of Cherbourg to launch attacks against Allied ships in the Bay of the Seine. Just as dawn was breaking, the E-boats returned to port, where the flotilla skipper reported the results of his mission to Admiral Hennecke, who was in a bombproof shelter at the harbor. The officer said that his boats had reached a point north of the Saint-Marcouf Islands at about 1:30 A.M. and fired three spreads of torpedoes at destroyers and a cruiser. Three hits were scored, the E-boat leader claimed.[4]

Later in the day, Radio Berlin told the home front of the daring attack on the Allied warships by the Cherbourg E-boats, and how at least three vessels had been severely damaged or sunk. All this came as news to John Bulkeley and his men along the Mason line, none of whom had as much as spotted an E-boat that night. And the Allied naval command reported no ships hit by torpedoes in the Saint-Marcouf region.

Just before 8:00 A.M. on June 8—D day plus two—Comdr. Clifford A. Johnson was on the bridge of the destroyer *Glennon,* which was approaching her gunfire-support position about three miles northwest of the Saint-Marcouf Islands. Suddenly a tremendous blast shook the ship; her stern had struck a delayed-action or magnetic mine. A sailor standing on the fantail was tossed high in the air before splashing down into the water with both legs broken.

After a rapid check of the damage, Commander Johnson passed word over the loudspeaker: "This ship will not sink. All hands remain aboard. Repair parties proceed with rescue and salvage work." [5]

Lt. Comdr. Edward A. Michael, Jr., of Jamestown, New York, brought his 1,400-ton destroyer escort *Rich* to the wounded *Glennon*'s side and called out, "Do you need any assistance?"

Over a bullhorn Commander Johnson responded: "Negative. Clear area cautiously. Live mines." [6]

Just as the *Rich* was pulling away, a near-miss shell from a shore battery knocked out her generators, broke the steam lines in the torpedo tubes, and put the ship's antimagnetic mine equipment out of commission. Moments later a blast rocked the *Rich;* she had struck a mine.

Patrolling on the Mason line, Lt. Calvin R. Whorton, skipper of PT 508 (*Mairzy Doats*), saw that the *Rich* was in distress, and he radioed Commander Bulkeley aboard his flagboat for permission to rush to the *Rich*'s aid. Permission was granted, and the 508 boat was the first to arrive on the scene, followed by Bulkeley's 504 (skippered by Lt. Harold B. Sherwood, Jr.), Lt. Charles E. Twadell's 502, and Lt. Jaquelin J. Daniel's 506.

Bulkeley ordered his boat to pull alongside the disabled *Rich,* and in response to his megaphoned shouts, officers on the destroyer's bridge replied, "No help needed."

Then it came—the big one.

There was a muffled roar as a second blast ripped the crippled warship, sending skyward a fountain of saltwater mixed with oil, bodies, and pieces of steel.

Commander Bulkeley's PT boat was only about fifty yards away, and the explosion seemed to hurl the fifty-ton plywood boat from the water as if slapped by a mighty hand. All but the smaller pieces of debris missed Bulkeley's boat, and as the great green wall of water dropped like a theatrical curtain, it revealed the *Rich* torn almost in two.

Oil gushed from the rent seams of the warship, and the air was filled with moans and screams from the injured. Their faces and bodies blackened by oil, mutilated dead and dying were everywhere, floundering or floating in the water or pinned in the twisted wreckage.

John Bulkeley now headed his PT boat toward the *Rich,* and had gone perhaps fifty feet when a third blast ripped apart what was left of the sinking hulk. This explosion—another mine—was on the side of the *Rich* away from Bulkeley's craft, so the PT boat was shielded from its full force.[7]

With her back broken, with bodies and parts of bodies draped from her radar mast, the *Rich* was a scene from a holocaust. John Bulkeley's four PT boats made fast to the sinking ship, and the Sea Wolf led rescue parties aboard.

ADMIRAL BULKELEY:
Most of the wounded men on the *Rich* were being removed by our boys to the PT boats. Many of our fellows played heroic roles in this rescue operation by lowering to safety some of the victims pinned under heavy piles of debris, knowing that depth charges, which formed part of the debris, might be armed and blow them to hell at any moment.

One of our boys rushed up to me and said that the *Rich*'s captain and executive officer were on the bridge, bleeding badly with their legs broken by the big blast, and they'd refused efforts by our boys to take them off the *Rich.* Both apparently wanted to go down with their ship.

I picked my way around wreckage and bodies to the bridge. Both officers were sitting on the deck, forty-fives [pistols] out, and threatening to shoot anyone who tried to carry them off the ship.

Commander Michael was a gallant officer. I'd known him as an old shipmate on the *Indianapolis* in the mid-30s. So I began sweet-talking the two men, and finally grabbed them and, with the help of one of our crewmen, carried them to where they were lowered to my flagboat.

Elsewhere on the doomed *Rich,* EM1c George E. "Ted" Lucas, of Port Huron, Ohio, a crewman on the *Rich,* and the ship's pharmacist's mate (medic) were administering heavy doses of morphine to men pinned under the wreckage so the trapped men would not know that they were going to their deaths when the *Rich* went under.[8]

Meanwhile, Lt. Cal Whorton, the 508 boat skipper, who in peacetime was a sports writer for the *Los Angeles Times,* spotted an injured crewman floundering in the water. Whorton plunged into the Channel, swam to the man, and towed him back to his PT boat.

CALVIN WHORTON:
The impulse that prompted me to dive into the Channel was formulated several days earlier while our PT boats were escorting minesweepers to

the landing beaches. One of the sweepers was hit by a German torpedo. Desperate survivors were everywhere in the water, and we succeeded in rescuing some of them. One young victim was within arm's length of my boat, and I desperately tried to make contact to pull him to safety. But before I could do so, he slipped from my grasp and sank. So I thought that had I jumped into the water I could have saved him. This scenario flashed through my mind when, without a second thought, I plunged into the Channel to rescue the *Rich* crewman, although I realized later that if the ship sunk she could have sucked me under with her.

Casting off lines only after the decks of the *Rich* were awash, men on Whorton's boat spotted a lone figure bobbing by under the overhanging bow of the PT. The bow line was rapidly coiled to rescue this last *Rich* survivor, but before it could be tossed the man raised his face to the 508's crewmen staring down at him from on deck, and in a firm, calm voice, said, "Never mind, fellows, I have no arms to catch it." [9]

He disappeared under the water.

John Bulkeley's four boats took off sixty-nine wounded men, who were stretched out on the decks and in the tiny compartments below.

Two men in the rescue parties, QM2c R. W. Gretter of PT 504 and SN1c Paul E. Cayer of PT 506, were so busy trying to dig men out from under the debris that they failed to hear the order to abandon the *Rich* and went down with the ship. However, they disentangled themselves from the twisted wreckage, popped up to the surface, and were picked up by a Coast Guard cutter. (Cayer would be cited for removing nine *Rich* crewmen who would have died without his aid.)

The pile of smoking, contorted junk that had been the sleek destroyer escort *Rich* had sunk within fifteen minutes of the first blast. Out of her crew of 215 men, 27 were killed, 52 were missing, and 73 were wounded.[10]

In the meantime, destroyer *Glennon* had become stuck, her fantail apparently firmly anchored to the bottom by her starboard propeller. For forty-eight hours she resisted the efforts of grunting tugs to dislodge her. Then, on the morning of June 10, a German battery north of Utah Beach began pounding her. Its second salvo crashed into the *Glennon* amidship and cut off all power. Then more shells struck the sitting duck and an enormous explosion cut her in half.

Her skipper, Commander Johnson, ordered her abandoned. In the fireroom, where the "black gang" sweated to keep up steam and put out a fire in the aft sections, word was not received. Chief Water Tender William Venable of Mayodan, North Carolina, Water Tender Second Class Francis Dauber of Elizabeth, New Jersey, and FN1c John Valkenberg of Patterson, New Jersey, remained at their posts.

On a rescue ship, Commander Johnson discovered that three of his men were missing. John Bulkeley roared his PT boat up to the stricken ship, which then was barely afloat. He spotted the ''black gang'' members standing calmly on deck and shouted, ''Get the hell in here in a hurry!'' They needed no urging and clambered down the ladder and into the PT boat.[11]

Bulkeley raced away, for the ship could have exploded.

A short time later, *Glennon,* in her death throes, rolled over and sank. Twenty-five of her crew were lost and thirty-eight wounded.

Vastly outnumbered by Allied warplanes, the Luftwaffe chose the wee hours of the morning to raid the ships anchored off the invasion beaches. German air leaders had developed a new tactic in which a plane with precise navigational gear would drop flares in the center of a group of ships. The flares were equipped with a device that permitted them to float on the water. Then German bombers would arrive and use the floating iridescent light to drop their explosives accurately.

John Bulkeley quickly provided a countermeasure to this new tactic. As soon as the flares began to drop, his PT boats would race to the scene and sink the flares by riddling them with machine-gun fire, leaving only the black seascape for the approaching Luftwaffe bombardiers.

Meanwhile on land, foot soldiers and tankers of Maj. Gen. J. Lawton ''Lightning Joe'' Collins's VII Corps were driving northward from Utah Beach to seize the crucial port of Cherbourg. Until the invaders captured Cherbourg in order to rapidly bring in guns, troops, tanks, ammunition, vehicles, fuel, and rations, they were in danger of withering on the vine and being cut to pieces by German forces converging on Normandy from all over Europe.

17

A Dash into Cherbourg Harbor

Navy Capt. John "Pappy" Ford was growing restless on the *Augusta,* and for several days he had been pacing the deck like a caged panther. The command ship was too far from the action, Ford thought, even though black-bodied Dorniers had been winging over nightly to pay their explosive respects to the invasion fleet. So Ford radioed Mark Armistead on John Bulkeley's PT boat patrolling the Mason line and asked him to come over to the *Augusta* and pick him up. He said that he had some "important matters" to take up with Bulkeley.

The Sea Wolf, a fighting man, was not too thrilled over the request. He didn't want rear-echelon types, especially rear-echelon types who outranked him, looking over his shoulder. But Armistead assured him that Pappy Ford would not get in his way, so Bulkeley took his boat alongside the *Augusta.*

Bulkeley had pegged Pappy to be a true eccentric—perhaps one in need of professional therapy. He recalled his first and only encounter with the Hollywood legend back in London at Claridge's when Pappy, stark naked, had stood at attention and saluted him. Now Bulkeley's original impression was reinforced. The figure being lowered from the *Augusta* in a bosun's chair was so disheveled, he looked to Bulkeley more like one of the infantrymen ashore than a captain in the United States Navy Reserve.

However, Bulkeley greeted the Hollywood refugee warmly, holding out his hand and saying, "Captain Ford, welcome aboard!" Pappy, who apparently had not shaven since before D day, a week earlier, glared at the skipper he outranked and grunted, "It's *Jack* Ford! Call me Jack!"[1]

The Sea Wolf briefed Ford on the operations of his task group and showed him the charts. Almost at once, Bulkeley's evaluation of the movie director began to shift—for the better. Pappy asked intelligent questions, and his manner was subtly deferential to the professional navy officer who was his junior.

Back on the Mason line, Ford began talking about plans of the big Hollywood studio Metro-Goldwyn-Mayer (MGM) to produce an epic movie, *They Were Expendable,* based on a late 1942 best-selling book by William L. White. "This isn't going to be some goddamned, two-bit propaganda flick," Pappy barked. Rather it would be a stirring film about the delaying actions fought by John Bulkeley, his warriors, and a handful of PT boats in the Philippines early in the war.

Hollywood moguls, Ford explained, had been after him for more than a year to direct the epic, and they would pay him the astronomical sum (for the time) of $300,000. That aspect bothered Pappy. How would it look, he mused aloud, for him to take off from the Navy to earn that kind of money when American boys were fighting and dying for a pittance all over the globe?

Ford said that Secretary of the Navy Frank Knox wanted the movie to be made, and would put him on inactive status to direct the film. "But I'm going to solve the situation by waiting until the war is over," Ford exclaimed. "Then I'll make *They Were Expendable.*"

Pappy remained aboard Bulkeley's PT boat for five days. At one point they bumped into an E-boat off Cherbourg and, plunging along at more than forty knots, the PT boat and the E-boat engaged in a running machine-gun shootout. Ford stood in the cockpit to get a better view of the action, but mainly he wanted to observe the famed John Bulkeley under the stress of battle so that one day he could direct *They Were Expendable* with realism.[2]

Ford never flinched as the PT boat's automatic weapons chattered furiously and raised an earsplitting din, nor when tracers from E-boat machine guns zipped overhead and one burst stitched Bulkeley's hull just above the waterline.

After the fireworks ended, Pappy, with a straight face, accused Bulkeley, who carried a camera strapped around his neck, of being prepared to take the first picture of him sprawled out on deck—dead.

Ever since the name John Bulkeley had burst like a meteor across

America after the rescue of General MacArthur from Corregidor, Ford had admired the young navy officer from afar. Now he had grown to admire him up close. "Say, John," Pappy said evenly, "who do you think ought to play your part in *They Were Expendable*?" Bulkeley shot back, "How in the hell would I know. You're supposed to be the movie genius!"

On the afternoon of June 18 (D day plus twelve) Mother Nature began to show signs of her anger. Winds picked up to twenty-two knots with gusts up to thirty-two. By midnight, gales and driving rains lashed the Normandy beachhead and vessels offshore. It was the launching of the worst June storm over the Channel in forty years, and one that threatened to disrupt, even jeopardize, the invasion.

A raging surf pounded the landing beaches, halting all unloading operations. Small boats, landing craft, and barges were hurled onto shore and smashed. Pontoon runways leading to land from ships offshore were buckled and twisted like pretzels. Derelict vessels careened about, crashing into other ships and ripping apart temporary steel piers.

Relentlessly, for four days and nights, the storm demons shrieked, and along the Mason line, John Bulkeley's PT boat and twenty others remained on station and were pitched about by the huge waves as though they were toys in a child's bathtub.

EDWARD SLATER:
Being caught in the English Channel on a torpedo boat in a Force 7 sea or better is a horrible experience and a fight for survival. All hands are wet to the skin. Men are smashed to the deck plates and have to fight to get to their feet. Water pours in ventilators, which have been stuffed with dungarees. Guns break loose of their breeching. Wires are shorted and shock those on the bridge.

Galley plates, cutlery, food, pots, and pans fly about. Batteries jump out of boxes and make fumes in the engine room. Crewmen are ordered below for fear that they will be washed overboard. Only one man remains at the helm—the skipper or his exec, in relays. Saltwater and wind blind them, their bodies are black and blue from being slammed against surroundings, and tension on board heightens with the crash of each mountainous wave. Even atheists pray.

All of Bulkeley's boats rode out the ferocious gale and never left positions. But the storm nearly destroyed the temporary unloading facilities at the Allied landing beaches, so the prompt capture of Cherbourg now became SHAEF's number one urgent priority. However, on June 25—D day plus nineteen—Lightning Joe Collins's exhausted foot soldiers and tankers were bogged down outside Cherbourg, where 40,000 German troops were holed up inside concrete bunkers in a fortified network that surrounded the city on three sides.

Cherbourg would be a tough nut to crack. Before D day Adolf Hitler had declared the port to be a fortress, and had forced its commander, hulking Lt. Gen. Karl Wilhelm von Schlieben, to sign a document pledging to defend Cherbourg "to the last man and the last bullet." Without a major port, both the Fuehrer and the Allied high command knew the invasion could fail.

All down the Allied chain of command, from General Eisenhower at Southwick House to the machine gunner at a front-line outpost, the heat was on: *seize Cherbourg!*

ADMIRAL BULKELEY:
Admiral Morton Deyo called me to his flagship, the heavy cruiser *Tuscaloosa.* He was very grim. The Germans had eight dual-purpose 88mm guns at Fort des Flamand, at the eastern end of the breakwater in Cherbourg, Deyo said, and these weapons were holding up a 4th Infantry Division regiment.

Deyo said he had a mission for me that was very simple. The eighty-eights wouldn't fire and disclose their positions, so they couldn't be pin-pointed. So I was to take a pair of PTs and charge up to within a thousand yards of the Nazi guns. The theory was that the Germans could not resist opening fire on us at point-blank range, and they would give away their positions.

In other words, my two PT boats were to be clay pigeons.

A curious mixture of haze and smoke rolled over embattled Cherbourg as the sun began to sink behind the western horizon. Commander Bulkeley, in PT 510 (skippered by Lt. Elliott B. MacSwain), and PT 521 (under Lt. Peter S. Zaley) were racing across the choppy blue water toward the line of concrete encasements that housed the 88mm guns at Fort des Flamand. Four PT boats were held in reserve if needed.

Bulkeley's two boats charged to within a thousand yards of the enemy guns, and when the Germans refused to swallow the bait the PTs bolted onward, pouring withering bursts of machine-gun fire at the concrete enclosures. Apparently, the PT boats' impudence angered the German gunners behind the thick walls, for they opened fire.

For thirty-five minutes, the clay-pigeon boats raced at high speed back and forth in front of Fort des Flamand, as shells from the high-velocity 88mm guns hissed into the water around them. "They're disclosing the hell out of their positions!" a gunner on Bulkeley's boat called out dryly above the deafening din.[3]

Suddenly, Lieutenant Zaley's boat was in trouble—big trouble. Two shells had exploded near the craft, stopping all of its engines, bending the throttle rods, loosening the deck planking, and jarring the port torpedo halfway out of its rack. For ten frightening minutes Zaley and his crew made emergency repairs while their boat lay dead in the water virtually under the muzzles of the German guns in the fort.

All the time, John Bulkeley's boat was circling the disabled craft, partially concealing it with smoke. Shells continued to explode next to both PTs. Sighs of relief were almost audible on the clay pigeons as the engines on the crippled boat began to sputter and cough, then broke out in a full-throated roar.

Bulkeley ordered Zaley to launch his dangling torpedo toward Fort Flamand, after which he shouted, "Let's get the hell out of here!" The PTs zigzagged at high speed toward the open sea, and shells continued to splash into the water around them until they were far out into the English Channel.

That same day, which the Cherbourgois would call their Day of Liberation, General von Schlieben was trapped in his underground command post inside the city and surrendered to gleeful, disheveled GI foot soldiers. But von Schlieben, wearing at his throat the Iron Cross he had been awarded on the Russian front, refused to order the Cherbourg garrison to lay down its arms. Die-hard Nazis continued to resist bitterly in isolated pockets within Fortress Cherbourg as Lightning Joe Collins's infantrymen, tankers, and engineers rooted them out, street by street.

ADMIRAL BULKELEY:

Admirals [Alan] Kirk and [John] Wilkes called me in and said they wanted to go into Cherbourg harbor to inspect the damage done to the port facilities by German demolitions. I wasn't too keen about the idea, for Cherbourg was heavily mined and had not been swept. Anyone who went directly into the harbor would be asking for it, but I made no protest, of course.

So with Admirals Kirk and Wilkes aboard, I raced my PT into the harbor at high speed, keeping close to the breakwater and certainly not in the middle of the channel where German mines would be. Sure enough, acoustic mines in the middle of the channel exploded when ticked off by the noise of the propellers on our boat. We'd all been blown to hell had I come in that way.

I tied up at the mole, and the admirals jumped out and ran to the fort [des Flamand] . . . looking for souvenirs. Not me. I was afraid of booby-traps. When they finally came out, a couple of die-hard Nazi snipers opened up with rifles to pot the two admirals. What I didn't need on my hands was a couple of dead American admirals.

I grabbed my rifle—always carried one on the boat—leaped on the inside of the mole at the waterline, and slipped along it to get into place behind these two Krauts. I got a bead on them and dropped them with two rounds. They never knew what hit them. Now my two admirals suddenly lost their desire to hunt for souvenirs, so we got the hell out of Cherbourg—fast.

With the capture of Cherbourg, the Neptune part of Operation Overlord was considered to be concluded, and Admiral Kirk's Western Task Force was dissolved on July 10. Before he departed, Kirk sent John Bulkeley a personal letter:

I cannot leave without congratulating you and all your men on the very fine job done by the PT boats during the campaign. Your boys have fully justified our very high expectations. . . . You have all done yourselves proud.[4]

These were bittersweet days for John Bulkeley, professional navy officer. Gen. Charles de Gaulle, the elongated leader of Free French Forces, pinned on Bulkeley's tunic the croix de guerre (cross of war) with star, and the citation spoke of the recipient's "conspicuous gallantry and extraordinary bravery in action" as commander of motor torpedo boat squadrons operating off France. At age thirty-two, Bulkeley had received all the military decorations his country had to offer (some of them two or three times), and now he was promoted to full commander. But his gratification was tempered with receipt of orders that would separate him from the PT-boat service that he had loved for more than three years. He would become skipper of the destroyer *Endicott*.

DR. MAX VAN DEN BERG:

Before John Bulkeley came aboard, the *Endicott,* on which I was a lieutenant, had been something of a jinx ship. Back in Maine, a few of our

> seamen stole a submachine gun and pillaged across the United States. Then, before D day in Normandy, General Eisenhower fell on the *Endicott* while preparing to go ashore, and the entire ship's complement was confined to quarters. And finally, we missed the invasion because we were rammed by an out-of-control Liberty ship in the Irish Sea, and our skipper was relieved. That's when John Bulkeley took charge.
>
> As soon as Bulkeley came aboard, many *Endicott* men wrote home excitedly about their famed new skipper with the Medal of Honor and all the other medals. Knowing of Bulkeley's reputation as a fierce and bold warrior, however, some of the fellows were a little leery. They wondered if someone would have to write a new *final* chapter to *They Were Expendable,* on how the *Endicott* went down with all guns blazing while attacking ten German warships.

The *Endicott*'s engineers and crewmen, with help from the British, had labored around the clock to repair the ship, and when Bulkeley boarded her on July 18, 1944, she was again seaworthy and ready for action. That action would not be long in coming. The *Endicott* would participate in Operation Dragoon, a massive invasion of southern France. Second in scope only to Overlord, Dragoon would involve an initial force of 300,000 men, 1,000 vessels, and 2,000 airplanes. A 10,000-man airborne contingent would spearhead the operation by jumping and landing behind German coastal defenses along the fabled Riviera.

Dragoon was designed to seize the vitally needed major ports of Toulon and Marseilles and to liberate the southern two-thirds of France by driving northward up the Rhone River Valley to link up with Overlord forces breaking out of the Normandy bridgehead. Overlord and Dragoon would be General Eisenhower's one-two punch to help bring Adolf Hitler to his knees.

18

Sudden Death for Two Nazi Warships

Operation Dragoon was the worst-kept secret of the war. Throughout the vast Mediterranean, people were openly discussing the looming invasion of southern France. Axis Sally, the sultry-voiced propagandist on Radio Berlin, had been taunting American fighting men about the "warm reception" they would receive. The Allied high command could not conceal the massive preparations for Dragoon—the thousand vessels of diversified shapes and sizes assembled at ten Mediterranean ports. It would be the largest sea armada ever known to this part of the world.

Winston Churchill, who had vigorously opposed Dragoon, told confidants: "It may well prove to be another bloody Anzio!" [1] U.S. Rear Admiral Lyal A. Davidson, a task force commander, declared in a briefing aboard his flagship *Augusta,* "If surprise fails, this attack is going to be very bloody!" [2]

If Col. Gen. Johannes Blaskowitz, commander of Army Group B and defender of southern France, were to learn or deduce the true Allied landing beaches along the Riviera, he could concentrate his forces and possibly drive the invaders back into the sea. So at Naples, Lt. Comdr. Douglas E. Fairbanks, Jr., a special operations officer on the staff of Vice Adm. H. Kent Hewitt, commander of Dragoon naval forces, and other officers hatched an intricate sea-and-air scheme to hoodwink the Germans about the precise location of the actual assault.

Before being called to active duty by the Navy, Douglas Fairbanks had been a popular movie star, so those involved with him in planning the hoax wryly called it "The Hollywood Nightmare."

The decoy operations would be under the overall command of navy Capt. Henry C. Johnson. His Western Diversion Unit (code-named Operation Ferdinand) and his Eastern Diversion Unit (Operation Rosie) were to stir up such a racket to either side of the true invasion site that the German generals would be uncertain about Allied intentions and hesitant to rush all reserves to the Riviera.

Operation Dragoon D day was set for August 15, 1944.

In due course, Comdr. John Bulkeley arrived at Naples on the *Endicott*, which would play a key role in Ferdinand, the Western Diversion Unit operation.

JACK W. WATSON:
I was on the staff of Capt. Henry Johnson, the Diversionary Group commander, and took part in Ferdinand as a special communications officer on the *Endicott*. When John Bulkeley was being briefed on the *Endicott*'s role in the decoy operation, he grew bored and finally blurted out: ''To hell with all this hocus-pocus stuff—just show me where I'm supposed to fire my guns!''

On the afternoon of August 14—D day minus one—the *Endicott* sailed out of the harbor at Calvi, Corsica, bound for the southern coast of France. Seated next to John Bulkeley on the bridge was Penny, the big, brown, gum-chewing dog that her master had found near death a year earlier in New Guinea. In some mysterious manner, Bulkeley had managed to get Penny shipped to England from Alice Bulkeley's apartment in New York City.

DR. MAX VAN DEN BERG:
Before departing on the Operation Ferdinand decoy mission, Admiral Bulkeley told us officers on the *Endicott* that ''the Germans might believe that we are actually a large landing force and send everything they've got our way. Or we might get away with it.'' Bulkeley said, ''But remember, we'll take on anything that they've got. *Nothing* is too big for us! And one of two things can happen. Either the other fellow will stop firing—or we'll be sunk. And maybe we'll be sunk—but we'll never stop firing. In either case, our decoy mission will be accomplished.''

Just before 2:00 A.M. on D day, Commander Bulkeley was on the bridge of the *Endicott* as the Operation Ferdinand naval force steamed toward the bay of La Ciotat, a break in the rugged coastline midway between Marseilles and Toulon, and sixty miles west of the nearest Dragoon beach. A warm breeze was sweeping gently over the dark Mediterranean, and a billion stars twinkled in the sky.

Deployed over an area eight miles wide and twelve miles long around the *Endicott* were eight PT boats, four British MLs (motor launches), and eleven air-sea rescue craft (sixty-three-footers). Each vessel trailed reflector balloons made of a substance that would garble German radar screens and convey that the Ferdinand flotilla was a much larger force.

All the while, Lt. Jack Watson, a Council Bluffs, Iowa, native, was periodically sending out coded radio signals from the *Endicott*. These were short messages—and meant absolutely nothing. Watson himself had created the codes, which could not be broken, for he had more or less conjured them up out of thin air. The purpose of the electronic high jinks was to support the illusion that this was a large armada preparing a landing operation at the bay of La Ciotat.

Circling over the decoy little naval force were three Wellington bombers of the Royal Air Force. They dropped "window," a metallic substance that caused images to blur on enemy radar so that the precise number of vessels could not be counted.

At 2:15 A.M. a German radar station on the coastal heights passed along a report that a large convoy was steaming directly toward the bay of La Ciotat, whose smooth, sandy shores were ideal for a major amphibious landing.

Meanwhile as part of Operation Ferdinand, a flight of American C-47 transport planes, flown by British pilots, knifed over the coastline near the La Ciotat radar station. Flying at 600 feet, the C-47s were spaced at five-minute intervals and their crews pitched out "window" in order to indicate to German radar that the flight was a large one.

At a point fifteen miles north of Toulon, the dark sky was awash with blossoming white parachutes; C-47 crewmen had pitched out 300 lifelike rubber dummies dressed in precise replicas of the helmets, boots, and other battle gear worn by American paratroopers. The hoax was to make it appear that there had been paratrooper landings in support of an amphibious assault in the bay of La Ciotat.

In the meantime, the Ferdinand naval force had reached the mouth of the bay of La Ciotat and, at 4:05 A.M., the *Endicott* and a few other vessels began bombarding the shore. Forty minutes later, according to plan, Bulkeley's destroyer and the remainder of the flotilla withdrew.

All the while, a similar scenario—Operation Rosie—was unfolding to the right of the true landing beaches. Edging into position not far from Cannes was a small force consisting of two decrepit British gunboats, the *Aphis* and the *Scarab,* fighter-director ships *Antwerp* and *Stuart Prince,* and three motor launches. Lieutenant Commander Doug Fairbanks was on one of the gunboats. The vessels began lobbing shells inland and raised sufficient racket to simulate a large armada, presumably one preparing to send troops storming ashore.

Shortly after dawn, elements of thirty-seven-year-old Brig. Gen. Robert T. Frederick's 1st Airborne Task Force bailed out behind the Riviera, and at 8:00 A.M. assault troops splashed ashore at Saint-Raphael, Saint-Tropez, and Saint-Maxime. German resistance to the seaborne attack was mixed, ranging from nonexistent to tenacious at points. But clearly the Wehrmacht commanders had been taken by surprise.[3]

Within a few hours, evidence surfaced that Operations Ferdinand and Rosie had played major roles in hoodwinking the Germans. In the Third Reich on D day morning, Josef Goebbels's Radio Berlin broadcast: "The Allies are landing troops on a broad front from Toulon to east of Cannes. . . . Thousands of enemy paratroops are being dropped in an area northwest of Toulon."[4]

At 8 o'clock that night, Radio Berlin reported that "a large Allied assault force attempted to breach defenses near Toulon [at the bay of La Ciotat] but the first waves were wiped out by mine fields, and the rest lost heart and fled."[5]

On the night of D day plus two, Commander Bulkeley's *Endicott,* along with a small supporting cast of PT boats and motor launches, returned to La Ciotat bay for an encore decoy performance. Also getting into the act were Douglas Fairbanks's gunboats *Aphis* and *Scarab.* Although the Riviera beachhead was steadily being widened and deepened, it was not yet secure. So the La Ciotat encore was to cause German commanders to believe that a secondary landing might be taking place and not rush remaining reserves to Alpha, Camel, and Delta beaches.

It was 1:15 A.M. Suddenly, the tranquility was shattered and the dark seascape was illuminated by muzzle flashes as the guns of the *Endicott, Aphis, Scarab,* and motor launches pounded the shore. At the same time, the PT boats scurried around madly like waterbugs on a farmer's pond, their sound projectors giving off noises like guns, small-arms fire, and amphibious assault boats.

At 5:45 A.M. Commander Bulkeley received an urgent call for help; the *Aphis* and the *Scarab* reported that they were under attack by two

Nazi corvettes (ships slightly smaller than destroyers) and were badly damaged and in imminent danger of sinking. One gunboat was out of ammunition, the radioed report stated, and the other's fire-control system was out and it had no electric power. The corvettes were the *Capriolo,* armed with 4.7-inch guns, and the *Kemid Allah,* a converted Egyptian yacht with 3-inch guns. *Endicott* raced to the scene at full throttle.[6]

> ADMIRAL BULKELEY:
> We [the *Endicott*] came charging through a pall of smoke to 3,000 yards of the German corvettes. We had fired at La Ciotat so rapidly and for such a long period that we were knee-deep in shell casings and the barrels of three of our four five-inch guns were literally red hot. They were too hot to fire. But as long as we had even one gun left, I was going to attack the sons of bitches—that's what's expected of a United States Navy officer and warship.
>
> "Commence firing!" I ordered, meaning the usable gun. Nothing happened. "Commence firing!" I repeated. Still nothing happened. So I rushed a note down to our gunnery officer, Lt. Charles Rogers: "*Please* commence firing!"

After three minutes passed the single gun barked—but not in the usual rapid tempo. The gun crew had no time to repair a damaged rammer and had to load the shells by hand. During the engagement, big, strapping Leonard Barge of Sutherland, Oregon, loaded eighty shells, then drove them home by hand in lieu of the rammer, until his burned hands looked like raw hamburger. His mates had to open and close the breech lock with leather mallets.

GM1c William Russell, the captain of the firing crew, kept the gun going throughout the action. Once when the loaded weapon refused to fire, Russell opened the gun breech, pulled out the powder, and reloaded—a ticklish job that could have blown the crew to smithereens.

Meanwhile, shells from the Nazi corvettes were seeking out the *Endicott.* Now, as each round left the ship, Bulkeley's gun crew cheered loudly, hit the deck when an enemy shell came close, and rose again for the next cheer.

Suddenly the *Endicott* quivered as a German shell gouged a six-inch hole in the bow just above the waterline, rupturing a steam line and setting bunk bedding afire. The projectile was a dud and came to rest, smoking, on a bunk. CM1c Lewis Fisher and SF Lewis Ashe wrapped an underwear top around the hot, heavy shell, carried the bunk gingerly up the ladder to the deck, and pitched bunk and shell into the Mediterranean.

In the finest tradition of the Navy, the repair party reported tersely to Commander Bulkeley on the bridge: "Hole plugged, fire out, shell overside!"

Hand loading meant a rate of fire of only one shell per minute, but the aim was accurate. *Kemid Allah* was hit numerous times, causing her to list to port and shudder from internal explosions. Like a swarm of ants, the *Kemid Allah*'s crew began scrambling down the sides into rafts, and others leaped from the doomed ship's deck into the water. Ten minutes later, the 1,600-ton corvette plunged to the bottom.

ADMIRAL BULKELEY:
Now we took out after the *Capriolo,* which was trying to flee back to Toulon. We kept rounding her bow to cut her off. But the *Capriolo* kept firing at us, and shells were splashing around us. We dodged several straddles, then took a direct hit on a forward turret. The canvas bloomer atop one gun caught fire, and Ens. Stanley Watts jumped in to put out the blaze with an extinguisher. But our only casualty was a sailor named Verdier who was knocked out when bopped on the head by one of our own shells, which was jarred from a loading place by the impact of the German hit.

We closed to within 1,000 yards and began raking the *Capriolo*'s deck with every 40mm gun that would fire. The result was devastating. Prisoners told me later that the 40mm fire either killed or wounded almost all the Germans manning their guns topside.

Commander Bulkeley ordered his ship to bore in closer for the kill, and at 800 yards—PT-boat range—the *Endicott*'s lone five-inch gun poured two more shells into the *Capriolo,* causing her to go dead in the water and her crew to abandon ship rapidly.

The *Capriolo* was smoking, parts of her superstructure were twisted wreckage, and muffled explosions were heard in her bowels; nevertheless, John Bulkeley decided to board the crippled vessel. Perhaps she could yet be salvaged and, after extensive repairs, turned against the Nazis. A boarding party from the *Endicott* quickly concluded that there was no hope of saving the *Capriolo,* so Bulkeley and his men scooped up armloads of the ship's papers and scrambled over the side. At 7:07 A.M., one hour after the *Endicott* had begun dueling with the two German warships, the *Capriolo* disappeared under the waves.

Back on the *Endicott,* Bulkeley was poring over the documents taken off the *Capriolo*. Suddenly he felt a surge of exultation. In his hands were blueprints of all the German mine fields off the coast of southern France. He could not believe his eyes. Never would he know why the officers on the doomed vessel had not destroyed these ultrasecret blueprints, for they had at least twenty minutes before giving the abandon-ship order.

The blueprints were rushed to a Dragoon command ship, and the next morning minesweepers were clearing out the concealed explosives. Bulkeley's startling discovery no doubt played a major role in the fact that not a single Allied warship, troop transport, or freighter would be sunk by mines in the months ahead when some 1,000,000 men, their weapons, and supplies would pour over the landing beaches and through the ports of southern France.[7]

DOUGLAS FAIRBANKS, JR.:
My two old tubs [*Scarab* and *Aphis*] were manned by willing, tough, and high-spirited crews as ever I saw, and for an hour and a half they fought their buckets as well as possible. Then John Bulkeley came charging up at the last minute, just like the United States cavalry in movies of the Old West. Bulkeley fought a masterly fight in a truly professional manner, which gave my old layman's heart a big and proud thrill. If it hadn't been for Bulkeley and the *Endicott,* we would have been goners.

Now the *Endicott* was joined by Doug Fairbanks's pair of shrapnel-scarred gunboats, *Aphis* and *Scarab,* and the three vessels began cruising around to rescue the couple of hundred Germans bobbing about in life jackets, perched on life rafts, or clinging desperately to pieces of debris. In the meantime, a motor barge edged alongside the *Endicott* and from it stepped Fairbanks, who scrambled up the net ladder and was escorted to the bridge.

ADMIRAL BULKELEY:
Doug [Fairbanks] had a damned rough time of it, as the two German corvettes were larger, faster, and outgunned his two old boats. Doug was the perfect picture of an old sea dog. His helmet was cockeyed, chin strap dangling, and a forty-five [pistol] was hanging almost to his knee—just like the gunslingers in our frontier days—and his battle jacket was wrinkled and stained with salt spray.

After Bulkeley and Fairbanks shook hands and briefly discussed the battle action, the movie actor asked for a sheet of paper, sat down, and began writing in longhand:

> We few, we happy few, we band of brothers;
> For he today who shares his blood with me
> Shall be my brother; be he e'er so vile,
> This day shall gentle his condition.
> And gentlemen in England, now a-bed
> Shall think themselves accursed they were not here,
> And hold their manhoods cheap, whiles any speak
> That fought with us upon Saint Crispin's Day.[8]

Doug Fairbanks handed the sheet to John Bulkeley, who was amazed that anyone could spontaneously create such sophisticated verse, especially in the wake of the battle action that both men had endured. Fairbanks grinned and said: "Shakespeare, *Henry V,* Act 4, Scene III."

Using long-handled hooks, netting, and lines, crewmen on the *Endicott* fished out of the Mediterranean 164 of Adolf Hitler's sailors and 5 officers, including the captains of both sunken warships. Fairbanks's battered *Aphis* and *Scarab* hoisted out 41 more survivors. About 200 Germans had been killed.[9]

CAPT. STANLEY BARNES:
One of the captains of the Nazi corvettes was bobbing around in the Mediterranean and insisted on being hauled out of the water last, and then when he was brought aboard he refused to salute the U.S. flag flying over the *Endicott.* John Bulkeley booted the German officer back over the side and made a wide circle before coming back. The German was hauled aboard once more, and again he refused to salute the colors, and John pitched him back in. Then Bulkeley left for an hour or so [to pick up survivors] before returning once more to fish out the German, a chancy thing for the odds of finding a single survivor are not good. It became quite clear to the Nazi captain that this was his last chance, and he did indeed salute this time around.

Forty wounded prisoners were treated in the *Endicott*'s wardroom, and the remainder were herded into the forecastle and guarded by a junior officer and two bluejackets. Bulkeley issued written orders to the guards: "Shoot to kill if prisoners try to escape, commit sabotage, or endanger ship." [10]

The captains of the *Kemid Allah* and *Capriolo* were taken below. Bulkeley personally selected the two men who would guard them: MoMM Henry Schwartz and TM1c Joe Finkelberg. Concealing his glee, Bulkeley introduced his crewmen to the German officers as "two American patriots from the Bronx, Mr. Schwartz and Mr. Finkelberg." (Actually, the latter was from Los Angeles.)

ADMIRAL BULKELEY:
I looked down on occasion, and it was the funniest thing I ever saw in my life. The two Jewish boys were holding tommy guns, and the Nazis kept facing the bulkhead [wall], afraid to say one word back to Schwartz, who was jabbering at them in German. One word of reply, the Krauts probably figured, would make them dead ducks.

At 11 o'clock that morning, Radio Berlin gave the *herrenvolk* (people) Goebbels's version of what had taken place during the night at the bay of La Ciotat where the *Endicott* and supporting vessels had raised such a ruckus to draw German attention away from the Riviera invasion site. Said Radio Berlin, "An additional and futile attempt of the American forces to land large bodies of troops west of Toulon [at La Ciotat] has failed miserably."

Then Lord Haw Haw, a British traitor (real name, William Joyce) who served as a zealous Nazi propagandist, took to the Berlin airways to explain that the American convoy (Bulkeley's force) was twelve miles long, and that for a second time in three nights "the Allies have learned of the determined resistance of the Wehrmacht, to their heavy cost." [11]

On the afternoon of the nineteenth—D day plus four—Bulkeley's *Endicott* joined with other destroyers, PT boats, and British motor launches in a screen designed to protect the landing beaches and the unloading operations there from surface and U-boat attack. It would be a period of tedious watching and sudden, sharp flashes of action. Twenty-four hours after the *Endicott* moved into position, a force of three E-boats tried to dash through the picket line, but a few destroyers opened fire and forced two of them to beach and sank the other one.

A week after D day, the Dragoon bridgehead was considered to be secure, and during the next week the major objectives of Toulon and Marseilles were seized. Then American and French forces drove north-

Comdr. Bulkeley Decorated For Sinking 2 German Warships

Heavily decorated Comdr. John D. Bulkeley, U. S. N., of PT-boat fame, has done it again. A second Silver Star was presented to him recently in ceremonies at the Naval Operating Base here for action off the southern coast of France during the invasion. Bulkeley is now at sea again.

Commanding the destroyer Endicott instead of patrol torpero boat squadrons, Bulkeley tackled two German warships off Ciotat which lies between Marseille and Toulon on August 17, and sank both, although his own ship was very badly crippled.

"We were assigned to bombard Ciotat as our part in the invasion," he said, "and after completing that job, which included sinking a ship in the harbor, we ran down to convoy two British gunboats then under the command of Lieut. Comdr. Douglas Fairbanks, U. S. N R.

"While on the way we received a message from the gunboats that they were being attacked by two German warships believed to be corvettes."

"Hold them until we get there," was the Endicott's reply.

The Endicott arrived in time to see the two gunboats retiring under a smoke screen and identified the two German vessels as the 1,600-ton Kemid Allah and the Capiaullo, an ex-Italian destroyer of 1,100 tons.

Guns Red Hot

All four of the five-inch guns aboard the Endicott were red hot because of the previous bombardment and three of them refused to work at all. However, one gun could be hand-loaded, and Leonard Barge, seaman first class, of Sutherland, Ore., had already loaded 400 five-inch shells after the loading mechanism had gone bad. During the fight with the German ships he

COMDR. BULKELEY

Silver Stars, the Purple Heart, the Army Distinguished Unit Badge and the Philippine Distinguished Conduct Star.

Lieut. (jg) Stanley S. Watts, U. S. N. R., of Richmond, in charge of the 40-mm. and 20-mm. guns, began alternating his fire between the two opposing vessels, and at 1,500 yards the German gun crews began to jump overboard.

The batteries of German forces ashore failed to fire, although they were in easy range of the U. S. S. Endicott.

Five-inch shells were plunging into the Capiaullo and at 7 o'clock in the morning

—The Virginian-Pilot

ward along each side of the Rhone River for nearly 300 miles. Near Dijon, 140 miles southeast of recently liberated Paris, on the morning of September 12, a historic junction occurred. Dragoon forces linked up with units that had broken out of Normandy. Dragoon and Overlord had merged into one.

Bulkeley's *Endicott* was still on picket-line duty on October 20 when electrifying news reached her radio room: Gen. Douglas MacArthur had kept a sacred pledge and returned to the Philippines. It had been thirty-three months since MacArthur had escaped from surrounded Corregidor in John Bulkeley's battered, 77-foot PT 41. Now he had come back aboard the 10,000-ton, 614-foot cruiser *Nashville* at the head of a powerful sea and air force and a veteran army that would number 200,000 men.

"Are you surprised over MacArthur's return to the Philippines?" an *Endicott* officer asked Bulkeley. "Surprised? Hell, no, I'm not surprised! General MacArthur always said he would return, and by God, he's returned!" [12]

Bulkeley was half a world away from the Philippines and performing an important task. But secretly, his spirit was in Leyte Gulf, going ashore with Douglas MacArthur, with whom the name John Bulkeley would forever be linked.

ALEXANDER W. WELLS:
I was skipper of PT 525 and had been named to take General MacArthur and his party ashore. Around 11:30 A.M. my boat edged up to the *Nashville*, and General MacArthur scrambled down a rope netting with a dexterity that belied his sixty-five years. He shook hands with me. Also coming aboard my PT were his chief of staff, General Sutherland; General George Kenney, his air corps chief; General Walter Krueger, commander of the Sixth Army; and other brass.

General MacArthur was quiet while heading for the beach. He sat at a corner of the cockpit on the port side. Clearly, this was a highly emotional moment for him, and he was deep in thought.

General MacArthur went ashore—this was on Leyte Gulf—and gave his famous "I have returned" speech. My crew and I had remained on the boat, and presently here come MacArthur and the generals in three jeeps. General MacArthur was in a great mood. As he stepped aboard my PT 525 for the trip back to the *Nashville*, he walked up to me, clasped my right shoulder, smiled broadly, and said: "Well, Lieutenant Wells, it isn't Paris, but it will have to do!"

In late 1944, the *Endicott* received orders to sail to the United States. En route, the ship made a stopover at Tangier, French Morocco, a city lying opposite Gibraltar at the western opening to the Mediterranean Sea. Most of Tangier's residents were Moslem Berbers and Arabs.

CAPT. STANLEY BARNES:
While ashore on liberty in Tangier, two *Endicott* sailors were badly beaten up in a sleazy bar by a pair of Moroccan thugs. John Bulkeley knew that an official protest through diplomatic channels would be futile. So John put on civilian clothes, went alone into Tangier in this disguise, identified the two native hoodlums who had mauled his boys, and beat the hell out of them.

A few days later, the *Endicott* was knifing through the Atlantic toward the United States. On December 16, her radio room received a news flash. Hordes of German tanks had broken through thin American lines in Belgium and were racing hell-bent for Paris. The bloody pitched fight that erupted would come to be known as the Battle of the Bulge.

Midshipman Bulkeley at Annapolis. (U.S. Navy)

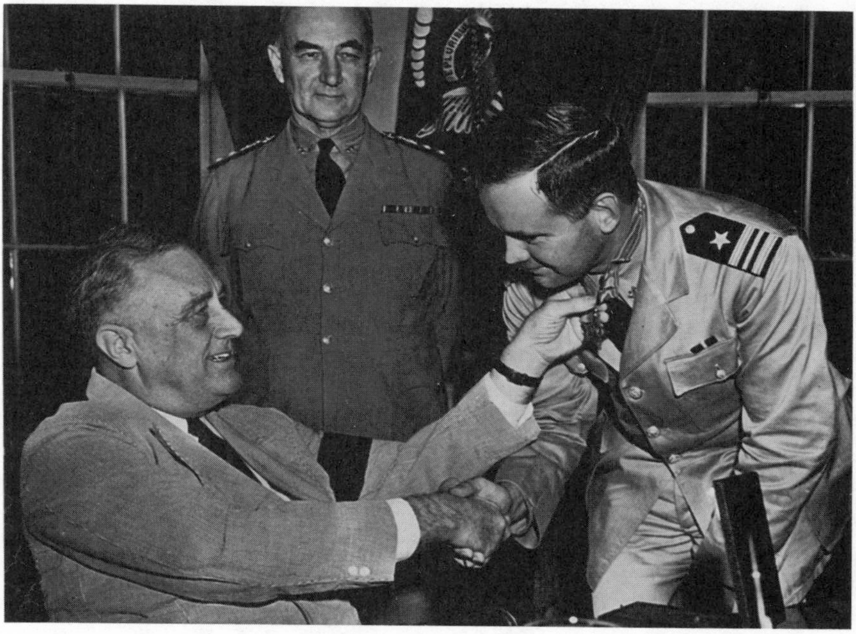

Lieutenant Commander Bulkeley receives Medal of Honor from President Roosevelt, July 1942. (U.S. Navy)

Lieutenant Bulkeley (naval uniform) with General MacArthur at ceremonies honoring Australian war dead shortly after the breakout from Corregidor. (courtesy of Alice Bulkeley)

Bud Liebenow (left) and Ed Slater, two of Bulkeley's earliest PT boat skippers, shown here inspecting a 38mm bow gun at Dartmouth, England. (courtesy of Edward W. Slater)

Lieutenant Commander Bulkeley with King George VI of England. (U.S. Navy)

Lieutenant Harold B. Sherwood, Jr., skipper of Bulkeley's flagboat PT-504, rescues a survivor of USS Rich, sunk by mines off Normandy, June 3, 1944. (U.S. Navy)

Commander Bulkeley chats with actress Donna Reed at the Naval Academy, Annapolis. (U.S. Navy)

Drawing fire from the German fort at Cherbourg, France, June 1944. (U.S. Navy)

Captain Bulkeley and his wife, Alice, with President Kennedy.

Captain Bulkeley (center) with famed movie director and Navy Reserve Rear Admiral John Ford (right) and his aide, Captain Mark Armistead.

Admiral Bulkeley watches as a section of pipe is removed from the water line at Guantanamo. The dry pipe refuted Castro's claim that Bulkeley had been stealing Cuban water. (*U.S. Navy*)

Mindful of Cuban propaganda, Admiral Bulkeley had a movie camera perched on a hillock overlooking the main gate manned 24 hours a day. (*courtesy of Norfolk* Ledger-Star)

Memento of the Cuban water incident sent to President Johnson.

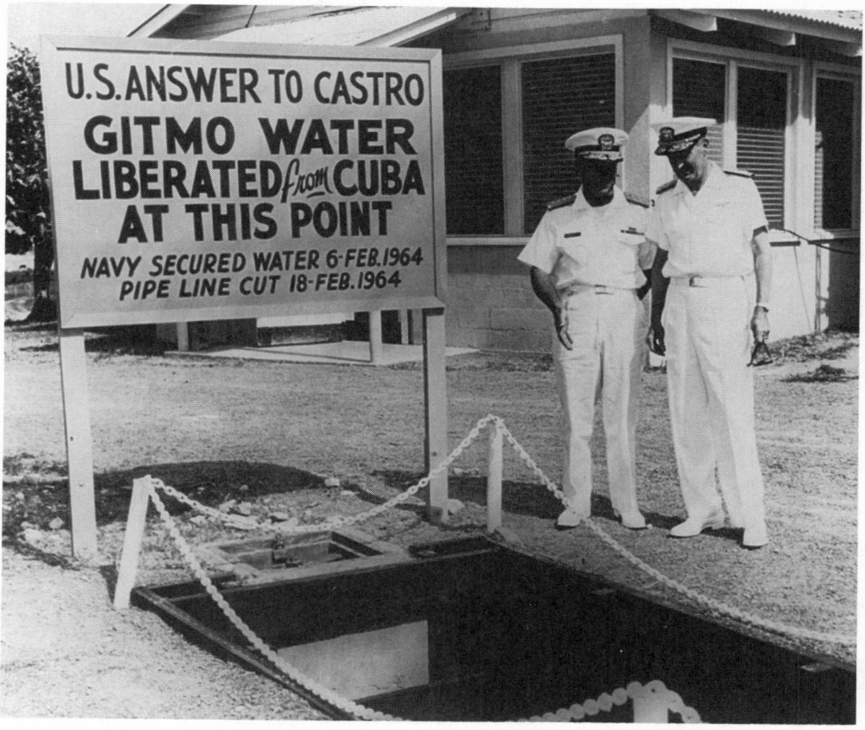

Rear Admiral Bulkeley explains his triumph over Castro to Chief of Naval Operations Admiral McDonald. (U.S. Navy)

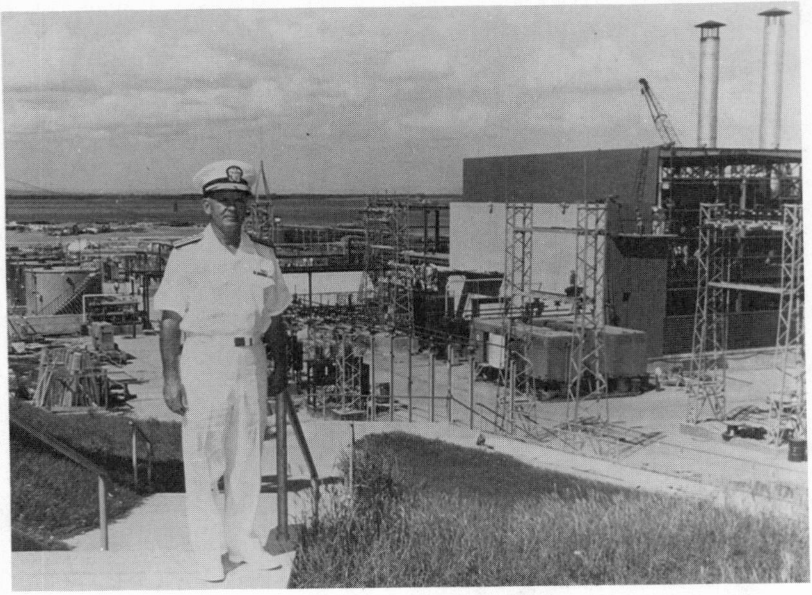

Rear Admiral Bulkeley standing in front of the water desalinization plant, built in record time to thwart the water cut-off by the Cubans. (*U.S. Navy*)

The Norwegian cruise ship Viking Princess *on fire. Using every ship in Guantanamo Bay, Bulkeley performed "one of the great sea rescue missions of the century."* (*U.S. Navy*)

Admiral Bulkeley prepares to take Secretary of the Navy Paul Nitze on a helicopter tour of the Guantanamo Bay naval base. (*U.S. Navy*)

Bulkeley Hall, Guantanamo

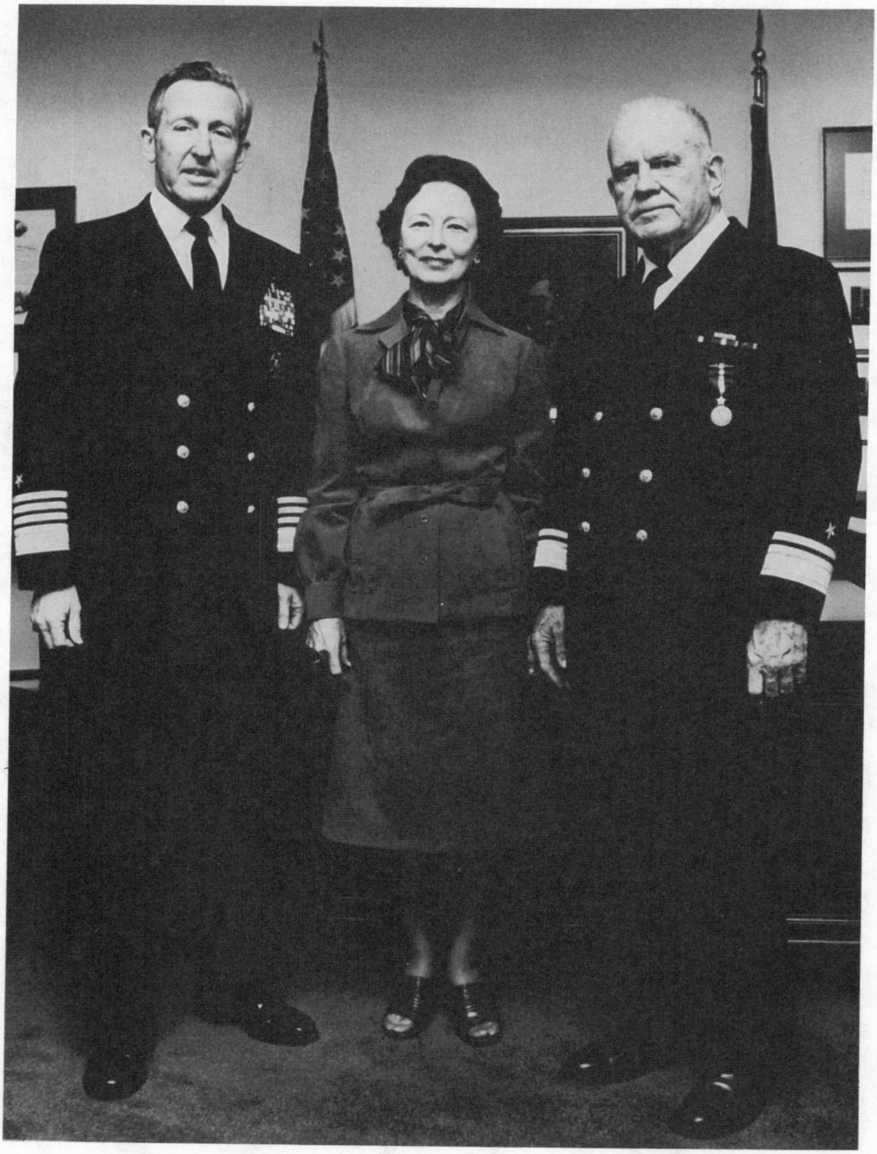

Rear Admiral Bulkeley and his wife, Alice, with Chief of Naval Operations Admiral Thomas Hayward. (U.S. Navy)

The Admiral and two of his inspectors check an electrical switchboard during an INSURV inspection in January, 1988. (U.S. Navy)

Fifty years of Naval service—INSURV—January, 1988. (U.S. Navy)

19

Duty Tour with the Nuclear Geniuses

Shortly after New Year's Day 1945, Comdr. John Bulkeley and the *Endicott* were back in the States. The Sea Wolf's new orders left him racked with frustration. Bloody battles, including monumental naval actions, were raging in the far Pacific, and the *Endicott* and the U.S. Navy's most famed warrior had been assigned to routine antisubmarine patrol along the eastern seaboard. It was a job Bulkeley found to be boring—there had been no real U-boat threat to the United States Atlantic coast since early 1943.

While Bulkeley was searching for periscopes, navy Capt. John ''Pappy'' Ford was nearly ready to commence filming *They Were Expendable,* the epic movie on the destruction of Bulkeley's PT Squadron 3 in the early bleak days in the Philippines. In the fall of 1944, Ford had had a change of heart. The Hollywood director had told Bulkeley that he would wait until the war was over to make the movie. But his viewpoint had been altered after having spent five days on the Sea Wolf's PT boat during the Normandy invasion. A genuine rapport (one that would endure for a lifetime) had developed between the two men after Ford had watched Bulkeley lead his squadrons with a calm professionalism, even under intense enemy fire. He had been mesmerized by the rough but always cool Bulkeley.[1]

Late in the fall of 1944, Captain Ford had flown from London to New York, and after resting briefly and visiting show business people, left for Los Angeles. Pappy telephoned MGM Studios executive James McGuiness, who had been prodding Ford for eighteen months to make

They Were Expendable, and said that he was ready to go—"provided 'Spig' is permitted to write a final version of the script."

Spig was Comdr. Frank Wead, who had retired from the Navy with a disabling injury and had written the original script in early 1943. Ford had been enthralled with Spig's efforts. As a navy man himself, Wead had a feel for his subject, and produced a moving blend of drama, excitement, heroism, self-sacrifice—and disaster.

However, the MGM moguls had imported Budd Schulberg, a New York screenplay writer with impeccable credentials, to rewrite Spig's script. Schulberg, despite his literary skills, didn't know a rowboat from a battleship, and his script infuriated Pappy Ford. He pitched the revised work onto the desk of Jim McGuiness, shouted "This is an abomination!" and went back to the war.[2]

The MGM honchos knew that Ford, with his flare, cinema genius, and navy background, was the only director who could hope to turn *They Were Expendable* into a box-office smash. So now they granted his demands. Pappy's qualms over the "obscenity" of accepting the whopping $300,000 fee "while our boys are dying all over the world for a few bucks a month" were resolved. He would use the money to purchase a clubhouse and grounds outside Los Angeles for the postwar recreation use of his Field Photographic veterans and their families.[3]

Much to the astonishment of those involved with the production of *They Were Expendable,* Ford cast the suave, gentle star Robert Montgomery in the role of John Bulkeley (who would be John Brickley in the film). Montgomery was not the gung-ho, action type, but he had unique qualifications for the role of the Sea Wolf. Before being sent home after contracting malaria, Montgomery had been executive officer in Bulkeley's PT-boat Squadron 7 during combat in the Southwest Pacific in 1943, and many persons thought that Montgomery and Bulkeley bore a facial resemblance to each other and had similar mannerisms.

Both Captain Ford and Lieutenant Commander Montgomery had been placed on inactive duty by Secretary of the Navy Frank Knox, who enthusiastically cooperated in the *They Were Expendable* project. Due to the film's story, the big budget, the top Hollywood stars, and the direction of John Ford, Knox felt that *They Were Expendable* would be a navy public-relations bonanza.

Lanky, hard-drinking, hard-swearing John Wayne, a rising star known to friends as Duke, would play Bulkeley's number 2 man in the Bataan days (Lt. Robert Kelly). Wayne would be cast in the film as Lt. Rusty Ryan. Beautiful young Donna Reed would be Sandy Davis, an army nurse on Corregidor, who falls in love with Rusty Ryan (Kelly) while he is a patient in the hospital bay in Malinta Tunnel. (The real-life Sandy Davis was Peggy Greenwalt, who, along with other American nurses, had been captured by the Japanese when Corregidor fell in the spring of 1942.)

On February 1, 1945, after two years of squabbles, script changes, and delays, actual shooting got underway at Key Biscayne, Florida. The Pentagon furnished (on loan) a number of PT boats and their crews, most of whom were Pacific veterans already in the States.[4]

John Ford, always an intense, painstaking man, directed the movie with unprecedented zeal. On the set, Pappy stormed about, ranted and swore like a mule skinner when an actor or an episode displeased him. He was particularly hard on Duke Wayne. Ford shouted to Wayne that he was a "clumsy bastard" and a "big oaf," and at one point the two high-strung men nearly came to blows.

To Pappy Ford, *They Were Expendable* was more than just a movie; it was a crusade to achieve a silver screen masterpiece and to do justice to MacArthur's Pirates.

Throughout the filming, a stream of navy officers and assorted straphangers trekked to Key Biscayne to watch and kibitz. John Bulkeley was not among them. He felt that his appearance at the scene would be interpreted by the public as his endorsement of the movie, and since *They Were Expendable* was a commercial venture, that would be unseemly for an officer in the United States Navy.

Two days before shooting was completed on *They Were Expendable,* Pappy Ford was rendered *hors de combat*. He took a spill off a camera scaffold and plunged twenty feet to the cement floor, fracturing his left leg. It was a painful injury, and he was flown to Los Angeles where he spent two weeks in traction at Cedars of Lebanon Hospital. Bob Montgomery, whom Duke Wayne liked but considered to be Pappy's "pet" during the shooting, directed the last few days of the picture.

Early on the morning of March 2, 1945, some 11,000 miles from where Commander Bulkeley was on guard against phantom U-boats, Gen. Douglas MacArthur led an entourage of army brass onto four PT boats for the twenty-mile ride from Manila to Corregidor, the war-worn rock in the bay. This was an emotion-charged moment in history. MacArthur was coming back to the antiquated fortress he considered to be a symbol of the honor of America.

In what the supreme commander would describe as "one of the boldest actions in military history,'' young Col. George M. Jones's crack 503d Regimental Combat Team had jumped on The Rock two weeks earlier and, aided by a seaborne battalion of the 24th Infantry Division, had wiped out the 6,000-man Japanese force.

Now, at the Manila pier, Douglas MacArthur was in a buoyant mood, remarking jovially to his PT-boat skipper: ''So this is the 373. I left [Corregidor] in John Bulkeley's 41.''

Two months later, on May 2, Adolf Hitler shot himself in the head in his Berlin bunker while Allied armies were closing in from all directions and the Russians were only a few blocks down the street. At 2:41 A.M., inside a red brick school building that served as Gen. Dwight Eisenhower's advance headquarters at Rheims, France, Gen. Alfred Jodl signed Nazi Germany's unconditional surrender to the Allied powers.[5]

In the United States, President Harry S Truman, the peppery Missourian who had succeeded to the nation's highest office when Franklin Roosevelt died less than a month earlier, proclaimed May 9 to be Victory in Europe (V-E) Day. Tumultuous celebrations erupted across the land.

CECIL SANDERS:
I happened to run into my good friend from the Melville PT-boat training center, Jack [John F.] Kennedy, in San Francisco when the war in Europe ended. We were both lieutenants now, and I hadn't seen Jack since we had had dinner together in Jacksonville, Florida, in spring 1943.

Jack and I celebrated V-E night with a few drinks and talked over old times at midshipmen's school at Northwestern, where we had both been recruited into PT-boat service by John Bulkeley. We recalled how proud we were to have been selected from so many applicants, even after Bulkeley had told us that we wouldn't come back from the war.

There were a number of Russian soldiers on the streets in San Francisco, and Jack remarked that sooner or later, we would have to deal with Russia. Seventeen years later, he did—as president of the United States during the Cuban missile crisis.

Ever since he had arrived back in the States in January 1945, John Bulkeley had been itching to take his third crack at the Japanese. That fervent hope seemed to have translated into reality in July, when he was detached from command of the *Endicott* and ordered to report to the Bethlehem Steel Corporation's yards in Staten Island, New York. There he would assist in fitting out the spanking new destroyer *Stribling*, which was destined for the Pacific with Bulkeley as her skipper.

Staten Island was but a stone's throw from 45–42 Forty-first Street, Long Island, where Alice Bulkeley and the couple's growing family still lived. A new son, Peter, was born on July 20, 1945, to join Joan, now five years old, and John, Junior, now three.[6]

"That makes me quite a staff, counting Admiral Jasper," Bulkeley quipped to reporters who called on him at the Bethlehem plant. Admiral Jasper was the family cat.[7]

Wearing eighteen ribbons—"all earned the hard way," a scribe would write—topped by the Congressional Medal of Honor, Bulkeley was escorting a bevy of journalists over the Navy's newest warship, a slim but sturdy beauty weighing 2,250 tons. Standing under a five-inch gun—the *Stribling* had six of them—the skipper was asked if Japan was on the verge of surrendering.

"I can't talk about that," Bulkeley countered. "I'm just a junior officer—I'm not being paid to think." [8]

Yet the Sea Wolf allowed as how "the Jap warlords will still take a lot of killing."

On August 6, 1945, at precisely seventeen seconds after 8:15 A.M., a blinding, bluish white light cut across the sky above Hiroshima, Japan, followed by searing heat, a thousandfold crash of thunderlike noise, and finally an earthshaking blast that sent a mushroom-shaped cloud of dust and debris towering 50,000 feet. History's first atom bomb had been unleashed. When the Japanese warlords ignored President Truman's call to surrender and pledged to continue to fight, a second A-bomb exploded over Nagasaki.

On September 2, just before 9:00 A.M., a Japanese delegation came aboard the battleship *Missouri,* anchored in Tokyo Bay, and signed the instrument of surrender. Presiding over the proceedings was five-star General of the Army Douglas MacArthur. All over the vast Pacific, the guns fell silent.

Back in the United States, MGM moguls had planned to release *They Were Expendable* in September, but decided to postpone the unveiling due to the historic event that had taken place in Tokyo Bay. Finally, on December 19, amid an avalanche of media hype and Hollywood hoopla, the world premiere of *They Were Expendable* was held at Loew's Capitol Theater in Washington. A glittering array of the high and the mighty turned out. John and Alice Bulkeley were theater guests of five-

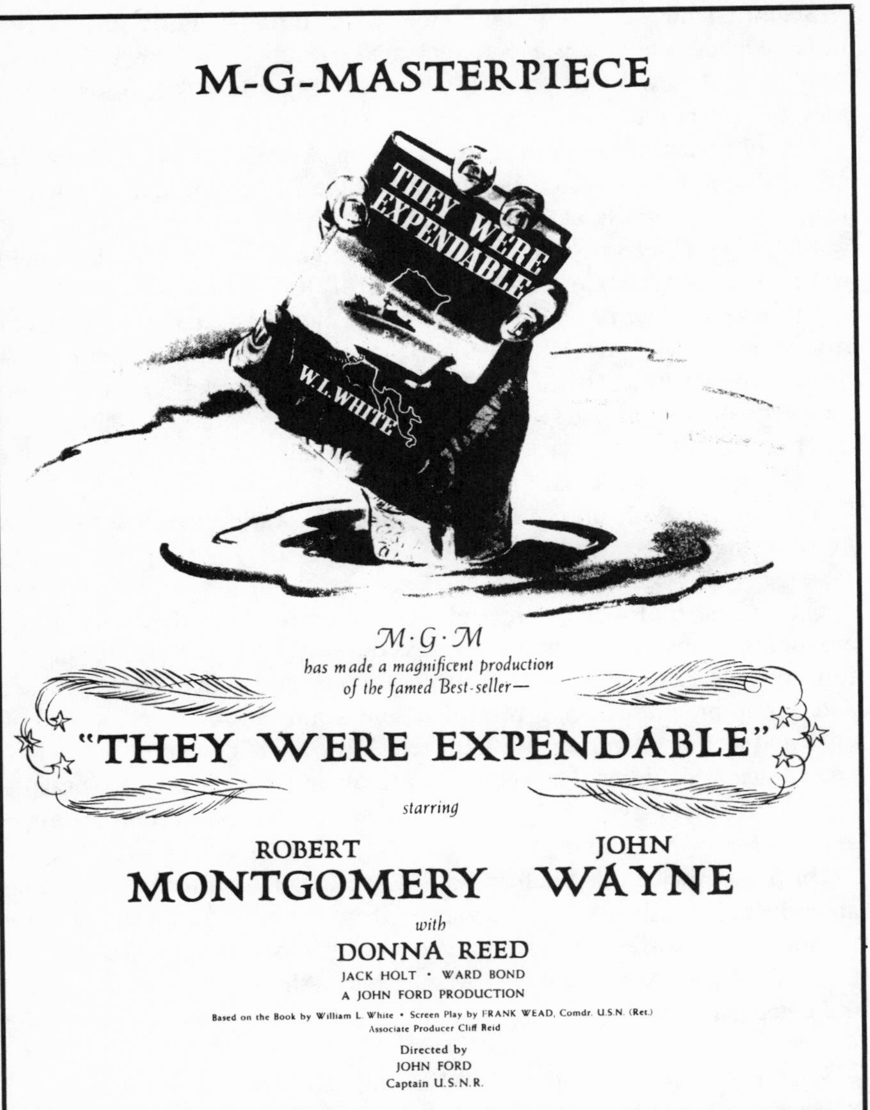

M-G-MASTERPIECE
THEY WERE EXPENDABLE
W. L. WHITE
M·G·M
has made a magnificent production
of the famed Best-seller—
"THEY WERE EXPENDABLE"
starring
ROBERT MONTGOMERY
JOHN WAYNE
with
DONNA REED
JACK HOLT • WARD BOND
A JOHN FORD PRODUCTION
Based on the Book by William L. White • Screen Play by FRANK WEAD, Comdr. U.S.N. (Ret.)
Associate Producer Cliff Reid
Directed by
JOHN FORD
Captain U.S.N.R.

(Advertisement in *New York Times*)

star Admiral of the Fleet Chester W. and Mrs. Nimitz. The white-haired, soft-spoken Nimitz had been Supreme Commander of the South Pacific, headquartered in Hawaii, a similar post to that held by General MacArthur in the Southwest Pacific.

Before the curtain went up at Loew's Capitol, famous personalities were introduced from the stage—John Bulkeley, Admiral Nimitz, Robert Montgomery, Donna Reed, and other luminaries. The most boisterous cheers and applause went to Commander Bulkeley.

Later that week, *They Were Expendable* opened at movie houses across America, and Pappy Ford's epic was acclaimed by most media critics. The *New York Times* called the film "a stirring account of a small but vital aspect of the war." Said the *Washington Post:* "This is a film packed with historical excitement, steeped in the pathos of war, rich in courage as it reenacts our bloody retreat from Manila and Bataan."

Despite the rave reviews, patrons were not stampeding the box offices as no doubt they would have been earlier in the year when there was a national thirst for vengeance against the Japanese. But now the war had been over for three months, and Americans were on an unprecedented binge of self-indulgence and pursuit of pleasure. Bataan was ancient history, and many didn't want to be reminded of all that nasty business.

Commander John Bulkeley emerged from World War II as perhaps the most-decorated, and certainly among the best-known, fighting men in American history. Like millions of others around the world, he rejoiced over the cessation of the butchery that had raged for sixty-eight months. Yet the Sea Wolf knew that peacetime, historically, was but an interlude between armed conflicts, so he pledged to work tirelessly to prepare himself and those serving with and under him for America's next call to arms.[9]

Bulkeley, now thirty-five years of age, began speaking out publicly on the challenges confronting the nation's security. Seared indelibly in his mind was the spectacle of army and navy leaders in the Philippines squabbling bitterly with each other while Japanese hordes had been running roughshod over the islands in early 1942. His candid remarks often aroused the ire of some Pentagon brass, particularly when he committed flagrant heresy by publicly calling for the unification of the Army and Navy, whose interservice skirmishing had endured since 1798.

"The nature of warfare today demands the closest cooperation among all our forces," Bulkeley declared in a speech.[10]

Commander Bulkeley finished his tour as skipper of the *Stribling* in

July 1946, and was banished to a desk job at the United States Naval Academy at Annapolis. There he chafed over the lack of challenge in the administrative assignment that he described to wife Alice as "boring paperwork held together by cheap paper clips."

In 1947, peace broke out—theoretically, at least—between Army and Navy after a century and a half of intense rivalry. Despite strident opposition from a wide array of sources and heavy bloodletting on the floors of the Senate and House, Congress passed the National Security Act, unifying the services under a Department of Defense. President Harry Truman appointed James V. Forrestal, a former president of Dillon, Read & Company, a Wall Street investment firm, to be secretary of defense. Forrestal had been secretary of the Navy since 1944.[11]

> ADMIRAL BULKELEY:
> Jim Forrestal, a good man, fancied himself to be a boxer and often went to the Washington Athletic Club to work out with the gloves. Since I was in the spotlight while commanding the *Stribling,* Forrestal sent for me, and during our visit he learned that I had fought on the Naval Academy boxing team. He asked me to spar around with him a little. Then, whenever he wanted to work out, he would send his plane to New York [where the *Stribling* was based at the time] and I would fly down to Washington, box a few rounds with him, then fly back to New York.
>
> Jim was pretty good with his dukes, but there were numerous openings when I could have coldcocked him. However, I always resisted the temptation. I could just see the newspaper headline: "Bulkeley Coldcocks Secretary of the Navy."

For two years, Comdr. John Bulkeley had been yearning for a return to his first love, sea duty; so he was elated when, in May 1948, orders came through to report to the USS *Mount Olympus,* flagship of Amphibious Group Two, as executive officer. The Sea Wolf's exile to Annapolis as a paper shuffler had been lifted.

When Bulkeley was detached from the *Mount Olympus,* in July 1949, his boss, Capt. Jackson S. Champlin, concluded a fitness report with the observation:

> This officer [Bulkeley] is the finest leader and, professionally, the most competent officer I have ever served with in over twenty-three years of service in the Navy. He leads by his superior example of tireless energy and selfless devotion to duty.[12]

A month later, Commander Bulkeley reported to the Armed Forces Staff College, a coveted assignment. Students at the Norfolk facility were largely middle-level navy, army, air force, and marine officers judged to be destined for admiral and general rank. This was the first class at the college that had been established under the combined armed forces concept.

In January 1950, after a successful completion of the staff college course, Bulkeley received orders that mystified him. He was to report for duty at the Atomic Energy Commission (AEC) in Washington. Atomic energy? What did he know about atomic energy? On arrival at his new post, the skipper was gripped by excitement. His working partners would be some of the scintillating figures in atomic energy development: navy Capt. Hyman Rickover, an irascible genius whom Bulkeley had known in the China days in the late 1930s; world-renowned physicists Dr. E. L. Lawrence and Dr. J. Robert Oppenheimer; and beetle-browed Dr. Edward Teller, credited with being the father of the A-bomb.

When John Bulkeley enthusiastically told Alice of his prestigious associates, she smiled and replied: "That's wonderful, dear, but please allow them to express their opinions on atomic energy before telling them where they can go." [13]

ADMIRAL BULKELEY:

What a time that was! There I was, a piddling navy commander, with a list of titles as long as your arm, and I didn't know what hardly any of them meant. I was supposed to be chief of "this" and assistant to "that." I did my damnedest, but on occasion was thoroughly confused—just like everyone else. Remember, nuclear energy was in its infancy.

There were towering egos to contend with. Most of the "brains" got so hung up on lofty titles and job descriptions that few could even understand, that I often wondered whether we would ever get anything done.

Teller, Oppenheimer, and the other physicists were geniuses, of course, but sometimes I got the impression that they were floating around somewhere in outer space. Like the prominent physicist who came to me and wanted to know his home address—had forgotten where he lived.

Well, somehow, despite the muddling, the eccentricities, and the king-sized egos, we got a hell of a lot done. Atomic developments in those early years were mind-boggling.

In September 1952, John Bulkeley was promoted to captain, his first elevation in rank in more than eight years. A month later he flew to the Far East and took command of Destroyer Division 132, deployed in the Sea of Japan off Korea. Perhaps with the exception of PT boats, Bulkeley's first love was the sleek, swift destroyers, and he looked forward to conducting the slashing attacks for which he had become famous in World War II. But he would never have that opportunity.

For two and a half years, a nasty, bloody fight had been raging in South Korea between United Nations forces (mainly American) and those of Soviet-backed North Korea and (later) Communist China. It was largely a foot soldiers' struggle, so American naval forces were used primarily to shell shore targets, escort troop and supply convoys, and launch fighter planes off aircraft carriers.

Fighting ceased on July 27, 1953, when an armistice was signed, and the two Koreas remained divided at the 38th Parallel.[14]

In mid-March 1954, Captain Bulkeley became chief of staff to the commander of Cruiser Division 5, whose mission was to patrol Korean waters in the event fireworks were to break out anew.

20

Prelude to a Naval Base Confrontation

In January 1956, Capt. John Bulkeley was back home, primed for a prestigious post on the staff of the Joint Chiefs of Staff (JCS) in the Pentagon. Chaired by Adm. Arthur W. Radford, a keen-witted, forthright officer who had been appointed by President Eisenhower, the JCS served as the principal military adviser to the nation's chief executive.

Admiral Radford selected Bulkeley to be his morning briefing officer, a task that required the Sea Wolf to reach the Pentagon at 4:00 A.M. or earlier each day. There he would sift through a mountain of top-secret messages that had arrived overnight from all over the world, pick out the most significant ones, boil down the information into a concise summary, and brief Admiral Radford at 9:00 A.M.

Even though JCS staff officers had to be on duty or available around the clock, Bulkeley was fascinated by the job. He found it exciting to be among the first in Washington to know what global events had taken place, and to be involved to a degree in helping to reach decisions that were often of major significance to America's security. Radford had instructed Bulkeley to voice his own action recommendations on certain matters that would surface during the briefings.

After two years of shore duty with the JCS in the Pentagon, the Sea Wolf returned to his natural habitat—the sea. He was to take command of the USS *Tolovana,* a Pacific Fleet oil tanker based at Long Beach, California. It would be a short-term troubleshooting assignment. Before departing for the West Coast, Bulkeley was told by navy brass that the *Tolovana* was a "naval disaster waiting to happen," and that his job was to whip her and her crew into combat readiness.

In February 1958, Captain Bulkeley landed on the *Tolovana* with all guns firing. He was appalled by what he found. Equipment and machinery had been neglected and were on the edge of operational failure. Worse, perhaps, crew morale had hit rock bottom.

Bulkeley could barely control his anger. He assembled the *Tolovana*'s officers in the wardroom and read them the riot act. "You are a disgrace to the navy uniform!" he thundered. "None of you will leave this ship until your own division or department is brought up to *my* standards—and those standards are goddamned high!"

Bulkeley paused. Silence reigned. "Apparently you think you're members of some highbrow society club," he barked. "Each of you needs a haircut, and those with the Hollywood beards and mustaches will have them removed by oh-eight-hundred tomorrow."

The new skipper said that the *Tolovana* was to depart Long Beach in ten days for operations with the fleet. "This ship will meet its commitments—even if those of you in this room have to use oars to row us there!" [1]

Six months later, Captain Bulkeley's troubleshooting mission was completed, and he reported to higher headquarters that the *Tolovana* was shipshape and ready for unrestricted operations with the Pacific Fleet.

Bulkeley flew back to Washington for a reunion with his family, and in September 1958 he began a tour of duty with the Bureau of Personnel, a necessary step on the ladder leading up to flag rank. Then, in April 1959, he took command of Destroyer Squadron 12 in the Atlantic Fleet. One year later his seven-ship force received the navy's coveted "E" award (for battle efficiency excellence).

In June 1960, Bulkeley eagerly opened orders that would disclose his next assignment—and challenge. He was stunned. America's most-decorated warrior was being sent to command the supersecret Nuclear Modification Center outside Clarksville, Tennessee, about as far from the ocean as a navy man could get. There was no solace in knowing that experiments crucial to national security were being conducted at the center.

ALICE BULKELEY:
I had never seen John so disheartened. He even toyed with the idea of resigning from the Navy he had always loved so dearly. John was convinced that the navy brass were putting him on a back burner, that at age forty-eight he was being sidetracked to a job as a paper shuffler and had reached

a dead end in his career. The admiral's stars he had coveted since boyhood now seemed to be fading away.

After two weeks of reflection, Bulkeley decided to report to the Nuclear Modification Center. Located fifty miles north of Nashville on the Kentucky border, the 5,000-acre facility was a self-contained navy enclave nestled within sprawling Fort Campbell, Kentucky, home of the 101st "Screaming Eagles" Airborne Division.

The nuclear center was surrounded by a sturdy chain-link fence and guarded by a contingent of 700 marines. Inside the enclosure was a huge building that was used as a weapons modification laboratory, and many igloo-type structures in which scientists, physicists, and technicians worked.

Hardly had Bulkeley driven through the front gate for the first time than he realized that there was a major disciplinary problem at the Nuclear Modification Center. Almost at once he isolated the cause—the daily monotony of peacetime duty that steadily eroded many officers' sense of leadership and responsibility.

ADMIRAL BULKELEY:
The entire complex was a festering sore. Accidents, booze, and brawls were the norm. The snot-nosed, middle-rank officers, who had never come any closer to armed combat than their boot camp training, had established little rings of power. For the most part, they weren't kids; they were misguided twits who needed a kick in the caboose.

Abuse of authority was rampant—and no one seemed to give a damn. Plain and simple, all this monkey business was going to grind to a screeching halt.

Bulkeley's task to correct the situation would be even more difficult due to the fact that the overall installation was a joint armed forces operation, with Fort Campbell and the Nuclear Modification Center each having its own commander. The navy skipper soon learned that a rivalry between the Fort Campbell airborne men and the nuclear center's marines had gotten out of control. A certain amount of spirited contention was normal and even beneficial to both services, Bulkeley knew, but brutal clashes could result in a hazardous climate for working and living on and around the military facility.

Captain Bulkeley worked with the Fort Campbell commanding general to set up joint marine-army military police patrols to make the rounds of the sleazy saloons clustered outside the gates and in adjacent towns. When marines or navy men were hauled in by the MPs, Bulkeley threw the book at them—and made certain that the offender's fate was widely publicized at the center.

Bulkeley asked military-surplus stores to stop selling handguns and knives to servicemen, and most outlets complied. Those that ignored the "request" were visited by navy officers, who reminded them of their financial loss should their outlets be placed on the off-limits list. Each reluctant store owner fell into line.

Security had always been Captain Bulkeley's number one priority. He was fond of citing the case of the fabled Trojan horse as proof that an unbeatable foe can be vanquished by its enemy through tricks that penetrate a military position. Within hours after taking command at the nuclear center, Bulkeley called in the colonel in charge of the marine force to be briefed on the facility's security system.

The center's security was "tight as a drum," the marine officer assured Bulkeley, and could not be penetrated by any human. Surrounding the center were four sets of fences, one of which was charged with electrical voltage sufficient to kill a man several times over, the marine explained. As an added security measure, vehicles carrying heavily armed marines, who had orders to shoot to kill, passed any given point at thirty-minute intervals on a road that ran just inside the fence line.

Captain Bulkeley was unconvinced that the fence line could not be penetrated by a dedicated person bent on reaching the highly sensitive buildings inside the perimeter. Hardly had the marine colonel departed than the navy skipper hatched a plot to put the security system to a test. If he, John Bulkeley, could sneak through the four fences and avoid being electrocuted or shot by patrolling marine guards, then so could an enterprising enemy saboteur.

Shortly after midnight, Bulkeley stole up to the outer fence that ringed the nuclear center. He looked like the creature from the black lagoon. Before leaving home, he had dressed from head to foot in "guerrilla black," and smeared his face and hands with black greasepaint. Instead of the tommy gun and two pistols he had carried on guerrilla missions in the Philippines eighteen years earlier, the one-time Wild Man was armed with several hand tools. He had told no one of his caper.

Lying face down in the darkness, Bulkeley paused and listened. The only sounds were the gentle rush of a light breeze and the merry chirping of crickets. Peering intently into the night, the skipper sized up the outer fence; it was formidable—ten feet high and crowned with barbed wire. This would be touchy business: if he were to get hung up on the chain-link fence, a passing marine patrol might shoot the unknown intruder.

Working rapidly and as silently as possible, Bulkeley used a cutting tool to hack a hole in the fence and wriggled through the opening. He peeked at the luminous face of his watch. Right on time. The pseudosaboteur knew that the mobile marine patrol would soon be arriving on its regular thirty-minute schedule—a crucial fact that any resourceful spy could find out for himself by merely watching the fence line from the outside for a few days, Bulkeley reflected.

Moments later, about a mile away, the bright lights of the security truck split the blackness. As the vehicle neared, the intruder hid in a roadside ditch. Lifting his head cautiously, Bulkeley could discern the silhouette of a marine standing behind the cab and fingering a loaded machine gun. Inside the cab, he knew, were two other marines—a driver and a man riding shotgun—both of whom carried loaded rifles. Only a few yards from where Bulkeley was sprawled, the truck rolled past and was swallowed up in the dark.

Now came the acid test—penetrating the fence charged with electric voltage. Bulkeley would have to work fast; another marine security truck would be coming along in thirty minutes. If he as much as touched the "hot" fence he was dead, fried to a crisp. Using cutters with rubber grips, he snipped a power line that ran for three feet from a ceramic insulater to one section of the barrier. Here his knowledge of electricity paid off. Even though he had cut off the power to the fence section that he had chosen, there remained in the chain-link barricade a static charge that was sufficiently powerful to kill him. Using a technique he had learned as an Annapolis midshipman, Bulkeley grounded that fence section, then carved out a hole with his wire cutters and slipped through the opening.

Fences three and four were easy to negotiate. In two hours' time, including periods in which he had to hide from the marine patrols, Bulkeley had breached the "impenetrable" security system. But his task was not completed.

Like a giant black jungle cat, Bulkeley stole across the dark terrain and slipped into a paint storage shed, emerging with several empty five-gallon cans. These he placed at strategic points in the top-secret buildings. In each container he put a note that had been hand printed earlier: "This can represents a nuclear 'suitcase' weapon, radio fused to activate on a coded signal. *You're dead, dummy!*''

After the ''suitcase bombs'' had been found the next morning, Bulkeley told his staff, ''This stunt may seem ridiculous to some people, but there is technology here that is damned important to the security of this nation, and a successful attack on this center would be exceedingly harmful.''

Bulkeley's nocturnal caper had achieved the desired results: every military officer at the nuclear center, as well as the work force, became instantly security-conscious.

A short time later, the marine colonel's successor arrived at the center and, armed with Bulkeley's suggestions, began an exhaustive overhaul of the security system. A few weeks afterward, the navy skipper told him, ''Colonel, I don't think that even I can penetrate this damned place now!''

On a bitterly cold day in January 1961, more than eighteen years since the then-Lt. Comdr. John Bulkeley had recruited John F. Kennedy into the PT-boat service, Kennedy, now forty-three years of age, was sworn in as president of the United States. Therefore, he became commander-in-chief of the navy skipper who had recruited him. In the Washington inauguration parade, a PT boat was hauled down Pennsylvania Avenue, a reminder of the new president's wartime service.

Seated in a VIP box as guests of President Kennedy was a collection of his PT-boat comrades from the Pacific days, including William ''Bud'' Liebenow, skipper of PT 157 (*Aces & Eights*), who had rescued a marooned Lieutenant Kennedy from a desolate Pacific island in 1943.[2]

PAUL B. FAY, JR.:
In 1961 Jack Kennedy reinstituted the Presidential Medal of Honor reception at the White House, a gathering abandoned by President Eisenhower. Since I had been a PT boat officer in the Pacific after having been recruited by John Bulkeley and was now under secretary of the Navy, the president asked me to join him in the receiving line.

As would be expected, Bulkeley came through the line and was greeted warmly by the president. Even though there were people still in line, Jack spent at least two minutes talking to Bulkeley. The next morning President Kennedy called me and asked if John Bulkeley was still in town, and if so would he be able to come by the Oval Office at about 1:30 P.M. My office tracked John down at a hotel, and I said, ''John, can you and Mrs. Bulkeley join an admirer of yours for lunch at 1:30 this afternoon?''

''Mr. Secretary, I'm flattered,'' Bulkeley replied, ''but I'm due back to my command at Clarksville this afternoon and have our plane reservations booked.''

''Well,'' I replied, ''I'm sure your admirer, the president of the United States, will deeply appreciate your dedication to your command.''

There were a few moments of silence. Then John said, ''On second thought, I just cancelled my airplane reservations!''

John met with the president for a considerable length of time, during which I believe they refought World War II in the Pacific.

Later, as a result of that meeting, President Kennedy expressed to me, ''I have a certain concern that the military is giving too much recognition to those who have high qualifications in technical capability at the expense of officers who are recognized leaders under fire, such as John Bulkeley.'' No doubt President Kennedy was referring to the fact that Bulkeley was still a captain, while others in his Annapolis class and later ones, who had made their mark in technology, had already been promoted to flag rank.

On April 20, 1961, only two months into John Kennedy's presidency, a bombshell exploded on Washington. Operation Pluto, a CIA-conceived and orchestrated invasion of Communist Cuba by Cuban exiles, had been smashed a day earlier by troops led by thirty-five-year-old Fidel Castro Ruiz, dictator of the narrow, 746-mile-long Caribbean island.[3]

At the Bay of Pigs invasion site, Castro captured hundreds of the invaders, and promptly took to Havana television to blast ''the ignorant schoolboy Kennedy and all the sages of the Pentagon and the CIA.''

Stung hardest by the Bay of Pigs fiasco was the man who had given Pluto the green light, President Kennedy, and his scrappy younger brother, Attorney General Robert F. Kennedy, who was fiercely protective of his older brother. The Kennedys were hard-nosed Irishmen from Boston, and they were obsessed with settling the score with Castro, the man Bobby sneeringly called ''the bastard with the beard.''

President Kennedy put Bobby in charge of an ongoing program to eliminate Fidel Castro and his Communist regime, largely through CIA machinations. There was no title for Bobby's ad hoc job as the president's ranch foreman to ride herd on the CIA and the Pentagon hands the second time around. But Bobby had become the unofficial assistant president of the United States.

Before the CIA could reload for another shot at Fidel Castro, a new and frightening specter reared its ugly head. On October 10, 1962, a high-flying, black-bodied U-2 spy plane swept over Cuba at a height of thirteen miles, and its cameras detected forty Russian missiles. Each was armed with a warhead fifty times as powerful as the Hiroshima bomb, and all were angled skyward and aimed at Washington, New York, Chicago, and other United States cities.

President Kennedy reacted with a naval quarantine of Cuba, and announced that any Soviet ship trying to sneak missiles or related materials into the island would be seized. During a tension-packed week in which the United States prepared for war, Jack Kennedy and the pudgy, bombastic Soviet leader, Nikita Khrushchev, stood eyeball to eyeball. The Russian blinked first. On October 28, he informed Kennedy that the missiles were being dismantled and shipped back to the Soviet Union.

The world ceased holding its breath. But the United States and Communist Cuba were on a collision course, and navy skipper John Bulkeley would find himself in the eye of the hurricane.

In mid-August 1963, Bulkeley flew from his post at the Nuclear Modification Center in Tennessee to Albuquerque on an inspection trip, and while in the New Mexico city an important telegram (identical to ones sent to seventeen other navy captains) caught up with him:

> This morning I signed a selection list for temporary promotion to rear admiral. I was delighted that your name was on the list. I am sure that this is a richly deserved promotion and I offer you my congratulations.
>
> John F. Kennedy

Admiral's stars were the Holy Grail that John Bulkeley had pursued tenaciously since age twelve. But his elation was tempered by a gnawing doubt: had he truly earned flag rank, or had it been bestowed upon him partly due to wartime comradeship with the commander-in-chief?

PAUL FAY:
For reasons personal to John Bulkeley, he told me at that time if President Kennedy had anything to do with his promotion to rear admiral he would resign his commission in the Navy. I didn't understand his rationale, because it was the accumulative recognition of all of his superiors that resulted in his promotion to flag rank.

Jim [Admiral James S.] Russell, head of the Selection Board, told me, as undersecretary of the Navy at that time, that the Board knew of President Kennedy's interest in John Bulkeley, but that Bulkeley was promoted because he was a brilliant officer who was a leader under war conditions.

I told Bulkeley that it was not all bad to have the individual most concerned about the ability of the armed forces, namely the commander-in-chief, to want him in a high position of command.

Meanwhile, the simmering Caribbean cauldron was starting to boil. Fidel Castro, who had seized power on January 1, 1959, had confiscated one billion dollars' worth of American properties in Cuba, had labeled the United States Embassy in Havana "a den of thieves and spies" and demanded that it be closed, and now was agitating raucously for Uncle Sam to get out of the naval base at Guantanamo Bay—the last symbol of "Yankee oppression" in Cuba.

A United States flag had waved over Guantanamo Bay since 1898, when marines had stormed ashore during the Spanish-American War and helped the colony of Cuba gain independence from Spain. In 1903, after the United States pulled out her troops, the government of Cuba leased America "naval or coaling stations" at Guantanamo Bay, for which the U.S. agreed to make an annual payment in "lawful money." Known as the Guantanamo Treaty, the pact gave the United States "complete jurisdiction and control" over the 29,000 acres of land and water until the end of time—unless Uncle Sam "abandoned" the naval base.

ADMIRAL BULKELEY:
That rascal Fidel Castro had been harassing our naval base at Guantanamo in every devious manner that he and his henchmen could think of. So Bobby Kennedy told me [privately] that the president wanted me to go down there and take charge of the base, stand up to Castro, and show "that bastard with the beard who's boss in this part of the world," as he put it.[4]

On November 22, 1963, America and much of the free world were stunned and grief-stricken by a news flash: President John Kennedy had been shot to death in Dallas by twenty-four-year-old Lee Harvey Oswald. A month earlier Oswald had been in Mexico City trying to get a visa to visit Cuba.

In Havana that same day, Jean Daniel, a French journalist, was interviewing Fidel Castro, who now called himself the *Líder Máximo* (Maximum Leader), when word came of Kennedy's assassination. Daniel noted that Castro never changed expression or showed surprise over the sudden death of his hated foe. "I'll tell you one thing," the dictator said evenly, "at least Kennedy was an enemy to whom we had become accustomed."[5]

Less than two weeks after the thirty-fifth president of the United States was laid to rest under an eternal flame in Arlington Cemetery, Adm. John Bulkeley arrived at Guantanamo to take command.

21

"There'll Be No Pearl Harbor Here!"

Admiral John Bulkeley's mission was clear: defend the key United States naval base, stand up to Fidel Castro's threats, and avoid igniting World War III. The task would be formidable, for Guantanamo had become one of the cold war's flash points. In recent weeks, stateside media had been calling Gitmo a powder keg, a tiny American island in a red sea filled with sharks. *Life* magazine headlined a story: "The United States' Most Vulnerable Fortress." [1]

Since November 1963, Fidel Castro had been howling stridently for the "Yankee imperialists" to get out of the naval base. His television, radio, and newspapers had launched a barrage of charges, including a graphic (and phony) account by "eyewitnesses" that told how "bloodthirsty" marines at the base had beaten and tortured a Cuban civilian.

Castro had built the strongest armed force that the Caribbean had known. He had 250,000 Soviet-trained soldiers armed with modern weapons and backed by large numbers of Soviet-built tanks and MiG jet fighter planes. After the 1962 missile crisis, the Maximum Leader had installed Russian short-range SAM-3 missiles, primarily antiaircraft weapons, in a thirty-mile arc around Gitmo.

Contrary to Washington's view, Bulkeley and Gitmo intelligence officers were convinced that substantial numbers of Russian troops, many of them in civilian clothes, were in Cuba. President Johnson had only Nikita Khrushchev's "solemn pledge" to Secretary of State Dean Rusk that all Soviet soldiers and airmen had been pulled out after the 1962 missile brouhaha.

Only two weeks before Bulkeley arrived at Guantanamo, Khrushchev had noisily reaffirmed that, should an armed clash break out between Cuba and the "Yankee imperialists," Russian missiles would come to the aid of Castro.

Admiral Bulkeley had but 5,000 men with whom to defend the naval base: a crack marine battle group, sailors and Seabees (navy construction men) trained as infantrymen, a squadron of Crusader jets based at Gitmo's McCalla Field, a few heavily armed helicopters, and the guns of warships anchored in the bay. They were virtually surrounded, their backs to the sea and hemmed in on three sides by hostile forces. On surrounding hills, soldiers of Castro's Frontier Battalion, probably his best troops, peered down on the naval base.

Bulkeley was undaunted by the heavy odds against him. At his first press conference, he told visiting American reporters: "Gitmo is sure as hell not going to be another Pearl Harbor—for Castro . . . or anyone else!" The "anyone else" was the Soviet Union.[2]

Speaking with customary machine-gun rapidity, the Sea Wolf said that "in the event of attack" his mission was to hold Gitmo for forty-eight to seventy-two hours. This would buy time for marines to be rushed in from Camp Lejeune and Camp Pendleton in the States, from Roosevelt Roads in Puerto Rico, and from the Atlantic Fleet.

"Nothing fazes this man," a reporter cabled home. "Castro's going to find out he'll have his hands full—just like the Japs did."[3]

Gitmo, a forty-five-square-mile patch of land and water, was the anchor of American defenses in the Caribbean, a shield for the southeastern United States. It had long provided an unexcelled training center for Atlantic Fleet ships that came for shakedowns and refresher courses. Like a huge, grotesque hand, Guantanamo Bay stretches twelve miles inland to form one of the Caribbean's finest harbors. Lower Guantanamo Bay is part of the naval base, and is separated by a narrow land bottleneck (known as Water Gate) from the upper bay, which belongs to Cuba. Rocky, scrub-covered hills border the deep waters.

Under the terms of the 1903 Guantanamo Treaty, foreign ships had the right to sail between the Caribbean Sea and upper Guantanamo Bay, in Cuban territory. This provision had been intended to allow freighters to reach the Cuban sugar ports in the upper bay; but now, six decades later, it presented an alarming security problem; Soviet, Cuban, and Communist-bloc vessels, which could be loaded with sophisticated surveillance equipment or drop off frogmen to plant delayed-action explosives on the hulls of American ships, cut directly through the naval base.

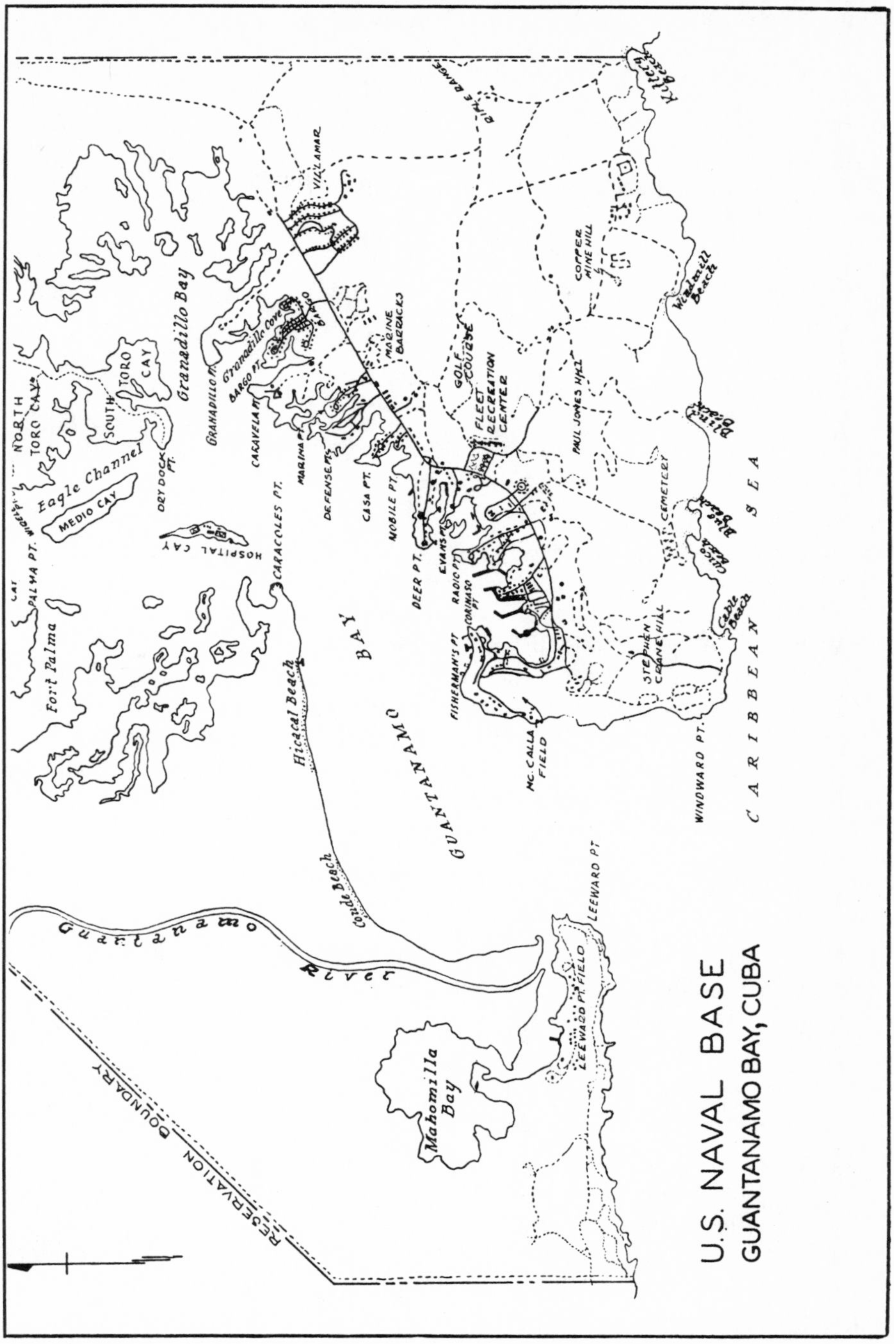
U.S. NAVAL BASE
GUANTANAMO BAY, CUBA
RESERVATION BOUNDARY
Guantanamo River
Mahomilla Bay
LEEWARD PT. FIELD
LEEWARD PT
Conde Beach
Hicacal Beach
GUANTANAMO BAY
CARIBBEAN SEA
Fort Palma
Eagle Channel
MEDIO CAY
NORTH TORO CAY
SOUTH TORO CAY
Granadillo Bay
Granadillo Cove
HOSPITAL CAY
CARACOLES PT.
DRY DOCK PT.
GRANADILLO PT.
BARGO PT.
CARAVELA PT.
MARINA PT.
DEFENSE PT.
CASA PT.
MOBILE PT.
DEER PT.
EVANS PT.
RADIO PT.
CORINASO PT.
FISHERMAN'S PT.
MC. CALLA FIELD
WINDWARD PT.
STEPHEN CRANE HILL
CEMETERY
PAUL JONES HILL
COPPER MINE HILL
FLEET RECREATION CENTER
GOLF COURSE
MARINE BARRACKS
VILLAMAR
Windmill Beach
Cable Beach
Blue Beach
Kittery Beach

Only a few days after John Bulkeley had taken command, an officer rushed up to him with a note that had been handed to a marine guard at the main (northeast) gate. Signed by Maj. Ramiro Valdez, Castro's minister of state security and one of the more rabid revolutionaries, the note said that 1,100 yards of the chain-link fence on the leeward (western) side of the base would be bulldozed down later that day. Valdez warned that it would be "imprudent" for the Americans to try to restore the fence.

Bulkeley's square jaw tightened. "Well, we'll see about that!" he snapped. "If the bastards tear down the fence, we'll put it right back up!"

ADMIRAL BULKELEY:
I knew precisely what Castro was trying to do by this bald-faced challenge—find out if the new Gitmo commander had a backbone. And tearing down the fence was a scheme to force the United States out of the naval base. Well, I wasn't going to let the bastard run us out of there.

While sailing to Gitmo, I had studied the Guantanamo Treaty, and it stated that if any portion of the perimeter fence went down, and was not repaired or replaced immediately by the United States, the base would be considered abandoned and revert to Cuban ownership. Castro thought that I, a new base commander, wouldn't be aware of that technicality.

I have always believed that when one is challenged, he must meet that challenge with appropriate action. Then if the other guy wants to talk, you can talk.

Major Valdez carried out his threat; that afternoon Cuban soldiers bulldozed the fence that divided the naval base and Cuban territory. Within the hour, Bulkeley fired off a note to Valdez: "That fence is going back up at ten o'clock in the morning."

At the appointed time the next day, Admiral Bulkeley jeeped up to the site of the destroyed fence. Wearing a steel helmet, combat boots, and battle fatigues, he packed a .357 Colt magnum pistol, and three hand grenades dangled from his web harness. Standing with hands on hips, Bulkeley glanced around at the muscle he had ordered to be present. Colonel George Killen, a veteran of Pacific battles and marine commander at Gitmo, had deployed 2,000 of his men along the three-quarter-mile stretch of downed fence. They were dug in, and their loaded machine guns, rifles, and rocket launchers were pointed toward the Cuban side.

High in the bright blue sky, Crusader jets circled like hawks ready to swoop down on prairie chickens. Hovering just behind the fence line were six helicopters, their automatic weapons ready for action. On board one chopper was a "snatch squad" of marines, a specially trained unit whose job was to rescue comrades who might fall into Cuban hands should violence erupt. Out of sight in Guantanamo Bay, crews stood by loaded guns on four destroyers.

It was an impressive show of force.

Now Seabees arrived with truckloads of fencing, cranes, and other construction equipment. Transits, double-checked for precise accuracy, established the true line of demarcation, and by 4:00 P.M. a new chain-link fence had been erected.

Not a single Cuban soldier had been seen throughout the day. But now a marine spotted a jeep, with two men in it, parked on a hill a mile away. Through high-power binoculars, Bulkeley saw that the passenger was standing up in the jeep and had his binoculars trained in the admiral's direction.

"I can't tell for certain," the Sea Wolf called out, "but I think it's that son of a bitch Major Valdez!"

Covered from head to foot with dust and grime, Bulkeley returned to his headquarters. Pitching his helmet on a table, he remarked to Capt. E. C. "Spud" Lindon, his chief of staff, "Well, Spud, there goes my navy career!" Lindon, a World War II submarine skipper, chuckled at the quip. Both men knew that Bulkeley had tiptoed a fine line between defense and provocation, and now nervous bureaucrats in Washington would be howling for the admiral's scalp.

Fidel Castro, a bitter enemy of the late President Kennedy and his brother Bobby, was now John Bulkeley's foe. He came from a wealthy family and was egotistical, shrewd, and impulsive. Castro had been a zealous revolutionary since his student days at the Jesuits' Belén College and at the University of Havana. At the latter institution, Castro had been involved with two terrorist groups, and kept a loaded revolver in his dresser. Twice he had been hauled in by police for questioning about political murders.

A lawyer by profession, the image-conscious Castro wore a long, scraggly beard as both a trademark and as concealment for a weak chin. He called his revolution the 26th of July Movement in order to give it identity. The name came from an ill-advised and disastrous raid he and his band of *barbudos* (bearded ones) had made against the Cuban army's

Moncada Barracks on July 26, 1953, an action the Maximum Leader considered to be the birth of his revolution.

When Castro had seized control of Cuba from longtime dictator Fulgencia Batista Y Zaldivar on New Year's Day 1959, segments of the United States media hailed the new ruler as the "Cuban George Washington" and the "Robin Hood of the Caribbean." But in Washington, CIA Director Allen W. Dulles told President Eisenhower that "the Cuban people have exchanged one bad apple for another." That evaluation seemed to gain authenticity in the weeks ahead when Castro's firing squads executed some 500 "criminals and enemies of the people" after brief kangaroo trials or no trials at all.

Hard on the heels of his victory in the fence-line showdown, Admiral Bulkeley made an alarming discovery: the naval base was perched on a time bomb of potential sabotage, one that could explode at any moment. There were 3,500 civilian workers, most of them Cubans, at Gitmo. A few hundred of them lived on the base, but most passed through the northeast gate twice each working day, coming from and going to their homes in adjacent towns.

Gitmo intelligence officers informed Bulkeley that 700 of the Cuban civilians were known Castro supporters and likely troublemakers and saboteurs. Large numbers of the base's male civilians were actually members of and drilled with Castro's militia of part-time soldiers. Hundreds of civilian workers were dues-paying members of Cuban labor unions, whose leaders had been harping for Uncle Sam to get out of Gitmo. Bulkeley was shocked on learning that civilians on the base were not required to wear identity tags and that they wandered in and out of the northeast gate as they pleased.

Furious, the admiral called in Comdr. Phillip Sheppard, chief of the Office of Naval Intelligence (ONI) detachment, and gave him orders: "I want every one of these foreign civilians identified. Each of these birds must wear an identity tag that gives his true name, nationality, and job on base. I don't want a bunch of goddamned Castro spies and saboteurs roaming around loose inside this base."

Due to his small staff, Commander Sheppard had been handed a difficult task. But within a few weeks he presented Admiral Bulkeley with a detailed record of all foreign civilian workers, including ones from twenty-two nations. Subsequently, Bulkeley had a large number of Cubans, suspected of being spies or potential saboteurs, kicked off the base. But not all of Castro's agents had been weeded out.

One evening three Cubans living on the base were grabbed by sharp-eyed marines while slipping hand-written notes through the fence to Cuban soldiers. The suspects were hustled off to the office of the provost marshal (chief of police, in essence) and grilled. They were frightened, but denied being spies. However, sheets of blank paper found in their pockets were sent to the United States for analysis, and a report quickly came back: there were messages written on the paper in invisible ink, and apparently referred to the movement of United States warships in and out of Guantanamo Bay.

ONI men searched the three suspects' living quarters and found more incriminating evidence: binoculars, compasses, and bottles of invisible ink. Bulkeley had the Cubans put in the brig.

Now the admiral was confronted with a complicated legal tangle. Terms of the Guantanamo Treaty stipulated that Cubans charged with crimes on the naval base were to be handed over to the Cuban government for prosecution. Castro was demanding their release. But it made no sense to Bulkeley to turn the three spies over to Castro, whose secret police had sent them into the naval base to spy. In Washington, the State Department pondered their fate.

Far west of Guantanamo on New Year's Day 1964, Fidel Castro was on the reviewing stand in the Plaza de la Revolucion in Havana, taking part in a massive celebration of the wooden anniversary of his revolt. High above screamed supersonic MiG-21 jet fighters, now flown by "Cuban youngsters," a loudspeaker voice blared out proudly. Below rolled a two-hour procession of Soviet-built tanks, artillery, armored cars, rocket launchers, and battalion after battalion of tough-looking Cuban troops.

Taking to the podium in his olive green uniform of the 26th of July Movement, Castro launched two hours of fiery oratory. "We alone could not have resisted Yankee imperialism—the blockades, the aggressions, the provocations. But with these [Soviet supplied] arms, we can fight against the best-equipped forces of the imperialist army of the United States!" Cheers rocked the plaza.[4]

A few hours later, Admiral Bulkeley was scanning the translated speech, which had been broadcast over Radio Havana and monitored on the naval base. The Sea Wolf pitched the document on his desk, shrugged his shoulders, and remarked: "So what else is new?"

MICHAEL L. INFANTE:
Castro's bluster and threats didn't phase Admiral Bulkeley one iota. He simply kept up his usual hectic pace, dashing all over the base, inspecting defenses and tightening security, often from before dawn until after midnight. When I came to Gitmo, early in 1964, as the admiral's new aide, I asked Lieutenant Ronald C. Rasmus, whom I would relieve, "Well, when does Admiral Bulkeley sleep?" Rasmus replied: "He doesn't!"

On January 9, 1964, Admiral Bulkeley was closely monitoring the bloody riots that had erupted that day 450 miles to the south at Balbao, adjacent to the United States–controlled Panama Canal Zone. Screaming mobs armed with guns and Molotov cocktails and led by hot-eyed men wearing red T-shirts and shouting *Viva Fidel!* were rampaging through the streets, burning and looting buildings that were "symbols of Yankee oppression." [5]

Gunfire broke out when American troops protecting the canal tried to restore order. Slowly, fitfully, the violence subsided. Three GIs had been killed, eighty-five wounded. Panamanian mob leaders claimed about three hundred casualties, including twenty dead. The Pentagon scoffed at those figures, pointing out that only nine rounds had been fired at snipers by American soldiers, and since that time blanks had been used, hoping to scare off the gunmen in the mob.

An uneasy peace settled over Panama and the Canal Zone. But one Panama radio station incessantly dinned the slogan: "A good Gringo is a dead Gringo!" [6]

Hard on the heels of the Panama riots, Admiral Bulkeley detected ominous signs that Fidel Castro would orchestrate a similar riot at the Guantanamo naval base. Radio Havana started appealing to Cuban civilians there to "return to the motherland" and railed that "drunken United States marines had indiscriminately fired their machine guns at Cuban workers on the base." [7]

The Sea Wolf shrugged off the Radio Havana rantings, but was concerned over the fact that Castro's soldiers along the Gitmo fence line were stepping up rock-throwing at marine sentries and had fired a machine-gun burst over the heads of a leatherneck squad. The marines retaliated by hurling rocks back at the Frontier Battalion soldiers.

Mindful of the extreme tension along the fence line, Bulkeley was determined to halt the agitation before a marine lost his head, killed a Cuban, and touched off a full-blooded shootout. So the admiral called in Marine Colonel Killen and ordered him to pull his men back 100 yards from the fence and to build a strong MLR (main line of resistance).

Colonel Killen responded to the "retreat" order with stone-faced silence. Sensing the scrappy marine's chagrin, Bulkeley said, "Colonel, my job is to defend this base without touching off World War III. That I intend to do!" The pullback order stood.

In the meantime, Cuban leaders were whipping up Yankees-get-out-of-Guantanamo hysteria. On January 13, thousands of Fidelistas rallied around the unoccupied U.S. Embassy building in Havana. Cheerleaders with bullhorns led the throng in a defiant chant: *"Pim pam fuera—abajo Caimanera!"* (Get out of Caimanera, the name Cubans from its nearest town gave to the naval base.)

The frenzied crowd screamed its approval when an effigy of Uncle Sam was strung up by the neck from the embassy balcony railing, and it roared when a United States flag was torched and the burned remnants were trampled underfoot.

More than 4,000 miles from Havana in mid-January, an Aeroflot TU-114 turboprop glided in for a landing in the twenty-one-degree cold of Moscow's Vnukovo airport. On board were Fidel Castro and his entourage. The aircraft came to a halt and out rolled a red carpet in the form of beaming Nikita Khrushchev to welcome the Maximum Leader when he came bounding down the ramp.

Khrushchev and his Cuban protégé hurried off to a secluded hunting lodge in a woods outside Moscow, where, on January 17, two Soviet bigwigs, Defense Minister Rodion Malinovsky and his deputy Andrei A. Grenchko, joined them in the winter wonderland. What subject was being discussed? "Matters of interest to both parties," reported *Pravda,* the Kremlin's mouthpiece.

Those matters of interest may well have been the United States Naval Base at Guantanamo, intelligence officers there conjectured.

Less than ten days after Fidel Castro returned to Havana, the simmering Caribbean pot boiled anew. On February 2, an American coast guard cutter was racing toward the *Lambda 8* and three other Cuban fishing boats lying one and a half miles off the Dry Tortugas islands, sixty miles west of Key West, Florida. The boats were violating the

United States three-mile territorial waters, and would be warned away.

Suddenly electronic equipment on the coast guard cutter picked up radio messages crackling back and forth between the *Lambda 8* and Cuba.

Lambda 8: "The American ships are the CG40438 and the CG95320 and the CG95312, all with thirty-caliber machine guns, and a destroyer."

Havana: "Keep the flag high. Cuba is with you!" [8]

It seemed curious to the coast guard commander that fishing boats would be in instant radio contact with Havana. His suspicions grew when his boarding parties saw that the thirty-eight crewmen on the four trawlers were clad in the olive green uniforms of Castro's revolutionary movement. The Coast Guard could not be certain what the Cuban boats were up to, so into Key West under escort went the flotilla.

The state of Florida, claiming that the Cubans had violated a 1963 law prohibiting ships of Communist powers from fishing within three miles of the Florida coast, released and deported seven boys fourteen to sixteen years of age. The remaining thirty-one Cubans were hustled off to the Monroe County jail in Key West to await trial.

In Havana, Fidel Castro took to the radio and sputtered indignantly: "A stupid, provocative act. . . . An intolerable act of cold-blooded aggression by Yankee imperialists!" [9]

On February 6, *Pravda* joined in the chorus of bitter attacks against Uncle Sam. "The [American] pirates who are flouting international law must be called to order," *Pravda* declared. The editorial was signed "Commentator" and therefore reflected the view of the chief honchos in the Kremlin.[10]

All over the world, Communist sheets, taking their cue from Big Bear Khrushchev in Moscow, lambasted the United States as "hijackers and pirates" for arresting the Cuban "fishermen."

At Guantanamo, Bulkeley recognized storm warnings when he saw them, and was ready to meet any threat against the naval base. Mindful that the instigators of the Panama riots had hollered incessantly that the Americans had initiated the bloody violence, the Sea Wolf arranged to get a filmed record of anything that might erupt. Since Gitmo's main gate was the logical site for a Castro-inspired civilian riot, Bulkeley had a movie camera with telescopic lens, manned night and day by navy photographers, perched on a nearby hillock and focused on the gate.

The admiral organized a riot-control force and had one-third of it on duty at all times. Two fire trucks, one filled with water and the other with sticky but harmless chemical foam, were hidden near the gate and manned by marines at all times.

If Castro, encouraged by pledges of support from Soviet leaders during his recent jaunt to Moscow, launched an armed assault against Gitmo, Bulkeley would be ready for that challenge also. Colonel Killen's marines had built a formidable main line of resistance 100 yards back from and all along the twenty-four-mile fence-line perimeter. The defensive positions included concrete pillboxes constructed during the 1962 missile crisis, all linked by trench systems, and a few hundred dugouts and countless foxholes. Between the MLR and the fence were mine fields.

Jet fighters were on fifteen-minute alert at McCalla Field. Each warship arriving for training was immediately given a combat assignment. Four destroyers berthed at El Toro Cay in Guantanamo Bay regularly plotted targets for their big guns. A large number of thirty-foot watchtowers were erected back from the fence, and new roads were bulldozed so that marines and sailors could be rushed to any Gitmo trouble spot.

On February 3, a reporter caught up with Bulkeley, in full combat gear, inspecting front-line positions. "What would you do if Castro were to charge the fence and overrun Gitmo?" The admiral glanced around the rugged terrain and replied, "Hell, this looks like a great place to fight!" [11]

Across the chain-link barrier, Fidel Castro was building up his positions, too. A security belt—patterned after the Communists' iron curtain in Europe—had been cleared of Cuban civilians to a depth of two to six miles. A network of roads had been built to provide greater mobility for Cuban tanks and motorized combat units. Trenches had been dug and tall observation towers built on hills surrounding Gitmo. Back of Castro's "battle zone" were artillery and mortars.

Admiral Bulkeley was confident that he could parry, blunt, deflect, or defeat any Castro action against the naval base. His lone concern was Gitmo's Achilles' heel—the fresh-water supply for some 10,000 Americans. Average daily consumption on the base was about 2,000,000 gallons—and Fidel Castro controlled every drop.

Since 1939 Gitmo's only source of fresh water had come from the Yateras River, four and a half miles from the northeast gate, in Cuban territory. Castro had kept the water flowing even during the Bay of

Pigs and missile crisis confrontations with the United States. Perhaps Cuba's anemic pocketbook needed the resuscitation provided by the $14,000 monthly that Uncle Sam paid for the fresh water.

It had long been the practice for a Cuban at the Yateras River pumping station to enter the base each week to collect the previous week's water bill. On the morning of February 6, 1964, he arrived in a highly nervous condition and demanded to see Admiral Bulkeley. The shaken man, who had long been on friendly terms with the Americans, was escorted into Bulkeley's office, where he dropped a bombshell: a few hours earlier, Castro's soldiers had taken over the pumping station and shut off the water flow to Gitmo.

In Havana, at the same time that the Sea Wolf was being tipped off, Dr. Raúl Roa, Cuban Foreign Minister, handed a diplomatic note to Swiss Ambassador Emil Anton Stadolhofer, who was representing United States interests in Cuba. It was 11:15 A.M. At noon, only forty-five minutes away, the note said, the Cuban government would shut down the Yateras River pumping station.

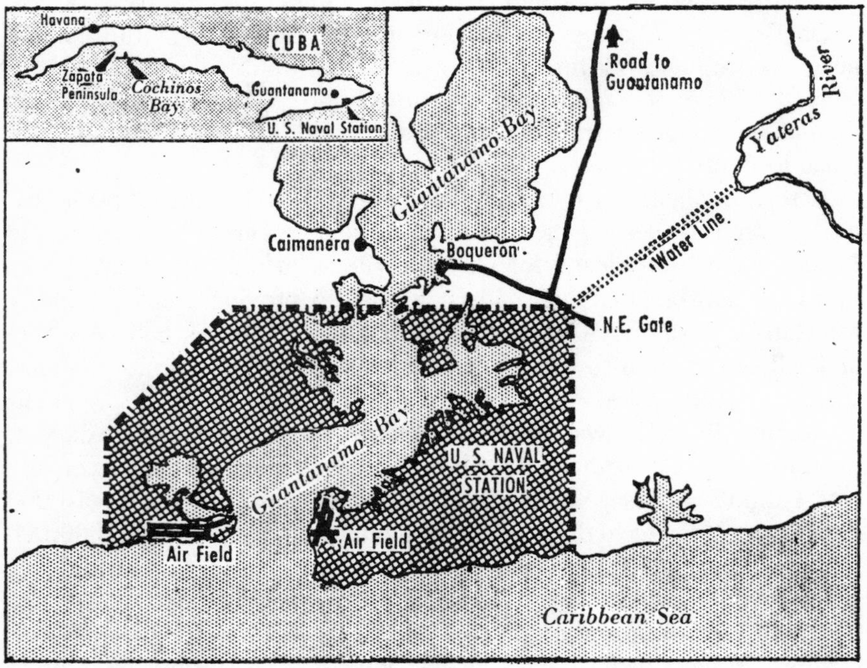

Water line between Yateras River and Gitmo

Castro's note stated: "In view of the unusual, arbitary, and illegal imprisonment of the Cuban fishermen forming the crews of the vessels piratically seized by the United States of North America in international waters, the flow of water will be halted . . . as a fitting reply to the imperialist insolence." [12]

Due to the grave significance of Castro's note, Ambassador Stadolhofer telephoned its contents, still in Spanish, to the Swiss embassy in Washington. At 12:05 P.M.—five minutes after the Yateras River water was shut off—the State Department received Castro's message.

PAUL FAY:

As undersecretary of the Navy, I was having lunch in the Pentagon with Paul Nitze, the secretary of the Navy, when in storms Admiral David McDonald, the CNO [chief of naval operations]. He wanted permission to send the marines off the base at Gitmo to capture the source of the water [the Yateras River pumping station] from the Cubans. When I asked on what legal or international law grounds he could justify such an action, he looked at me as though I were an unpatriotic flag-burner.

That day President Lyndon Johnson was in New York City for some politicking and a speech. Before leaving his suite at the Carlyle Hotel for the *New York Times* Building on West 43rd Street, where he would lunch with executives of the newspaper, Johnson received a telephone call from Secretary of State Dean Rusk: "The Cubans have shut off our water at Guantanamo."

Grim-faced, President Johnson replaced the instrument and left for his luncheon engagement.

A crisis pregnant with international ramifications had erupted at the mighty United States Naval Base in the Caribbean.

22

Ingredients for Nuclear War

On the hot seat at Guantanamo, Admiral Bulkeley promptly decreed Water Condition Alpha, a standby order to be implemented when "a serious casualty occurs in the water supply system that will require a shutdown for an extended period of time." Now each drop had to be measured. Marines with orders to shoot to kill were rushed to protect fresh-water reserves from sabotage.

But the Sea Wolf had to make certain that the nervous Cuban pumping-station official (who asked for and was granted asylum on the base) had been telling the truth. At 1:00 P.M., Bulkeley and navy Capt. Zabisco "Zip" Trzyna, the base engineer, grabbed a doctor's stethoscope and rushed to the point near the main gate where water from the Yateras River pipeline entered the base. A native of Poland, Trzyna had a sunny disposition, a dry sense of humor, and was one of the most popular officers at Gitmo.[1]

Bulkeley and Trzyna put the stethoscope to the ten- and fourteen-inch pipes and could hear water flowing through the intake valves of Gitmo's pumping station, which distributed the Yateras water on the base. It would require several hours for the water that had been in the pipelines after the cutoff to complete its four-and-a-half-mile downhill run.

Taking turns, the two officers listened for five hours. Just before 6:00 P.M. Captain Trzyna got to his feet, took the stethoscope from his ears, and with a straight face said, "Admiral, the patient has died." Bulkeley raced back to headquarters and informed Washington.

Three hours later in New York, a solemn President Johnson was speaking at a Waldorf-Astoria dinner to raise funds for the Chaim Weizmann Institute. Mindful of Castro's cozy alliance with Khrushchev and the Kremlin, Johnson interrupted his prepared speech to say, "This is a world in which in only a matter of moments we could destroy one hundred million people in Soviet Russia, and they could destroy one hundred million people in Europe or the United States." However, the president declared, "The United States will not be driven from Guantanamo!" [2]

At the same time that President Johnson was alluding to the dangers of nuclear war, Fidel Castro was holding court in Havana for a bevy of foreign reporters. Puffing on a long black cigar and basking in the afterglow of his water-shutoff coup, the Maximum Leader was in a generous mood. Despite the "extreme provocations" by the United States government, he told the press, he would permit water to flow into the naval base for one hour each day—"for the women and children."

A journalist quickly contacted Admiral Bulkeley for his response to Castro's offer. "To hell with the bastard and his water!" the Sea Wolf exclaimed. "We'll furnish our own water!"

Castro was unaware that Yateras River water could no longer flow into Gitmo. While at the pumping station with Zip Trzyna, the admiral had welded shut the intake valves because he was concerned that the Cuban dictator might try to poison the base's water supply.

Washington was in an uproar over Castro's bald-faced scheme to force Uncle Sam from Guantanamo by cutting off its water. At the Pentagon, the action was viewed as a threat as serious as the missile crisis of 1962. If Castro were allowed to grab Gitmo, the Soviets would base nuclear-armed warships and submarines only a stone's throw from the United States. Such an eventuality was described by a "high Pentagon official" as being "completely unacceptable." The military was ready to march.[3]

A White House spokesman, quoting a "high-level source," told the press, "If Castro thinks he can blackmail the Johnson administration out of Guantanamo, he has totally misread his adversary." That unidentified source was President Johnson himself.[4]

Democratic Senator Henry M. "Scoop" Jackson of Washington State urged the president to "protect our position at Guantanamo." Even dovish Senate Majority Whip Hubert H. Humphrey of Minnesota said,

"We have to be firm." Arizona Senator Barry Goldwater, an outspoken Republican and a major general in the Air Force Reserve, was in New Hampshire, politicking for his party's presidential nomination. Speaking before a packed house at the Hampton High School gymnasium, the silver-haired Goldwater declared that "Castro's action has made the United States the laughing stock of the world. . . . Our flag has been spat upon and torn to the ground, and as an American I am sick and tired of it!" [5]

When the cheering subsided, the fiery Goldwater peered through his horn-rimmed glasses and exclaimed, "I hope that President Johnson will have the courage to tell Fidel Castro, 'Turn it back on, or the marines are going to turn it on for you and keep it on!' " [6]

Nationwide headlines the next day blared: "Goldwater Calls for Sending in Marines."

Lyndon Johnson, fully aware that Senator Goldwater would likely be his foe at the polls in November, told newsmen, "I don't have to send in the marines. I've got a lil' ol' admiral [John Bulkeley] down there to handle things for me!"

In Havana, the Maximum Leader fired back. "If they [U.S. Marines] set one foot on Cuban soil, every last Cuban will die if necessary to defend the country," Castro told Tass, the Kremlin-controlled Soviet news agency. Tugging at his whiskers, he paused briefly, then bit off the words, "Let Goldwater come in the first line of combat!" [7]

Back in Washington the next day, February 7, Barry Goldwater was quick to reply, snorting to newsmen, "If Castro promises to be at the [Yateras River] pumping station, I'll lead the marines' charge!"

CAPT. LYNN M. CAVENDISH, USN, (RET.):

Just before Castro shut off the water, I was sent on temporary duty to the Navy Department in Washington from Gitmo, where I was operations officer under Captain Zip Trzyna. When the crisis broke, I became, by default, an instant expert on Gitmo in Washington. My assessment of all matters at Gitmo was sought by White House officials and by Department of Defense officers.

Rear Admiral Peter Corradi, chief of the navy's Bureau of Yards and Docks, immediately convened a study group of experts—including myself—to investigate and recommend an engineering solution to the water crisis. We worked all day and night investigating alternatives, talking by telephone with executives of major engineering, construction, and water desalinization equipment across the nation.

The next morning, February 8, we presented our ideas to Admiral

Corradi, maintaining that a fully operating plant to desalt water could be provided at Gitmo in about a year. Corradi agreed, and immediately made an appointment for he and me to see Secretary of the Navy Paul H. Nitze within the hour. I badly needed a shave. Admiral Corradi herded me into his private "head" and loaned me his electric razor.

Secretary Nitze puffed on a large [Cuban?] cigar and listened closely to our presentation. He gave us the go-ahead for building the plant, using available navy funds. I was designated resident officer in charge of construction.

Meanwhile at Guantanamo, Adm. John Bulkeley had immediately sprung into action to bring in fresh water. (There were already 14,000,000 gallons in base storage for an emergency.) Water barges were sent to Ocho Rios, Jamaica, and water tankers from Norfolk, Virginia, sailed for Gitmo. Two water tankers, the *Suamico* and the *Tallulah,* each with a capacity of 3,300,000 gallons, began operating a shuttle service between Port Everglades, Florida, and the naval base. And the water barge *Abatan,* moored at Gitmo, had the capacity to distill 200,000 gallons of fresh water from the sea daily.

Back in Washington, Assistant Secretary of Defense for Public Affairs Arthur Sylvester was trying in vain to smooth the ruffled feathers of a swarm of angry newsmen. The Pentagon had decreed that it was "not in the national interest" for American journalists to report on-the-scene activities at the potential tinderbox of Guantanamo.

"If that's the case," a furious reporter shouted at the beleaguered Sylvester, "what's that Englishman doing down there?"

That Englishman was genial Edwin Tetlow, correspondent for the *London Daily Telegraph.* Secretary Sylvester had to explain repeatedly that Tetlow had arranged to visit the naval base two weeks before the water cutoff and was there now by sheer happenstance.

At Gitmo, Ed Tetlow could not believe his good fortune: the only reporter at ground zero of a crisis situation. Yet there were obstacles. His stories had to be cabled to New York by navy communications, so his reports were being censored before they left Gitmo—and John Bulkeley himself was wielding the blue pencil. On water cutoff day plus two, the Gitmo commander deleted one sentence: "Guantanamo dependents might have to be sent home."

ADMIRAL BULKELEY:
Not for one minute was I going to give Castro the impression that anyone on the naval base had panicked. Particularly me. In every possible way, I made it plain that Castro was not going to run us out of there. I even went directly to our families by way of the base television to assure them that "we stay put!" That's what infuriated Castro—no one panicked.

I felt strongly that the Kennedy administration had made a serious mistake in pulling dependents out of Gitmo during the 1962 missile crisis. That action only encouraged Castro to try some other stunt at the base.

Shortly after noon on February 10, three Cuban teenage boys slipped into Guantanamo Bay at Water Gate. Their plan was to swim from Cuban territory a half mile across lower Guantanamo Bay and hope that Gitmo authorities would allow them to live on the base. Hardly had the boys begun swimming when they were spotted by Cuban soldiers, who opened fire on them. Two of the lads were hit and sank out of sight. With bullets hissing into the water around him, the surviving fifteen-year-old youth kept stroking and, nearly exhausted, was fished from the bay by the crew of a Gitmo patrol boat and taken to the base hospital.[8]

Admiral Bulkeley was furious over the murder of the two Cuban boys. "Those Castro bastards are real tough!" he growled to his staff. "It takes a hell of a lot of guts to gun down helpless kids!"

Bulkeley visited the surviving boy, Francisco Alveres, in the hospital, then arranged for the youth to be given a job and enrolled in the Gitmo high school. (A few years later young Alveres would attend Carthage College, Kenosha, Wisconsin, and was sponsored by the Guantanamo Scholarship Fund.)

Meanwhile, Water Condition Alpha had reduced daily consumption on the base from two million gallons to less than one million. Conservation was the battle cry. Armed marines stood by master valves and permitted limited amounts of water to flow through Gitmo three times daily. Swimming pools were closed. Baths were taken in saltwater. Hundreds of barrels of saltwater were distributed to homes and buildings for flushing toilets. Homes and canteens used paper plates and cups. Khakis and dungarees were worn at all times by navy men, because whites required frequent washings. Marines wore utilities on all occasions.

However, a solution to the fresh-water shortage was in the works. On February 10, Pierre Salinger, President Johnson's press secretary, announced a crash program to build a ten-million-dollar plant to convert saltwater into fresh water, making Gitmo ''forever independent'' of Cuban water—and Fidel Castro's machinations.[9]

Two days later, Bulkeley received word from a marine outpost that ''a big bunch of Commie soldiers are marching toward the main gate.'' This could be the start of the trouble Bulkeley had been expecting. He leaped into his spiffy Triumph sports car, a low-slung job decorated with the two stars of his rank and a model of a PT boat for a hood ornament, and sped toward the gate. Packing his customary .357 magnum, Bulkeley stood on a low hillock and watched events unfold on the Cuban side of the fence.

The hundred or so Castro soldiers gathered around a flagpole ten yards from the gate, and Commandant José Nivaldo Causse, chief of political orientation for the Cuban armed forces, hoisted the red flag of the Revolutionary Communist Party.

Then Wilfredo Lao Estrada, chief of the political section of the Eastern Army, delivered a fiery speech. He unloaded on ''the devious provocateurs of the [armed forces] at the naval base who had regularly been using blasphemy and had tried to bribe our incorruptible Cuban soldiers.''[10]

''Despite these provocations,'' Estrada bellowed, ''the Yankee beast [Bulkeley] has not obtained his objective,'' which was to bring about violence on the boundary between the naval base and Cuba.[11] ''In front of the Yankee enemy, we have raised the flag of our workers,'' Estrada shouted, waving his fist wildly.[12]

A hundred voices were raised in an off-key singing of the Communist *Internationale,* and the group marched away.

Bulkeley shrugged his shoulders, climbed into his Triumph, and sped back to headquarters.

At the same time that the Communist rally was in progress, grim marines were escorting 250 weeping, distraught Cuban civilians toward the main gate. This was the first batch of Gitmo workers to be sent back to an uncertain future in Cuba since President Johnson issued an order to fire and expel from the base some 3,000 of them.

Johnson's order was aimed at Castro's pocketbook. For decades, Cuban workers at Gitmo had been among the highest-paid native employees on the island, and, through their wages, Uncle Sam had been pumping five million greenbacks yearly into the sickly economy.

At Gitmo, Admiral Bulkeley viewed the mass expulsion order in simpler terms: ''Castro had taken a punch at President Johnson, and the President swung back.''[13]

CAPT. E. C. LINDON, USN (RET.):
Kicking the Cuban workers out was a gut-wrenching job for all of us. Most of the Cubans were loyal and hard-working employees, and for many the base had been their home. Often their fathers and mothers had worked and lived at Gitmo, as had their grandparents. Nearly all expelled Cubans blamed Castro for their plight, not the United States. They were angry at Castro.

Marine Colonel George Killen said to me in a sad tone, "Spud, it's damned tough having to order my boys to kick those poor bastards out of here!" I replied: "I know what you mean, George. I'm the one who has to select the ones to be booted out first!"

In Havana, Fidel Castro reacted angrily to President Johnson's mass expulsions of Cuban workers. He took to Radio Havana and harped for two hours that the firings were "illegal, arbitrary, and inhuman." [14]

Meanwhile, in Key West, the thirty-one Cuban "fishermen" with the four trawlers filled with sophisticated electronics equipment went on trial before a Florida judge. The twenty-seven crewmen were judged innocent, since they had been acting under orders. But the four captains were found guilty of poaching, were each fined five hundred dollars (paid by the Czechoslovakian embassy in Washington), and received suspended six-month jail terms. They were warned never to return to Florida coastal waters, then were put aboard their boats and sent home.

Fidel Castro's plot to drive the United States out of Gitmo was collapsing like a house of cards. A face-saving explanation was needed. So on February 13, water cutoff day plus seven, the Maximum Leader went on Havana television to charge that Admiral Bulkeley had been using suction pumps to slyly draw off some 114,00 gallons of water daily from the Yateras River pipeline. Had not Bulkeley been a water thief, Castro implied, the United States would now be in the process of pulling out of Guantanamo.

Earlier that same day, fourteen American reporters had flown into Gitmo after the Pentagon ban had been lifted. They rushed to Bulkeley for his response to Castro's accusation.

"Hogwash!" the Sea Wolf snapped. "We're bringing in our own water. Our mains were sealed tight right after Castro shut off the water, so it is impossible for us to draw off water by suction pumps or any other method." [15]

Despite Bulkeley's heated denials that he was a water thief, Cuban newspapers, television, and radio continued with a barrage of charges against the base commander. Castro himself joined in the chorus by howling over television that Bulkeley was "a member of MacArthur's warlike clique." The Yankee admiral would "stoop to any evil act to gain his goals!" the Maximum Leader exclaimed.[16]

Under the drumfire of Havana's charges against him, Bulkeley was getting angry. He told newsmen: "Castro's calling me a liar—and I'm mad!"

Ed Tetlow, the *London Daily Telegraph* reporter, cabled home that a lot of other Americans at Gitmo were also frustrated and incensed. One marine lieutenant told Tetlow: "There's nothing I'd love more than to lead a raiding party to the Yateras River and grab that goddamned pumping station back from Castro!"

> MICHAEL INFANTE:
> Those of us around Admiral Bulkeley began to sense that he was deeply frustrated at this point. He had not gained a chestful of medals in World War II by sitting back supinely and letting the other guy punch him in the nose. All of us around the admiral felt that, if it could be arranged, Bulkeley would like nothing better than to meet Castro in a one-on-one, no-holds-barred barroom brawl—winner take all.

At midmorning on February 17, water cutoff day plus eleven, Admiral Bulkeley received a call from Secretary of the Navy Paul Nitze over the secure-voice communications channel. Nitze, at the Pentagon, got right to the point: "Admiral, Secretary [of State Dean] Rusk just phoned and wants to know if you are taking water from Fidel Castro."

"No, sir, we are not," Bulkeley replied firmly.

"Are you sure?"

"Positive!"

As Nitze pressed the matter, Bulkeley felt anger surging through him. Now the Washington bigwigs seemed to be doubting his veracity.

"Do you know for a fact, Admiral Bulkeley, that the Guantanamo valves are closed?" Nitze asked.

"Mr. Secretary, I closed the valves myself and then welded them shut to keep Castro from poisoning our water supply."

"Well, how is it, Bulkeley, that Guantanamo, with ten thousand people, has lasted for nearly two weeks without getting water from the [Yateras] river?"

There was a long pause, then the Sea Wolf asked, "Sir, may I ask where the Department of State got the notion that I was stealing water from Castro?"

"From monitored reports over the Havana radio station."

Bulkeley was stupefied. The State Department had accepted as gospel the word of a Communist dictator against that of an admiral in the United States Navy whose integrity had never been questioned.

"Sir, that's it," Bulkeley said. "Unless I hear otherwise from Washington, I'm going to cut the pipe and prove to the world that it's dry!"[17]

The Gitmo commander promptly put in a call to Capt. Zip Trzyna, his public-works engineer. "Zip, I just got a call from Secretary Nitze," he said. "Nervous Nellies in the State Department are wringing their hands over Castro's latest squawk. I'm going to cut the damned water pipes and end all this nonsense that we're stealing water from the Cuban people."

Trzyna was instructed to rush an acetylene torch and two oxygen tanks to the main gate water-distribution station for the pipe surgery. He was shaken. Trzyna was fond of Bulkeley and knew that the Sea Wolf did not have Washington's approval for such a defiant act. Should the maneuver backfire, Trzyna was convinced, not only would Bulkeley be committing career suicide, but there could be serious international repercussions.

Despite the Polish-born Trzyna's deep concerns, an order was an order. So he sent up the acetylene torch and two oxygen tanks—but he would play for time. Both oxygen tanks were deliberately empty. Perhaps the lack of oxygen would delay the pipe-cutting operation and provide Bulkeley with an intermission to reconsider his planned action.

23

"Castro Can Go Straight to Hell!"

Only two hours after Navy Secretary Paul Nitze had called, John Bulkeley leaped into a jeep and raced to the main gate. Trailing in his wake were fourteen American reporters who had been notified earlier that "something big" was about to break.

At the water-intake station, about a hundred yards from the gate, Bulkeley ordered three Cuban civilian laborers to start digging. The first dirt was turned at 1:26 P.M. and by 3:45 P.M. a piece of the fourteen-inch pipe had been uncovered. Now the pipe-cutting could begin, but the oxygen tanks were found to be empty. Bulkeley radioed the Seabee commander to rush two full oxygen tanks to the site.

At 4:05 P.M. workmen started burning through the pipe, and at 6:17 P.M., at dusk, a three-hundred-pound section, thirty-eight inches long, was hoisted from the excavation. Across the fence line, Frontier Battalion soldiers watched curiously. Now was the moment of truth: who was the liar, Bulkeley or Castro? If the pipe was dry inside, no water could have flowed into the base since the February 6 cutoff. The reporters pressed forward and peeked into the pipe—it was bone dry.

Bulkeley hitched up his trousers and remarked, "That's it—and to hell with it!" [1]

On the following morning, Gitmo headquarters was buzzing with excitement. Not only had Bulkeley called Castro's bluff, but a report was circulating that the Maximum Leader, packing a .45 Colt, had been among the Cuban soldiers watching the pipe-cutting extravaganza. Castro had been nearby on an inspection tour, it was known, and had apparently been notified that the Americans were engaging in some kind of curious activity at the main gate.

"What a shootout that would have been!" a headquarters officer called out. "Bulkeley with his .357 magnum and The Beard with his .45 Colt!" [2]

Most of the night, the Sea Wolf, in combat gear and carrying a loaded rifle, trekked along the marines' main line of resistance, scrambling up one steep hill and down another. If Castro planned to retaliate for the humiliation that had been inflicted on him, Bulkeley was not going to be caught off guard. In the darkness, the admiral threaded past mine fields, some real, some dummies, with their triangular red warning signs. His bodyguard, a tommy gun–toting marine less than half Bulkeley's age, was hard put to keep pace.

On Suicide Ridge, a bluff not far from the main gate, the scene was World War II all over again. Foxholes and trenches honeycombed the rugged terrain. The moon was a luminescent fingernail paring, but by its mute rays Bulkeley could discern the helmets of marines crouched alertly in the excavations.

On foot and by jeep, the admiral covered the entire eastern perimeter, the most likely sector for any Cuban assault on the base. Just before 3:00 A.M. he drove to his quarters, a comfortable, two-level home perched at the tip of a spit of ground stabbing into Guantanamo Bay and known as Deer Point.

ALICE BULKELEY:
John had always kidded me about sleeping like a log. So I didn't even wake up when he climbed into bed with me at about three-thirty on this morning, after he had been on the go for twenty-four hours. After tramping for miles along the fence line, John was so exhausted that he hadn't even removed his uniform or muddy combat boots. The first clue I had that he had been in bed was when I awakened shortly after dawn and saw mud from his boots on the sheet. By then, he had already left for headquarters, having slept less than two hours.

Later he joked that I shouldn't sleep so soundly, that it might have been some marine climbing in bed with me.

News of the dramatic pipe-cutting had been flashed around the world. When John Bulkeley arrived at his office just before 5:30 A.M., a long-distance telephone call came in from Dan Bingham, military affairs

WATER PIPE
ADM. BULKELEY
To Adm. John D. Bulkeley
– full speed ahead!
CAL ALLEY

editor of a stateside newspaper. "What's the situation at Gitmo?" Bingham asked.

There was only one commercial line between the United States and the naval base, and that cable ran through Havana. At the telephone exchange there, Bulkeley knew, Castro's secret police monitored the Gitmo line around the clock. The Cuban sleuths were on the job, the admiral could tell, for the connection was weak.

"How are things going here?" Bulkeley repeated the question. "Fine, no difficulties whatsoever. If need be, we can hold out indefinitely!"[3]

That morning, a thin veil of apprehension hovered over the Gitmo housing area with its 2,500 women and children, a tension akin to waiting for the second shoe to drop. What action would Fidel Castro take to retaliate for the embarrassment he had suffered? At noon, Bulkeley was told that a rumor was sweeping the base that he expected all hell to break loose and had evacuated his family—Alice and children Johnny, Diana, and Regina—to the United States during the night.

Bulkeley was astonished. "I did *what?*" he exclaimed.

After the dinner hour, the admiral went on the Gitmo television station to squelch the potentially demoralizing rumors. "My family is at home, and they will stay put," he stressed. "There will be no official evacuation—repeat, no evacuation—of dependents and civil service employees." However, he added, "anyone who wants to leave Gitmo on their own will be furnished transportation back to the States."

Some two hundred civil service employees quickly packed their bags and left for the States. Not a single military wife departed. "God, I'm proud of our ladies!" Bulkeley told his staff.

In the wake of the pipe-cutting dramatics, the Navy was proud. Nervous members of the State Department were aghast. Castro's print and electronic media screamed "Foul!" United States publications had a field day. Scores of American newspaper editorials heaped praise on Bulkeley. Said the *Detroit News:* "He [Bulkeley] took action, not words. It was a language understood everywhere."

The Albany, New York, *Knickerbocker News:* "Hurrah and three cheers for Admiral Bulkeley—the first man to put Fidel Castro in his place since President Kennedy called his bluff."

The *Miami Herald:* "Admiral Bulkeley hit 'em where it hurts. He made Castro eat his lie, without any water to wash it down."

The *Arizona Republic:* "[Bulkeley] didn't present the all too frequent picture of the United States on its knees before some tin-horn dictator."

The Christian Science Monitor: "Admiral Bulkeley's action was indeed a refreshing change from the gobbledegook that emanates from the State Department when tense situations arise."

One editorial disapproved. The *Philadelphia Evening Star* cried out: "What on earth is going on down at Guantanamo? . . . Admiral Bulkeley's peevish action seems unbecoming for a war hero."

Almost overnight, John Bulkeley's hole in the ground near the main gate had become a sort of Guantanamo liberty bell. With the admiral's gleeful approval, Capt. Zip Trzyna concocted a scheme to enshrine the digging site. Trzyna's workmen erected a large, hand-lettered sign next to the hole:

> U.S. ANSWER TO CASTRO . . . GITMO WATER LIBERATED FROM CUBA AT THIS POINT

In the months and years ahead, no senator, congressman, movie star, navy secretary, chief of naval operations, general, admiral, or other VIP would visit Gitmo without having his picture taken next to the sign at the pipe-surgery excavation.

Castro's newspapers and broadcast stations were apoplectic over Bulkeley's propaganda bonanza, and began spewing out vitriolic attacks against him and other key figures at Gitmo. The latest issue of *Revolucion,* the Communist party newspaper in Havana, was smuggled into naval base headquarters.

> MICHAEL INFANTE:
> When *Revolucion* reached my desk I did a double take. On the front page was a large picture of Admiral Bulkeley, Commander Phil Sheppard [Gitmo G-2], and I being hung in effigy from a balcony railing in Havana. The caption explained that we were the "Yankee beasts" promoting Gitmo fence-line "violences."
>
> I couldn't figure how I, a lowly naval aide, was being hanged with an admiral and a commander. But I told Admiral Bulkeley that, if I had to be hanged, I knew of no one that I would rather be hanged with than him.

Hoy, the second Communist sheet in Havana, devoted an entire page of photographs (taken with telescopic lens) of marines guarding the fence line. "Marines are cowardly," the caption of one picture quoted a Cuban soldier as saying. "They are so frightened that they fire at anything that moves on the Cuban side after dark. . . . The marines have a constant turnover due to nervous breakdowns from fence-line tension." [4]

In the same pictorial story, a *Hoy* reporter described the scene on the United States side of the fence:

> An arrogant Yankee colonel [Admiral Bulkeley] stood facing the Cuban gate . . . and he was making wild gestures indicating that he spoke of bombs and explosives. He pointed toward our territory, his face inanimate, heavy with fat. Facing this Yankee beast and assassin stood the heroic fighters of the [Cuban] Frontier Battalion. One of our boys looked at the colonel [Bulkeley] and muttered, "Jump, fool, just dare to jump over this way!" [5]

Meanwhile, President Lyndon Johnson, the consummate politician, had been closely monitoring the press and public reaction to John Bulkeley's confrontation with Castro. Johnson liked what he saw and heard. Speaking at Los Angeles on February 21, the president, who was campaigning for reelection, declared: "We have dealt with this challenge and provocation from Havana. . . . We believe it is far wiser to send an admiral [Bulkeley] to cut [Castro's] water off than to send a battalion of marines to turn it back on."

It was not only praise for John Bulkeley, but also a jab at Barry Goldwater, who had been harpooning the president for "doing nothing" in the face of Castro's challenge to the United States. Actually, Johnson had employed some political sleight of hand in his remarks. It had not been him, but President Kennedy, who had sent the Sea Wolf to Gitmo to stand up to Castro, and Johnson had known nothing about the pipe-cutting operation until it had become a fait accompli.

In Havana, Cuban President Osvaldo Dorticós was quick to respond to Lyndon Johnson's Los Angeles speech. Castro's handpicked puppet took to television to declare that the Cuban government would "lay claim to the United States naval base at a time we consider convenient." [6]

Ten days after the celebrated pipe-cutting, Secretary of the Navy Paul Nitze flew to Gitmo to inspect the latest global hot spot. As Nitze's jet taxied to a halt at McCalla Field, Admiral Bulkeley walked forward to greet his civilian chief. This would be the first face-to-face meeting between the two men since their strained discussion over the secure radio channel.

Bulkeley knew that two-star admirals looking forward to coveted sea commands do not speak to the navy's top official in the tone that he had used. But Nitze greeted Bulkeley warmly, and the earlier conversation would never be mentioned.

Even as Secretary Nitze was touring the base by jeep, helicopter, and on foot, Capt. Spud Lindon, Gitmo's chief of staff, was beset by a major logistical task—how to respond to a blizzard of some 15,000 letters that had poured in from the States. The letter writers were a cross section of Americans.

George Stoddard of Chattanooga enclosed a dollar and asked Admiral Bulkeley to "have a drink on me." José R. Aguila of New York wrote: "The Virgin of Cobra [patron saint] looks with favor upon you." W. F. Potter of Buffalo declared that "it took a navy admiral to tell Castro that you can live without his water or anything else." Robert M. Carpenter of San Jose, California, was "grateful for your courage in cutting the pipe. . . . Helps answer our prayers." [7]

Bulkeley ordered a reply to be sent to each well-wisher, and over a period of several weeks he personally signed all 15,000 of the letters, often having to burn the midnight oil in order to finish the task.

Despite the threat of his puppet President Dorticós to take over Guantanamo at the "convenience" of the Cuban government, Fidel Castro appeared to have had a change of heart. On February 25, he met with foreign newsmen in Havana and said, "There is no special reason now that the [Cuban] fishermen have been released to keep the Caimanera [Gitmo] water shut off." Pausing briefly and tugging on his beard, he flicked the ash off his cigar and added, "Of course, restoring the water supply depends on the United States government requesting it." [8]

Contacted by a reporter for his response, Admiral Bulkeley snapped: "Mr. Castro can go straight to hell!"

In Washington, State Department bureaucrats were appalled. American admirals simply do not use such unvarnished rhetoric when referring to another nation's ruler. State suggested that it send an "expert in international relations" to serve as Bulkeley's political adviser. "No, thanks," the Sea Wolf replied, "I'll be my own political adviser." [9]

A few days later a Pentagon official asked Bulkeley for his views on a State Department study that claimed the United States Naval Base at Guantanamo Bay was no longer needed. Since Gitmo was primarily a training center for the Atlantic Fleet, Roosevelt Roads in Puerto Rico could serve that purpose, the study concluded.

Bulkeley was livid. "What State is saying," he exploded to his staff, "is that the United States should cave in to Castro!"

In his reply, the Sea Wolf minced no words. Gitmo was a United States military beachhead in "enemy territory" that could be used as a springboard to "wipe out Russian missiles," the admiral stressed. "With this beachhead and troops brought in by an amphibious force, we can take the whole island in two days. Or we can do the job ourselves with the marines already on board [at Gitmo]." [10]

Bulkeley's broadside was apparently right on target. No more was heard from Washington of thinly veiled proposals to abandon the navy base.

Meanwhile, the 10,000 Americans at Guantanamo were living in the front lines on this potentially explosive cold war battlefield. Bulkeley's pipe-cutting response to Fidel Castro's challenge to the United States had triggered an indefinable, yet quite real pride shared by all hands—navy men, marines, women, children, civilian employees. It was a kind of siege sentiment, a we're-all-in-this-together feeling. They realized the crucial significance of Gitmo in the scheme of things, and the necessity for their being present in what *Life* magazine had called "the United States' Most Vulnerable Fortress."

MRS. NATALIE LINDON:
Navy wives, especially those of us at Gitmo during this crisis period, were a close-knit family, but it was hard to overcome the feeling of isolation. It was necessary to keep busy, but periodic Defexes [defense exercises] on the base kept us reminded of our constant vulnerability.

Our daughter Gigi was attending the University of North Carolina at Chapel Hill [my husband was Gitmo's chief of staff] and my only communication with her was by amateur radio. We would set up a "patch" and try to talk to her at least once a month. "Hams" [in the United States] were the greatest, because without them it would have been very frustrating and frightening. We got in touch with Gigi through a ham at Camp Lejeune [North Carolina]. Two other hams in Birmingham and Fresno arranged "patches," as did a ham at Gitmo who arranged the whole thing. In this manner, we were also able to get in contact with my husband's and my mothers.

The view of the nearby Sierra Madre mountains, Fidel Castro's hideout during the early days of his revolution, was breathtaking. On days when the "debbil" claustrophobia would rear its ugly head, I would look toward the Sierra Madre and say, "I look to the hills, whence cometh my strength." It helped.

As March approached, Marine Corps Gunnery Sergeant Martin, a veteran of the Old Breed, was at Gitmo's main gate talking to a *Newsweek* reporter: "Admiral Bulkeley is out there on that little hill [by the main gate] whenever trouble is brewing before dawn, and he doesn't leave until after sunset each day." Martin shook his head in mock sadness and added: "Somewhere along the line Admiral Bulkeley took a wrong turn—he should have been a *marine corps general.*" [11]

On April 1, 1964—All Fools' Day—work began on the ten-million dollar desalinization plant that would forever free Gitmo from Castro's antics. The plant was being built at historic Fisherman's Point, where Christopher Columbus was said to have landed in 1494 on his second voyage to the New World, and where United States marines had stormed ashore in 1898 in the war that gained independence for the Spanish colony of Cuba.

The Navy had negotiated a prime engineering and construction contract with the Westinghouse Corporation, with the New York–based firm of Burnes and Roe Western Hemisphere Corporation to be subcontractor for field engineering and construction management. The plant would be large and complicated, and nearly every pound of materials and most of the hundreds of trucks, cranes, tools, and other equipment would have to be rushed in from the States.

Despite these formidable obstacles, July 31, 1964—only four months away—was the target date for completion of the first unit of the seawater conversion plant (two other units would follow). Admiral Bulkeley hoped to toast Fidel Castro with a glass of fresh water, produced right in the Maximum Leader's backyard, on the big Cuban holiday celebration of the 26th of July Movement. So at the Sea Wolf's urgent request, the target date was moved back from July 31 to July 26.

The construction pace was hectic; work continued around the clock. By mid-April, nearly two hundred skilled workers—civilians rushed in from the States and Gitmo military men moonlighting during off-duty hours—were employed. Progress was monitored daily all the way up the military chain of command and into the Oval Office of the White House. President Johnson had given the plant the highest priority, and he was briefed on developments every twenty-four hours.

Ground-breaking for the desalinization plant, hard on the heels of Admiral Bulkeley's blunt rejection of his offer to restore fresh water to Gitmo, touched a raw nerve in Fidel Castro. At once he launched a heavy bombardment of threats, harassment, and propaganda, all aimed at the United States Naval Base and its scrappy commander.

24

A $50,000 Dead-or-Alive Bounty

Although Adm. John Bulkeley had pulled back the marines a hundred yards from the fence line, Cuban soldiers loosed their heaviest rock-throwing barrage. Even slingshots were used to try to hit the marines. So many stones were hurled at Post 16 that a thirty-foot-high section of chain-link fence, like a baseball diamond backstop, had to be installed to prevent injury to the leathernecks.

Early in April, Cuban Foreign Minister Raúl Roa fired a propaganda salvo in the United Nations, charging bitterly that rock-throwing by marines was endangering Cuban soldiers and was "a deliberate act of aggression." Roa produced stacks of photographs to prove his charge. The pictures showed scores of rocks scattered over a patch of ground which, the Cuban claimed, was on the Cuban side of the fence.

Bulkeley scoffed at Roa's photographs. "Childish nonsense!" he told reporters. "More of Castro's gimmicks. Those pictures could have been taken anywhere in Cuba and are simply props for Roa's stage show. They're as phony as a three-dollar bill!"

On April 19, Havana's main plaza was packed with a few hundred thousand Cubans, many of whom had been trucked in from all over western Cuba, to hear a speech by Fidel Castro marking the third anniversary of his victory at the Bay of Pigs. The Maximum Leader was at his fire-eating best. "We are an armed people," he roared, shaking his fist. "The armed forces of Yankee imperialists cannot begin to compare [with ours]. If the Yankees don't take heed, a Bay of Pigs multiplied a hundred times [will] take place!" [1]

The plaza rocked with cheers and applause.

Wiping his forehead, the Maximum Leader continued: "The imperialists [at Gitmo] are not going to intimidate us!" He charged that "drunken marines" at the naval base "yesterday crossed over into Cuban territory . . . and broke down doors in two nearby buildings." [2]

Four days later, Foreign Minister Roa delivered an angry letter to United Nations Secretary U Thant of Burma, howling that there had been "1,161 provocations and violences by U.S. of North America forces" at Guantanamo since October 1962 (when the Soviet missiles on the island had been detected).[3]

Forty-eight hours later, Roa lambasted the United States on the floor of the UN, charging that the U-2 reconnaissance flights over Cuba were "intolerable." The U.S. was guilty, he declared, of "arbitrary, provocative, illegal, and irresponsible conduct that could bring the world to the brink of nuclear war!" [4]

Sleek, high-flying U-2 "spy planes," loaded with sophisticated photographic equipment, and low-level marine aircraft had been sweeping the island to guard against new Soviet missile sites and to detect any clues that Castro's armed forces were massing for an assault against Guantanamo.

Now the Maximum Leader sent his labor unions into action. On April 24, Admiral Bulkeley was handed a translated copy of a televised speech given by a high Cuban labor-union official:

> In view of the new provocations and threats by the Yankee imperialists at Caimanera [Gitmo], in view of the repugnant conduct of its marines, the [union] calls on its provincial and regional delegates to intensify preparations for May Day, the [Communist] international workers day.
>
> The Cuban Workers Central urges unrestricted support of the denunciations and warnings made to the Yankee imperialists and their lackey [Bulkeley] by our comrade, Major Fidel Castro.[5]

In the meantime, John Bulkeley, aware of Lyndon Johnson's delight with the pipe surgery, had a souvenir of the operation sent to the president. A one-inch ring sliced from the pipe that had been hoisted from the ground was mounted on a wooden plaque painted in navy blue, and from the center of the fourteen-inch ring protruded a water spigot. In gold letters was the inscription: "U.S. Naval Base, Guantanamo Bay, Cuba, February 6, 1964 [date of water cutoff]–February 17, 1964 [date of pipe cutting].'' In smaller letters was the time-honored phrase: ''Millions for defense, not one cent for tribute.''

After the souvenir had been dispatched to President Johnson, an officer at base headquarters made an off-hand comment: ''We ought to send another souvenir just like it to Castro.'' Bulkeley retorted: ''Well, why not?'' An identical memento was taken by courier to the Cuban sergeant at the main gate with a request that it be shuttled on to the Maximum Leader in Havana.[6]

John Bulkeley, it would appear, had gotten under Fidel Castro's skin, whether or not Castro received the souvenir. Late in April the Gitmo monitoring station recorded a speech that the Maximum Leader was giving in Havana. It was mainly a bitter tirade against Bulkeley, who was denounced as a ''beastly assassin.'' Castro topped off his diatribe by putting a $50,000, dead-or-alive bounty on the admiral's head.[7]

A few on Bulkeley's staff were mildly concerned. ''I've got two bodyguards,'' the Sea Wolf responded. ''One is my marine driver and the other is right here''—he patted the .357 magnum on his hip. It was his penchant for toting the large, powerful pistol that had resulted in the nickname coined by the marines—''Big Iron'' Bulkeley.[8]

On the night of May 2, five teenaged seamen from the amphibious assault ship *Boxer* were walking along a main road leading to one of Gitmo's swimming beaches. Before departing the *Boxer,* they had been warned to avoid taking shortcuts due to mine fields. Carrying swim trunks and bath towels, the youths climbed over a barbed wire fence and, due to the darkness, did not see several signs reading ''Danger—Mines.'' Marine sentries heard three explosions, and radioed base headquarters. Admiral Bulkeley was contacted at his home shortly after midnight and told of the mysterious blasts.

Dressing rapidly, Bulkeley raced to headquarters, leaped into a helicopter whose pilot had been alerted, and flew to the site.

While the chopper hovered low, the pilot switched on the searchlight, whose long, white finger picked up five clumps sprawled together in a field. Bulkeley knew at once that these men had stumbled into a mine field.

''Lower, get lower!'' the admiral called out. ''I want to see if any are still alive.''

''I can't get much lower, sir,'' the pilot replied. ''The air blast from our propellers might set off more mines and blow us to hell!''

Bulkeley insisted that the chopper get lower. When only thirty feet above the bodies, the admiral thrust his upper torso out of the door and leaned downward. Pulling back inside, he said, "No sign of life. They're all dead."

At first light, engineers with mine detectors began the delicate task of threading through the mine field. They worked all day and, one by one, dragged out the five mutilated bodies.

John Bulkeley had just sat down to dinner at his home on the night of June 28 when he was called to the telephone. The headquarters duty officer informed him that the Cubans had sneaked four large searchlights up to the fence and were blinding the marines with their powerful beams. The admiral put in a call to Col. George Killen, the marine commander, telling him that he would pick him up in five minutes.

Twenty minutes later, Bulkeley and Killen scrambled into an oblong concrete structure perched on a hillock a hundred yards from the gate. The building appeared to be a small warehouse, but it was a minifortress, with thick walls and sandbagged firing slots. Manned at all times by about thirty marines who ate and slept in battle gear, the building was crammed with machine guns and flamethrowers.

Bulkeley tried to see the Cuban side, but the searchlight beams in his eyes were overpowering. He and Killen discussed possible reasons for the Cuban action. It could be the forerunner of an orchestrated civilian riot at the gate, much like the bloody fracas in Panama, they conjectured. Or it could be to mask a charge by Castro's tanks through the main gate.

The admiral decided against calling a full-scale combat alert, an action that would have sent marines and sailors all over the base rushing to the fence line and possibly, in such a tense situation, touching off a shootout. Bulkeley and Killen stood by until dawn, when the searchlights were turned off.

Marines at the strong point were on full alert all day, but nothing out of the ordinary occurred. At dusk Bulkeley and Killen returned; again the searchlight beams flooded the strong point on the hillock. The leathernecks were angry, and had to be restrained from shooting out the lights.

As dawn neared, the searchlights flickered off, and Bulkeley prepared to leave. "It's just harassment," he declared. "Castro's version of psychological warfare." Going out the door, he added: "If that's what the bastards want, then I'll give them a dose of psychological warfare."

Later that day, John Bulkeley's improvised psychological warfare scheme began to unfold. Working on the slope in front of the strong point, Seabees laid out on the ground a circular concrete slab, thirty feet in diameter and six inches thick. When the concrete hardened, another crew of Seabees, this one armed with brushes and buckets of paint, began creating a design on the slab.

Just before dark, Bulkeley arrived to inspect his brainchild. He was delighted. So were the marines. When the Cuban searchlights came on, they bathed in iridescence the huge anchor-globe-and-eagle emblem of the United States Marine Corps that Bulkeley had instructed the Seabees to paint on the thirty-foot concrete slab. The stratagem foiled the Cubans: they could not shine their searchlights on the strong point without illuminating the marine corps emblem (said to be the world's largest).[9]

Two days later Admiral Bulkeley gleefully fired off a letter to Gen. Wallace M. Greene, Jr., commandant of the Marine Corps, in the Pentagon, telling of the episode and the enormous leatherneck emblem. He concluded on a laconic note: "There are no more Cuban searchlights!"[10]

In the meantime, construction of the desalinization plant at Fisherman's Point had been moving ahead at a spectacular pace. By July 1, only three months after the first dirt had been turned, Admiral Bulkeley and his engineers felt that the July 26 target date for completion would be met. Already, Bulkeley's staff had been drawing up plans for a huge celebration to mark the unveiling, for it would be a golden opportunity for the United States to dramatize an infrequent cold war victory.

Suddenly, Bulkeley's plans for a propaganda coup were shot down. On July 3, he received specific instructions from the State Department on how to handle visiting reporters when the plant was opened:

> Desalinization plant not (repeat not) to be played up. Treat it as casually as possible. Do not (repeat not) brag about our capabilities over Cuba in producing water. No (repeat no) flag waving of any sort. This has severe political overtones.[11]

The Sea Wolf was furious over the be-kind-to-Fidel order. State Department bureaucrats were roundly cursed at Gitmo headquarters. But the order may well have emanated from 1600 Pennsylvania Avenue, Washington, D.C.—the White House—and been tied to Lyndon Johnson's presidential election campaign. Johnson was projecting himself as a dove of peace, and spoke fervently of a need to "build bridges of understanding" to Communist nations. At the same time, he was painting Senator Barry

Marines Win Again

Eagle Puts End To Cuban Lights

Eagle Outshines Castro
. . . so Cubans turn off lights

Americans Squash Reds' Harassment

WASHINGTON — (AP) — Credit a huge Marine emblem with a Cold War victory over Fidel Castro's Cubans outside the gate of the Guantanamo Naval Base.

That's the way Rear Adm. John D. Bulkeley, the base commander, described the incident in a letter to Gen. Wallace M. Greene Jr., commandant of the Marine Corps.

It happened in early May, but went unreported until Saturday.

Ever since U.S.-Cuban relations deteriorated several years ago, Marine guards posted at the Guantanamo gates and along its fence have been subjected to harassment, including rock throwing and shouted insults.

Last spring, the Cubans hit on a new way to pester the American guards.

According to Bulkeley's letter, the Cubans put up flood lights outside the northeast gate on the base — then focussed strong beams on the guard posts. The aim: To blind the sentinels.

Medal of Honor Winner Bulkeley mulled this over for a while, then hit on a counter-stroke.

Bulkeley sent some Navy Seabees and Cuban workers employed on the base to the northeast gate.

They picked a site on a hill 75 yards inside the gate and began laying out a circular concrete slab 30 feet in diameter and six inches thick.

After the concrete hardened, they painted the anchor-globe-and-eagle emblem of the Marines in full red, gold and white color. A corps spokesman here said it's believed to be the biggest Marine emblem in the world.

The Cubans outside the gate found that when they turned on their floodlights at night, they couldn't aim them at the Marine sentries without illuminating the defiant Marine emblem at the same time.

So, reported Bulkeley, "there are no more floodlights."

Lead story in Miami Herald, *July 13, 1964*

Goldwater, his likely Republican opponent, as a wild-eyed fanatic seeking to destroy civilization by igniting a nuclear holocaust.

At this point, four months before Americans would select their next president, Lyndon Johnson's political pollsters indicated that he would win the election by a wide margin. So no action should be taken anywhere in the world that would sabotage his image as the "peace candidate," or torpedo his "bridges of understanding" to the Communist bloc.

On July 16, Admiral Bulkeley received even more precise instructions from the State Department:

> Talk as little as possible about Gitmo. Keep it out of the public news media. If it gets any notice, play it low key. Avoid all publicity and mute any that is received.[12]

Three days later, a third directive arrived, this one apparently aimed at the spunky Guantanamo commander personally:

> If newsmen from the United States or foreign come for [plant unveiling] avoid provocative attitude [toward Castro].[13]

On July 19, yet another directive came from Washington:

> Planned July 26 desalinization plant ceremonies must be postponed. Under no circumstances (repeat, under no circumstances) are you to take psychological advantage of Castro.[14]

Privately, Admiral Bulkeley exploded over the Washington edict that ordered him not to "take psychological advantage of Castro." But an order was an order, so he rescheduled to July 30 the celebration that would mark the unveiling of the world's largest plant of its kind.

CAPT. LYNN CAVENDISH:
I believe that it was early July 1964—when the plant was nearing completion—that the popular television game show "What's My Line" began discussions with navy officials in Washington for me to appear on the program. "What's My Line" was hosted by John Daley, and four celebrity panelists, through asking questions, would try to identify the nature of a guest's work.

I would be appearing as the navy officer in charge of construction at the Gitmo desalinization plant, which was Uncle Sam's answer to Castro.

Of course, I was excited over the prospect, for it would be an opportunity to inform millions of Americans what the Navy was achieving at Guantanamo.

Suddenly I received word that the Navy had broken off discussions with the "What's My Line" people—no reason given—so I never did appear on the show.

On the day that Admiral Bulkeley was reading the latest State Department directive, July 19, marine Pfc John T. Kozell III, of Cleveland, Ohio, was standing watch at sentry Post 9, located on a low hill about a hundred yards from the fence line. Kozell, eighteen years of age, could have been a football linebacker: he stood six-feet-four and weighed two hundred thirty-five pounds.

Standing above Kozell in a thirty-foot-high tower was marine Pvt. Michael J. Furillo, of Chester, Pennsylvania. The two leathernecks looked on casually as a Cuban army truck chugged up to the fence, for they had seen this routine many times. The truck would drop off two fresh guards and pick up two Cubans who had been on duty at that post, located about 175 yards from the pair of marines.

But this time the pattern changed. Instead of the two for two switch, five Cuban soldiers piled out of the truck, making seven men at the post. "Better phone the corporal of the guard and tell him about this," Kozell yelled to Furillo. "Reuben might be up to something!" (Gitmo military men referred to Cuban soldiers as Reuben.) Furillo placed the field-telephone call.

Now a Cuban officer wearing a beret (as opposed to the Soviet-style helmets worn by Frontier Battalion soldiers) began pointing around the nearby terrain, and the Cubans quickly scattered to take up positions. Some lay on the ground; others remained standing. Peering through binoculars, Corporal Kozell felt a cold chill at the sight of all seven Cuban soldiers aiming their rifles in his direction.

Suddenly there was a sharp crack. A bullet hissed past Kozell's head. He threw himself to the ground, shoved a clip of cartridges into his rifle, and shouted to Furillo, "Get the hell down from there!" Furillo needed no prompting; he had already started scrambling toward the ground. Kozell remembered his orders: he was to shoot to protect the life of a comrade. When Furillo was coming down the ladder, thereby becoming a vulnerable target, Kozell fired a shot, deliberately far over the heads of the Cuban soldiers, to give his comrade cover. Three Cubans flung themselves to the ground.[15]

Three to four minutes later, the marine officer of the day, Lt. John Palchak, of Denoree, Pennsylvania, barreled his jeep up the hill to sentry Post 9. He found Kozell shaken. Not only had he been shot at for the first time, but he was aware of the tinderbox nature of Gitmo and didn't want to be the one to touch off World War III.

Each marine's bullets were always counted before he went on outpost duty, so Lieutenant Palchak checked Kozell's and Furillo's ammunition and found that only one cartridge was missing. He told Furillo to remain at the post, and Kozell was taken to a guard shack.[16]

Now Capt. R. A. Widdows, of Hagerstown, Maryland, commander of the rifle company defending this sector, reached the outpost. Just as Widdows climbed from his jeep—six minutes after the Cuban rifle shot had been fired—he saw an ambulance pull up and halt on the other side of the chain-link barrier. Widdows, who at one time had commanded President Kennedy's marine honor guard, saw the Cubans buzzing around the ambulance as though they were treating someone lying on the ground.

Then another Cuban ambulance arrived. Captain Widdows, through binoculars, saw a man leap out of the second vehicle with what appeared to be a bottle of plasma. One minute later a motorcycle and sidecar roared up in a cloud of dust with Shutterbug Charlie, the name pinned on the Cuban photographers who for months had been dashing up and down the twenty-four-mile fence line, taking pictures of alleged marine "provocations and violences."

The Cubans loaded a stretcher into an ambulance while Shutterbug Charlie snapped away furiously, but Captain Widdows, Lieutenant Paychak, and two marine privates swore that the stretcher was empty.

ADMIRAL BULKELEY:

Fidel Castro had staged a masterpiece, one that would have made the famed Hollywood director John "Pappy" Ford green with envy. Intricate planning, delicate timing, and skilled acting had gone into Castro's fence-line scenario. Those birds sure put on a great show.

But this production did not bring down the final curtain on the Cuban extravaganza. Somewhere between the ambulances' departure from the fence line and their arrival in nearby Guantanamo city, a male cadaver had been placed in the back of one of the vehicles. Radio Havana identified the "martyr" as Pvt. Ramón Lopez Pena, nineteen years of age. In a communique, Defense Minister Raúl Castro, Fidel's younger brother, declared that "six shots were fired at Private Lopez Pena" and that "two of the bullets struck him in the neck and he died twenty minutes later." [17]

(From secret sources Admiral Bulkeley learned that the "martyr" was indeed a Cuban soldier, but he had been killed elsewhere the previous day in circumstances not connected with the naval base.)

In the meantime, a flatbed truck hauled Pvt. Lopez Pena—obscure in life, center stage in death—through the streets of Guantanamo city. As anticipated, the public display of the "martyr" whipped up an angry outburst against the Americans at Gitmo. That night, Raúl Castro gave the funeral eulogy in Guantanamo city cemetery. (His oration was broadcast throughout the Caribbean by the powerful Radio Havana.)

Poor Pvt. Lopez Pena was virtually ignored. Instead Raúl Castro launched a bitter diatribe against the United States, with special salvos aimed at Adm. John Bulkeley and Senator Barry Goldwater. What was needed, Raúl declared, was "a world front, a front of honest men, to face the war" that he predicted would result from the actions of "beasts" like Bulkeley and Goldwater.[18]

Twenty-four hours later, Castro charged that Gitmo marines had wounded two more Cuban soldiers, bringing his casualty toll at the fence to one Cuban killed and two seriously wounded.[19]

On the following day in New York, Cuban Foreign Minister Raúl Roa handed an official note to U Thant at the United Nations, charging that "the situation caused by provocations" at the Guantanamo naval base had created an "exceedingly grave risk" that could lead to an armed conflict that would endanger world peace.[20]

Translation: If United States forces at Gitmo were to clash with Cuban forces, the Soviet Union would leap into the fray and World War III would break out.

As the heated controversy raged over "the shot heard 'round the world," Fidel Castro flew to Santiago de Cuba, some eighty miles west of Gitmo, for a mammoth celebration marking the anniversary of his 26th of July Movement.

25

"A Gorilla of the Worst Species!"

On July 26, 1964, Santiago was bulging at the seams. Packed sardinelike into the main square were 250,000 campesinos (farm workers) who had been waiting in the broiling sun for hours to hear Fidel Castro speak on this Cuban national holiday. By truck and bus, they had been hauled into Santiago from all over the eastern half of the island. Seated on the platform was the Maximum Leader, wearing a .45 Colt at his hip; Che Guevera, a one-time Argentine physician turned die-hard Communist revolutionary; and Fidel's brother Raúl, the defense minister.

Seated in front of the podium were thirty American reporters who had flown in to cover the celebration. The Maximum Leader had banned Yankee scribes from Cuba three years earlier during the Eisenhower administration, except for a handful of sympathetic journalists who could be counted on to give a Castro-slanted pitch to their stories. Now the embargo had been lifted, for Castro wanted the Americans to report widely on what he would say.

The Cuban chief was somber as he strode to the microphone and unstrapped his .45 Colt. Cheers rocked the square. He promptly lashed out against a variety of pet targets, concentrating his heaviest salvos at Admiral Bulkeley, on whose head he had earlier posted a $50,000 dead-or-alive bounty.

There had been "extremely grave provocations" at the Guantanamo naval base in recent weeks, Castro thundered, "with U.S. Marines crossing the [fence line], outraging our flag, firing at a Cuban soldier and wounding him, then firing at another soldier and wounding him, and firing at a revolutionary soldier and killing him." [1]

Castro said that "we know who is behind all this. We do not believe that the United States government is ordering carrying out these provocations. . . . Something so absurd, so stupid, so illogical [had to be ordered by] elements in the [Guantanamo] naval base, probably the commander [Bulkeley], who is a gorilla of the worst species. This gentleman is responsible for the big provocations that have been taking place at the naval base." [2]

While the crowd cheered raucously, the Maximum Leader tugged at his beard. "From our point of view," he bellowed, waving his fist for emphasis, "the interest of that gentleman [Bulkeley] is that we return the fire and kill a few marines to aid Goldwater's campaign against President Johnson." [3]

Bulkeley and Goldwater would "stoop to anything" to "stir up trouble" at Gitmo, Castro declared. "But does that mean that we will have to bear their killing our men at the naval base?"

There were loud shouts from the throng: "No! No! No!" [4]

Castro continued to hammer at the theme that Bulkeley and Goldwater had joined in a diabolical plot to plunge the world into nuclear war. "We are willing to make sacrifices for peace," he exclaimed, "but we are not willing to turn into docile sheep who will enter the slaughterhouse [at Gitmo] on behalf of peace!" Heavy applause and cheering.

One of the massive crowd's greatest ovations followed Castro's warning that "our men will shoot back if these provocations continue [at the naval base]." A chant rose up to the effect that "Fidel will hit the Yankees hard! Fidel will hit the Yankees hard!"

The Maximum Leader pressed home his attack on Bulkeley and Gitmo. "It is very hard to bury a comrade who has been killed in a cowardly manner and to have to tell our soldiers to be calm and not to use the weapons they have in their hands to defend themselves. It is difficult to have to tell these men 'stay there and let yourselves be killed without firing a shot.' " [5]

The next morning, July 27, a carload of American reporters set out from Santiago for Guantanamo to get Admiral Bulkeley's response to Castro's saber-rattling oration. At a checkpoint beside a rusty railroad track leading to an abandoned sugar refinery just outside the naval base, Cuban soldiers refused to allow the reporters to continue. So the newsmen telephoned Bulkeley from nearby Caimanera.

"What is your opinion about Castro calling you a gorilla of the worst species?" one of them asked.

"He's entitled to his views," the Sea Wolf replied evenly.

"What do you think about Castro charging that you are the man responsible for the alleged shootings [at Gitmo]?" a second reporter inquired.

Bulkeley struggled to keep his composure. "First of all," he replied in his staccato style, "the so-called shootings were entirely phony. Since I have been in command, every bullet and shell on this base has been accounted for by me. Only one bullet had been fired—by the marine corporal [Kozell] shooting far over the Cubans' heads to give cover to his comrade whose life was being threatened by the Cubans' actions. . . . All of this is more of Fidel Castro's monkey business." [6]

Meanwhile, at 3:00 A.M. on July 26—Castro's big holiday—John Bulkeley, Lynn Cavendish, Zip Trzyna, and a few other officers had sneaked into the seawater conversion plant and, like mischievous schoolboys, drew several "unofficial" jugs and privately toasted the Maximum Leader. Four days later, on July 30, historic Fisherman's Point was the scene of a joyous celebration.

Several thousand navy men, marines, military families, American and foreign civilian workers, and Cubans living on the base joined in the unveiling of the plant. Bands played and huge amounts of hamburgers, chicken, beer, and soft drinks were consumed. Admiral Bulkeley had insisted that Barbara Cavendish, wife of the resident engineer in charge, turn a special valve that started the flow of fresh water from the plant. Thunderous cheers rocked the locale.

Now fireworks began exploding in the air over the plant, a dazzling pyrotechnic spectacular that one marine swore could be "heard and seen all the way to Havana." It was a typical, down-home American Fourth of July type of celebration—deep in the heart of Communist Cuba.[7]

Construction of the plant had been a near engineering miracle. From the first shovelful of dirt turned on April 1, it had taken three months, twenty-nine days, three and a half hours to build the facility—and not a single life had been lost despite the hectic pace.

No longer would Uncle Sam be susceptible to Fidel Castro's freshwater blackmail.

Six days after his Santiago diatribe against Admiral Bulkeley, Castro was holding court for a bevy of American reporters at Varadero Beach, his favorite seaside haunt. He was ensconced at the once plush Interna-

Cooling him off.

tional Hotel, which had deteriorated to the same shabbiness found in most public places in Cuba. Castro lit a long black cigar, then opened a lengthy monologue. "There are some who believe that an aggression against Cuba will not bring a world war," he declared. "But it will cause a world war, make no mistake about that."

In reply to a question, the bearded Cuban said, "I would take missiles again. . . . The Soviet Union is seriously compromised with Cuba." [8]

"But I don't think you would let an incident, a single incident or even several like you say happened at the [Guantanamo] naval base, start a third world war," pressed Bernard L. Collier, a correspondent for the *New York Herald Tribune*.

Flicking the ash off his cigar, Castro replied, "We must try very hard to avoid incidents [at Gitmo]." [9]

Fidel Castro manipulated certain elements of the United States media with the virtuosity that Jascha Heifetz had lavished on his Stradivarius. So it was duly reported in the States that the Maximum Leader was striving to preserve world peace by avoiding "incidents" at Guantanamo. Less than three days later, Castro launched a crash project to ring the naval base with pillboxes.

Thirty pieces of Soviet-built earth-moving equipment had suddenly been brought up to the fence line, and blue-clad "volunteer" Cuban laborers began clearing cactus and scrub brush to a depth of two hundred yards or more along the entire twenty-four-mile perimeter. Then six-ton flatbed trucks were used to haul up conelike pillboxes, which were lifted off by cranes onto the top of holes dug in the ground by hundreds of the "volunteers." [10]

Trenches having concrete sides and tops connected most of the pillboxes, the closest ones being about two hundred yards from the fence line. About one hundred yards from the dividing barrier, a triple fence of barbed wire about eight feet high was erected.

Most of the pillboxes (there would be 141 of them when the project was completed) were located on high ground. They were sunk deep into the earth, with only cupolas and firing slots showing. Mixed in with these prefabricated pillboxes was a second type built in the field from poured concrete and reinforced by steel rods. Their roofs appeared to be more than two feet thick.[11]

These formidable fortifications had a general pattern that followed Soviet military engineering practice, Admiral Bulkeley told Washington, and a Pentagon study would conclude that the Cuban Siegfried line had been built with Russian military and engineering advice and heavy equipment—along with fifteen million dollars poured into the project by Khrushchev.[12]

Stateside reporters bombarded Admiral Bulkeley for his views on the bunkers ringing the naval base. "Why are they building these pillboxes?" the Sea Wolf repeated the question of an Associated Press reporter who had telephoned from New York. Aware that Castro's secret police were eavesdropping on the line at the Havana telephone exchange, Bulkeley replied, "Well, you tell me. Castro knows that if we are ordered to break out of here that we'll go through his fortified belt like a hot knife through butter."

The admiral paused momentarily, then added, "So perhaps Mr. Castro wants his [Russian] friends to keep viewing him as a long-suffering hero, and I guess that this is one way for him to do it." [13]

Bulkeley told another telephoning newsman that "our marine artillery is zeroing in on each pillbox before it's finished, so if Castro starts a ruckus, we'll blow his pillboxes to hell in a hurry!"

Pentagon brass had grown uneasy about the ominous implications of the Cuban Siegfried line. So on August 20, Bulkeley fired off a letter to Comdr. Robert F. Hilton in the office of the chief of naval operations. "Napalm will take out any of the pillboxes, if necessary," he wrote, concluding his letter on a terse, upbeat note: "We have no problems at Gitmo!"

The pillbox ring was hot news in the United States, and Admiral Bulkeley was receiving so many telephone calls that he instructed base switchboard operators to refer media calls to his aide, Lieutenant Infante. On one occasion, Infante's phone rang while he was away from his desk. The Sea Wolf picked up the instrument and said, "Admiral Bulkeley's office."

"Lieutenant Infante?" a New York reporter asked. From the weak connection, Bulkeley knew that Castro's secret police were on the job in Havana, so he decided to have some fun at their expense. "Speaking," he replied. The reporter asked a series of questions about the fortified belt, and in his role of Lieutenant Infante, Bulkeley scoffed at the earth-moving activity and called it "Mother Castro's gardening."

A few days later the story appeared in the States, quoting the views of Lt. Michael L. Infante, Admiral Bulkeley's aide. In the Pentagon, the navy's chief of information was fit to be tied. He wrote an urgent letter to Bulkeley, requesting him to muzzle his talkative aide. Media inquiries on the delicate subject of the Cuban Siegfried line were to be handled directly by his Pentagon office, not by junior officers at Guantanamo, he pointed out.

Bulkeley handed the Pentagon official's letter to Lieutenant Infante (who knew nothing about his boss's shenanigans), chuckled, and said, "Mike, you always did talk too damned much!"

Later that day the color returned to Infante's face.[14]

In late August, George C. Gaudin and a small crew shoved off from a Florida port to bring a ninety-six-foot yacht around to Newport Beach, California, for use in his stabilizer business. As the vessel neared the south side of Cuba, Gaudin became alarmed from Miami radio reports that hurricane Cleo was bearing down on them at fifteen miles per hour. By midnight winds picked up to fifty or sixty knots, the yacht was buffeted about, and the radio went out, preventing Gaudin from picking up Miami weather reports.

Then the packing on the propeller shafts started leaking from the heavy pounding by the waves, and the yacht slowed to eight knots. Disaster loomed. Guantanamo was the only nearby friendly harbor, so Gaudin told the captain to head for it. "But civilian vessels aren't allowed there," the skipper protested. "They might open fire." Gaudin responded that they might just as well be blown out of the water by gunfire as to sink to the bottom in the approaching hurricane.

Dawn was breaking when the California businessman's yacht neared the harbor entrance, and two Gitmo patrol boats charged out to intercept the intruder. Navy officers on the craft told Gaudin that no civilian vessels could enter the bay, even in an emergency, without the personal permission of the admiral.

"Then radio your admiral," Gaudin pleaded. "We're taking on water, the hurricane is supposed to hit tonight, and we'll never survive it in the open sea."

GEORGE GAUDIN:

Moments later a reply was received—we could enter the harbor. The admiral said he'd been watching us on radar all night, ever since our yacht neared Cuba. We were escorted into the bay, where navy intelligence men came aboard and gave us a polite—but intense—grilling, concluding that we were law-abiding American citizens.

Hurricane Cleo was still headed in our direction, and some of Admiral

> Bulkeley's officers thought the large ships in the harbor should go to sea because their lines would not hold tied to the docks. The admiral told me not to worry, that he had done research on Caribbean hurricanes, and when they got close to Cuba the heat from the island caused them to veer off sideways. Cleo did just that.
>
> The next day the admiral came by and invited me to go with him in a helicopter to inspect the front lines. He said the Cubans shoot at him once in awhile, but they couldn't shoot straight. I begged off, telling him I had to work on my boat. He grinned and said that I didn't have enough guts to go. I replied, "Admiral Bulkeley, you are exactly right!"

Guantanamo was wrapped in an electronic cocoon to make it extremely difficult for a sneak attack to inflict a Pearl Harbor on the base. Admiral Bulkeley had been tracking George Gaudin's yacht on a sophisticated radar he had had installed on 493-foot Crain's Hill, the highest point on Gitmo. The radar could "see" Castro's jet fighters on the ground, when they lifted off and in flight. At the same time, the Crain's Hill station watched for missiles that might be fired from the island toward the naval base or in the direction of the United States. Gitmo intelligence officers knew that, despite the U-2 recon plane photos, there remained the possibility that the Soviets had hidden missiles in caves.

The Crain Hill radar also guarded against the threat of Cuban fanatics in explosives-laden suicide craft slipping into Guantanamo Bay to blow up an anchored aircraft carrier or other major ship by crashing into her.

Almost all Cuban wireless traffic was monitored from a post in the basement of Bulkeley's headquarters. Many Cuban military messages were in code, but most of the ciphers were so simple that base intelligence officers could break them on the spot. When the Cuban messages were in intricate codes, the intercepts were flown to Fort Meade, Maryland, home of the National Security Agency (NSA), to be deciphered.

Located midway between Washington and Baltimore, Fort Meade is a maze of buildings in which thousands of skilled mathematicians, scientists, cryptanalysts, and technicians constantly analyze and decode messages from scores of nations. These messages were intercepted by a network of hundreds of U.S. electronic listening posts scattered around the world.

Presumably unknown to Castro, the NSA had a hush-hush "navy" to help protect Gitmo from surprise attack. In the early 1960s, NSA decided to build its own flotilla of electronic eavesdropping vessels. What was needed, NSA decided, were "old tubs" that could slip along the Cuban coast and not attract undue attention.

One of the "old tubs" covertly selected and taken out of mothballs was the *Sergeant Joseph E. Muller,* a grizzled veteran of World War II coastal supply service. Ideal for electronic snooping, the *Muller* was secretly outfitted with sophisticated gear and put to work. Based at Fort Everglades, Florida, the *Muller* prowled the Caribbean, her bristling antenna pointed toward Fidel Castro's domain. If the NSA wanted a plodding "old tub," that is what it got. *Muller*'s crew quipped that a wave should have been painted on her bow to give the illusion that she was moving.

At almost the same time that George Gaudin had been seeking refuge for his yacht in Guantanamo Bay, the *Muller* was replaced by a much larger "spy ship," the *Georgetown,* which had a crew of 18 officers and 260 sailors.[15]

For years the Russians had been sending antenna-laden trawlers into Caribbean waters and along the United States' eastern seaboard, close to Gitmo and other sensitive military facilities. One Soviet trawler, the six-hundred-ton *Vega,* moseyed about twelve miles off the navy's big base at Norfolk, Virginia, from where secret wireless signals were regularly sent to Guantanamo and to the Atlantic Fleet. The electronic gear on the *Vega* reportedly could pick up signals at a distance of one hundred miles.

Despite the wealth of high-grade intelligence furnished Admiral Bulkeley through electronic surveillance and other means, the security-conscious skipper relied heavily on personal reconnaissance to guard against surprise attack or Cuban machinations. Despite the press of urgent business, twice daily the Sea Wolf climbed into a helicopter and, with crash helmet on his head and a high-powered rifle on his lap, flew along the entire twenty-four-mile fence line.

Each day Bulkeley tramped the marines' forward positions, packing a .357 magnum and toting a loaded rifle or tommy gun. Bulkeley wore battle gear when stalking the fence line, but not the two stars of his rank, a concession to the possibility of a lucky shot from a Cuban marksman. The admiral's seemingly constant presence along the forward positions spurred the marines' morale. The leathernecks coined a slogan: "They call it Gitmo—but we won't git!"

In mid-August John Bulkeley was delivered a shocker: the Pentagon wanted to know why marine positions had not been pulled back "out of Cuban rifle range." The Sea Wolf rushed back a reply:

> At this time, we are charged with maintaining surveillance [that is, defense] of the fence line. Since effective rifle range today is considered to be 500 yards [I can kill a man with a rifle at 1,000 yards] we would therefore not have surveillance of the fence line.
>
> I can then envision that Cuban soldiers would cut the fence to pieces undetected, enter, lay booby-traps and land mines, set fires, infiltrate, and in general raise particular Cuban hell to make this base untenable and drive us out, for that is [Castro's] aim.
>
> I am shocked and appalled at such a question.[16]

No more was heard from the Pentagon on the proposal.

26

The Great *Viking Princess* Rescue

One night in late August the telephone jangled incessantly in the bedroom of Admiral Bulkeley's home on Deer Point. It was 2:30 A.M. Picking up the instrument, he was greeted by the slurred voice of a youth who said he was a crewman on the nuclear-powered aircraft carrier *Enterprise* that was anchored in Guantanamo Bay. (Bulkeley's telephone number was listed in the Gitmo residential directory.) The sailor explained that he was on shore liberty, had been "hoisting a few with my buddies" at the Enlisted Men's Club, and had missed the last shuttle boat to the *Enterprise*. If he didn't get back to his ship soon, he would be marked down AWOL, the caller said.

The admiral concluded that the sailor had hoisted far more than a few, but he told the youth to be at a certain dock in fifteen minutes and that someone would pick him up and take him to the carrier. At the appointed time, Bulkeley himself, dressed in plain khaki shirt and trousers without the two stars of his rank, edged his private sloop up to the dock.

"Hi, ya, buddy!" the young sailor called out as he wobbled aboard, no doubt believing that his seagoing chauffeur was an overage enlisted man whom the base commander had rousted out of bed to take the stranded crewman to the *Enterprise*. Bulkeley steered toward the huge carrier, and his passenger was quite voluble. "What d'ya do in this man's Navy?" the tipsy one asked. "Oh, a little of everything," Bulkeley replied.

On reaching the *Enterprise*'s gangway, the sailor waved to Bulkeley, and, with a breezy, "Thanks, buddy," disappeared into the ship's interior.[1]

The Sea Wolf was angry. His little boat had pulled up to one of the navy's newest and most powerful aircraft carriers and had not been challenged. Where was the officer of the deck? Where were the lookouts? Why had not the ship's radar picked up his craft?

Bulkeley steered his boat along the entire length of the *Enterprise* (a distance of three football fields), around the bow, and back down the other side. Still he was not challenged. Taking an empty paint can from his boat, the admiral tied it to the *Enterprise*'s anchor chain, and in the container he placed a hastily scribbled note: "This is a bomb. You have just been blown up!" He signed his name and rank.

Then the admiral hurried to his headquarters and had an urgent message sent to the skipper of the *Enterprise:* "Enemy frogmen have been sighted in the bay."

Now it was nearly 4:00 A.M. Bulkeley rushed to the patio of his Deer Point home and, through binoculars, watched the hectic scramble on the *Enterprise* after the warning message arrived. Searchlights began sweeping the dark water. Small boats with armed crews were lowered. All hands rushed to battle stations.

Four hours later, the daily commanders' conference at Admiral Bulkeley's headquarters was a heated affair. The Gitmo skipper raked the *Enterprise* captain over the coals for the security lapse, and was unmoved by an explanation that the carrier was on a shakedown cruise, had a new crew, and all the kinks hadn't been smoothed out yet.

"You've got a major security problem," Bulkeley declared. "Get it fixed!"[2]

AMELIA S. FALES:
Admiral Bulkeley had built his personal sailboat himself, and on the few occasions when he had free time he puttered around with it or sailed it on Guantanamo Bay. There were times when the admiral asked my husband [navy captain] Bill and I to go sailing with him. Bill always enjoyed this, but I became wary about going along. Every jaunt was an adventure. Admiral Bulkeley would chase Russian cargo ships, then sail out to see if his vessels guarding the bay entrance were alert. I had visions of someone blasting us out of the water, so I started coming up with excuses not to go.

Admiral Bulkeley had a strict procedure for handling Soviet ships that cut directly through the naval base to load sugar at Caimanera, on upper Guantanamo Bay. Each time a Soviet freighter headed toward the bay's entrance, Bulkeley sent two gunboats to escort her. One American boat kept its guns trained on the bridge of the Russian ship, and the other trailed to make certain that the vessel in transit did not drop mines. There was no doubt that Soviet intelligence knew precisely where Admiral Bulkeley and his family lived, for when the Russian ships sailed back down Guantanamo Bay toward the open sea they invariably dumped their garbage into the water near the Bulkeley home on Deer Point.

In mid-August 1964, husky, forty-seven-year-old Col. Anthony "Cold Steel" Walker routinely relieved Colonel Killen as commander of Gitmo's marine battle group. A 1939 graduate of Yale University, Walker had seen heavy action in the Pacific in World War II. At one time he had conducted a bayonet school, and from that function gained the enduring nickname Cold Steel. Later he fought in Korea with the 1st Marine Division.

COL. ANTHONY WALKER, USMC (RET.):
On my first night at Guantanamo, I decided to let the Cubans know that I was on board. We brought up two tanks near to the fence line, where they shone their powerful searchlights on the Cuban positions. This provoked gratifying reaction, with lights going on all along the Cuban lines. Loma Picote on Reuben's side lit up like a Christmas tree. At least we had waked them up.

Once in awhile we would seek to break the monotony by flying helicopters along the fence at night, with their landing lights on, looking like enormous lightning bugs.

All this was more than frivolous behavior. We wanted Reuben to know that we were alert, active, and ready if the Cubans wanted to take us on. If that would have happened, our mixed bag of marines, sailors, and Seabees would have halted his infantry, our mine fields would have stopped his tanks, and the 2d Marine Division would have rushed in [from North Carolina] and driven the bastards all the way back to Havana.

Of course, Cuban artillery might have smashed things up a bit on the base.

Meanwhile, in the States, the campaign bloodletting between Lyndon Johnson and Barry Goldwater was drawing to a close. When the votes were counted in November, the "peace candidate" Johnson scored a knockout, winning by a whopping margin of sixteen million votes, the widest victory span in totals and percentage of any presidential contest up to that time.

A month later, on December 4, 1964, the third and final unit of the plant that converted saltwater from the sea into fresh water began operations. (The second unit had been completed in September.) At a ceremony marking completion of the entire project, Comdr. Lynn Cavendish, the navy resident engineer, presented Admiral Bulkeley with a large plaque that proclaimed him to be the "King of the Water Makers." In his response, the king's first official edict was to call for "turning on the water and turning off Castro." Now Guantanamo had the capacity to supply 2,250,000 gallons of fresh water daily, more than the base had been getting from the Yateras River.[3]

The Christmas season was at hand, and Bulkeley searched his mind for an appropriate greeting to Communist Cuba. His focus turned time and again to the main gate, where Castro's soldiers, armed with submachine guns, strolled about. Just behind them, in large letters painted on an arch, was the phrase: *República de Cuba: Territorio Libre de América* (Republic of Cuba: Free Territory of America). Now the admiral ordered his Seabees to erect a large sign a few yards back of the main gate, facing the Cuban soldiers and floodlighted at night. Marines guarding the fence line rubbed their hands in glee over the subtle wording: Peace on Earth to Men of Good Will.[4]

As the curtain fell on the tension-racked, one-year confrontation between John Bulkeley, representing the prestige of the United States, and Fidel Castro, the standard-bearer for the Kremlin and the Communist bloc of nations, Edwin Tetlow, the veteran correspondent for the *London Daily Telegraph,* was astonished that Washington had not fully exploited the dramatic story. Tetlow, who had covered Cuba for years, wrote:

> There was nothing for the United States to hide but a tale of triumph. The U.S. has won a tactical victory in its tussle with Fidel Castro and in a more significant struggle with world communism. Such victories [for the free world] have been scarce enough.[5]

In the wake of his failure to drive Uncle Sam from the naval base, Fidel Castro kept a low profile during the early months of 1965. However, Cuban soldiers indulged themselves with periodic fits of rock-throwing at the marines, many of whom retaliated in kind. Now and then at night, a shot or two was fired into Gitmo. Despite the relative tranquility, Admiral Bulkeley never let down his guard for one moment, even though he found time for some semblance of family life.

COL. ANTHONY WALKER:
All of us marines at Gitmo felt an affection for Admiral Bulkeley. On his birthday [August 19], at oh-six-hundred (6:00 A.M.), some 400 of us marines jogged to his quarters on Deer Point and gave three cheers for the Bulkeleys. The admiral and his family came out in various sorts of dress, and we presented him with a present, suitably engraved, a memento of our serving with him. Then we jogged off to the hills. This sort of thing pleased Bulkeley, I believe, but most admirals would have blanched.

In early September, Bulkeley called in Col. Richard S. Johnson, who had just routinely relieved Cold Steel Walker as commander of Gitmo's marine battle group, to discuss what action to take against Cuban patrols that were slipping over the fence at night and prowling about the rugged terrain inside the naval base. Johnson, a veteran of World War II's bitter fights at Guadalcanal, Peleliu, and Okinawa, and the base's skipper settled on a response: marine patrols would be stepped up along the fence.

Colonel Johnson was delighted. Stalking armed Cuban bands in the darkness over the hilly, brush-covered terrain provided realistic jungle training for the marines, who never knew when they might clash with the infiltrators.

COL. RICHARD JOHNSON, USMC (RET.):
One of our marine guard posts was located in upper Guantanamo Bay and had a good view of the towns of Caimanera and Boquerón. My boys were particularly watching at night for Cuban army infiltrators onto the naval base. In the blackness one night, this outpost reported that they had heard heavy automatic-weapons fire in the dock area of these towns.

After daylight, the bodies of ten or twelve Cuban civilians floating in the bay were recovered by us. They had been gunned down by Castro's soldiers while trying to swim to the naval base.

Furious over the ''senseless murder'' by what he called ''Castro's thugs,'' John Bulkeley contacted Cuban authorities by shuttling a message through the main gate, asking if they wanted the bodies of their countrymen. There was no reply. So the Sea Wolf had the Cuban corpses outfitted in presentable suits, placed in steel caskets, and given dignified burial in Gitmo's civilian cemetery.

Time marched on at Guantanamo. Almost daily there was some sort of fence line or other Cuban-inspired machination to contend with. Then big trouble broke out from an unexpected source. Shortly before midnight on April 8, 1966—Good Friday—Admiral Bulkeley received a telephone call at his home from the headquarters duty officer. ''Just got an SOS from the *Viking Princess,*'' the caller said. ''Had an explosion at sea. Cruise ship, Norwegian registry. Hundreds of passengers.''

Bulkeley scrambled several jets to search for the stricken ship. Every second counted, for a fire at sea could be disastrous in loss of lives. In less than a half hour, the jets radioed the *Viking Princess*'s precise location and reported that she was afire. Bulkeley ordered every available navy vessel—seven of them—to rush to the scene at flank speed.

As dawn broke over the Caribbean, the first rescue ship returned to Gitmo. Bulkeley—and three chaplains—were at the dock, as were scores of military wives who had volunteered to help and comfort the survivors of the 17,600-ton luxury liner. The *Viking Princess* had been en route from Aruba to Miami.

By happenstance, the first survivor to step off the rescue ship was the Norwegian skipper, who sported a handlebar mustache. Wet and shivering, the captain was wearing a tuxedo—a formal festivity had been in progress. For the next several hours passengers debarked from other rescue ships. Most survivors were badly shaken. Many were in sleeping garments; others were wrapped in bed sheets. Some of the women were covered with expensive furs.

At midafternoon, fifteen hours after the SOS signal had been received at Gitmo, all but two of the *Viking Princess*'s 494 passengers and more than 100 of the crew were safely ashore at the naval base. The only loss of life had been that of two elderly persons who had died of heart attacks while in lifeboats.

It had been one of the great sea rescue missions of the century.

By evening a flock of reporters, photographers, and television crews had flown in from the States. They descended on Admiral Bulkeley, pushing, jostling, and shouting that they had deadlines to meet and demanding a list of the passengers and their home towns.

ADMIRAL BULKELEY:
No list had been brought off the *Viking Princess,* so identifying 494 passengers was a time-consuming and tedious task. I refused to release a single passenger's name until we had identified each one. Under Captain Ben Cole, we worked throughout the night.

After I released all the names to the press the next morning, the TV boys from the States collared the *Viking Princess* captain. Although I had ordered the club manager at Gitmo to provide no booze for passengers or crewmen, someone had slipped the Norwegian skipper a bottle, and by ten o'clock that morning he was drunk as a lord. He put on quite a show in front of the TV cameras. Told wild tales about how he had saved nearly 500 passengers. A few hours later, the president of the charter line flew in and whisked the skipper and his entire crew away from Gitmo.[6]

One month after the once-glittering *Viking Princess* had been turned into a blackened hulk, Gitmo's fence line tension burst into flame once more. On a dark night in the first week of May, a band of Cuban soldiers scrambled over the chain-link barrier at a remote locale and into a large bunker on the American side. There were not enough marines to man all the bunkers at all times, as the Cubans had long been aware.

ADMIRAL BULKELEY:
Our electronic surveillance would later pick up information that told us that this was a plot cooked up by Raúl Castro to stir up trouble. If possible, Raúl was an even more vicious son of a bitch than Fidel. Raúl's scheme was for his soldiers who had infiltrated Gitmo to open automatic weapons fire from our bunker toward the Cuban side, so that Fidel could howl from the rafters that our marines had opened a murderous fire on Cuban positions and that the United States was in the act of "invading" Cuba from Gitmo.

As part of the secret deal that President Kennedy had struck with Khrushchev to get the Russians to pull their missiles out of Cuba in October 1962, Kennedy had verbally promised not to invade Cuba. So Raúl and Fidel apparently hoped to get the Russians back by screaming "invasion."

By pure happenstance, Raúl's scheme was squashed. Before the Cubans in our bunker could start shooting toward their side of the fence, a couple of squads of marines on routine night exercises happened to approach the bunker and the Castro boys hightailed it for the fence, and one of them was shot and killed while scrambling over the barrier.

The next day our security group was eavesdropping on Cuban army radio traffic out of Santiago (some seventy miles to the west), so we learned about the plot. Raúl was mad as hell. Claimed that some turncoat Cuban had tipped me off about the scheme, and that marines had been lying in wait and had "stormed" the bunker.

I passed word of the aborted Castro plot to Washington.

Fidel Castro and his media seized on the shooting of the Cuban to scream about the "latest provocative act by bloodthirsty marines." Admiral Bulkeley told the press that the way for Castro to avoid such incidents was to cease trying to infiltrate the naval base.

A few days later, U.S. intelligence reported a Cuban military buildup around Gitmo. Bulkeley responded by having the marines conduct large-scale training exercises in the vicinity of the fence line, a reminder to the Maximum Leader that American forces were alert and ready.

His mission accomplished, John Bulkeley departed Guantanamo on July 25, 1966, after a two-and-a-half-year confrontation with Fidel Castro and his Kremlin mentors. As ordered, he had defended the base and avoided touching off World War III.

Bulkeley left Gitmo in body only, for his indelible imprint would endure for decades to come. The marines, who could fault the man they called Big Iron only for "making a wrong turn along the way and becoming an admiral instead of a marine general," had given the name Bulkeley Hill to the strong point near the main gate. There, during countless hours of exceptional tension, Big Iron Bulkeley had stood guard side by side with the leathernecks.

The marine barracks area on the base was christened Camp Bulkeley, and in the Officers' and Enlisted Men's Clubs voices would long be raised in singing "The Ballad of Big Iron," a popular tune composed by marine Capt. Donald Knepp, who was on duty at Gitmo.

In the year ahead, Bulkeley commanded cruiser-destroyer Flotilla 8 and the fast-attack carrier Task Group 60.2, components of the Sixth Fleet in the Mediterranean. At Marseilles on February 17, 1967, he was joined on the cruiser *Columbus* by an old pal going back to the Normandy preinvasion days, Hollywood director John Ford. Now seventy-two years of age and decked out in dress blues identifying him as a rear admiral, United States Navy Reserve, Ford had arranged to put out with the Sixth Fleet on three weeks of active duty.

A genuine old salt with combat duty in World War II and the Korean War, Ford could have waited three more years back in 1951 for his promotion to flag rank and become a twenty-year man in the reserves, thereby qualifying for a substantial pension. But Ford had chosen early retirement and waived the pension so that he could become an admiral that much sooner. The two stars on Pappy's collar meant more to him than all the Oscars in Hollywood.

In the spring of 1967, John Bulkeley returned to Washington from his year of operational command duty with the Sixth Fleet. Now, at age fifty-five and after thirty-seven years of service, he would face perhaps the most significant challenge of his career—one in which the nation's security in a volatile and dangerous world would be at stake.

27

Black Hat Admiral

One of President John Kennedy's final acts, in October 1963, had been to appoint fifty-six-year-old Paul H. Nitze to be secretary of the Navy. A cum laude graduate of Harvard, Nitze had become deeply concerned about the moribund Naval Board of Inspection and Survey * (InSurv) almost from the beginning of his Pentagon tour.

InSurv's mission was to make certain that the United States Navy had ships that were ready for sustained combat action at any time. But Nitze quickly discovered that this crucial board had, in recent times, become largely a dumping ground for marginal officers and those burdened with serious personal problems.

Nitze was determined to correct this alarming situation. What was needed was an admiral who was both a technical expert and a proven combat leader, an astute, incorruptible officer to take charge of InSurv, grab it by the neck, and shake it violently. An admiral with all those qualifications would be difficult to find.

Scanning a list of candidates, Nitze had one name leap out at him: Rear Adm. John Bulkeley. The secretary recalled his inspection tour of the naval base at Guantanamo during the 1964 water-crisis showdown with Fidel Castro, and he had been impressed by the spirit of the personnel there and by the competence with which Admiral Bulkeley had handled

* InSurv had been established in 1868 under Adm. David Glasgow Farragut, who won immortal fame during the Civil War naval engagement at Mobile Bay with the battle cry: "Damn the torpedoes! Full steam ahead!"

the situation. He offered the Sea Wolf the post of president of the Board of Inspection and Survey.

At a Pentagon conference Secretary Nitze briefed Bulkeley on the monumental problems that he would encounter at InSurv. Federal law requires InSurv to conduct "an independent evaluation" of every navy vessel, including submarines, at least once every three years and to report to the secretary of the Navy deficiencies that might adversely affect a ship's combat readiness. Even when InSurv had reported deficiencies in the past, Nitze pointed out, on many occasions little or no corrective actions had been taken, due mainly to inertia and default.

Nitze's orders instructed the Sea Wolf to "revitalize and make effective" the Board of Inspection and Survey. Bulkeley was told that his job would be of enormous importance to America's security, and therefore his official status would be one held by no other navy officer. Bulkeley's ship-inspection reports—many of them would prove to be searing—were to bypass the normal chain of command and go directly to the chief of naval operations (the senior uniformed officer) and on to the secretary of the Navy. There would be no customary fitness reports on Bulkeley or any evaluation of his work, giving him the freedom to speak out and report deficiencies candidly and completely without fear of retaliation by outraged admirals senior in rank.

On the debit side, Bulkeley was told that he could expect no promotions in his InSurv post, and that he would remain on the job there until the board was "squared away."

> ADMIRAL BULKELEY:
> Many of our warships had become floating dogs. Guns that wouldn't fire, machinery that malfunctioned, equipment that was faulty. Flags [admirals], including myself, were responsible for the ships' problems. I blame all of us. We were the navy's leaders who either helped to create the problems or did not take immediate forceful action to correct them. I was determined to damned well do something about that situation.

Fired up by the challenge, Admiral Bulkeley descended upon InSurv's Washington headquarters with all the delicacy of a blockbuster bomb. He was appalled by the situation: it was even worse than Secretary Nitze had led him to believe.

ADMIRAL BULKELEY:
I had inherited a collection of misfits. Several officers on the board were alcoholics, one was undergoing psychiatric treatment, most were unprofessional, unmotivated, and simply didn't give a damn. Few were inclined to hard work, or any work at all. Disgraceful!

The whole organization was clumsy and wasteful. There were subboards all up and down both the east and the west coasts. Each subboard commander was overlord of his own little fiefdom, operating independently and using his own inspection standards—if indeed there were any standards.

I immediately paid a visit to each subboard. At one, the captain had disappeared for ten days on a drunk—and worse, had taken his executive officer with him. Another subboard commander had ceased inspecting ships that required of him any travel. At yet another, the captain was drunk most of the time, and had disgraced the Navy by engaging in a number of fistfights at the Officers' Club. A subboard captain in the West had been on the golf links almost constantly, then had the gall to complain to me that he didn't have enough stewards to pamper him at his quarters.

But I really exploded when I found out that some of these officers, whose sacred duty was to see that the Navy was ready to fight at all times, had received gratuities from contractors whose ships or equipment InSurv had to evaluate and approve for acceptance by the Navy.

Bulkeley promptly cleaned house. Eight InSurv captains and twenty-six lower ranking officers were "relieved for cause," and those whom the new boss felt had committed serious transgressions were given two options: immediate retirement or court-martial. All chose retirement.

Secretary Nitze, verbally and in writing, had promised to give Bulkeley his full support and backing, so when the Sea Wolf asked the Naval Bureau of Personnel for approval to handpick his own officers (rather than to have them assigned to him) the request was quickly granted. Within a relatively short period of time, professionalism returned to InSurv. Bulkeley surrounded himself with dedicated, energetic, and skilled technology experts. InSurv ceased being a dumping ground: rather it became a prestigious duty post for those who could measure up to Bulkeley's exacting goals and standards.

COMDR. SAMUEL J. ALEXANDER, USN (RET.):
When I received orders to report to InSurv for duty, my thoughts were akin to panic. I feared there was no way I could meet Admiral Bulkeley's

exacting standards. But I knew that he had personally reviewed my record, had approved my transfer, so he must have thought I could do the job.

When I reported for duty I was scheduled for an appointment with the admiral. I presumed that this would be a discussion in his office or the conference room. Our appointment turned out to be a thirty-second Bulkeley monologue in the passageway, which went something like: "I know who you are. They say you're pretty good. We'll see about that. You'd better be good. You'd better get on the ball and get after those guys at NAVSEA [Naval Sea System Command] and NAVELEX [Naval Electronic System Command] where you came from. Sometimes I think they don't know what they're doing over there."

Admiral Bulkeley went on to tell me that the Navy had lost the art of designing ships for combat, and we wouldn't have time to fix them when the next war started.

End of interview. I never got in a word. He turned and walked out of the building.

InSurv's subboards, which had grown like Topsy over the years, were streamlined to four: the submarine board based in Washington; the aircraft board at Patuxent River, Maryland; and boards at Norfolk for the east coast and San Diego for the west coast. Each of these boards was manned by technical experts in their particular fields.

Now, with InSurv's decks cleared for action, John Bulkeley plunged into the task of inspecting all fleet ships, submarines, aircraft, and equipment to determine their fitness for prompt, sustained, and reliable combat operations. "If they're not able to fight, the ships should be 'surveyed' out to the scrap heap or razor blades made out of them," the Sea Wolf was fond of saying.

Bulkeley established a grueling inspection routine that would be his own and InSurv's pattern. Forty-six weeks out of the year, he hopped around the globe, traveling in excess of 150,000 miles annually. His hectic pace left junior officers hard-pressed to keep up with their boss. His itinerary would take Bulkeley to the Mediterranean, to the Hormuz Straits in the Persian Gulf, to Pearl Harbor in Hawaii, to Subic Bay in the Philippines, to Yokosuka in Japan, and countless points in between.

On weekends, the InSurv chief tried to get back to his Washington office (which was not in the Pentagon) to handle the mountain of paperwork that had piled up in his absence.

Depending upon the size and complexity of the vessel, aircraft, shipyard, or equipment to be inspected, Bulkeley would take on his trips from two to a hundred skilled navy and civilian specialists.

COMDR. SAMUEL ALEXANDER:
Admiral Bulkeley never wears any rank or insignia when he is conducting an inspection, in order not to inhibit skippers and seamen alike from giving him their frank evaluation of problems that might affect their ship's performance. He roams the ship at will. Woe unto the C.O. who assigns an officer or senior enlisted man to escort the admiral. On large ships where an officer of his rank is provided a marine orderly, he delights in moving quickly, ducking in and out of compartments until he has evaded the poor soul, who now expects to be court-martialed for losing the admiral.

It is not at all unusual to go looking for Admiral Bulkeley on a ship only to be told by a crewman, "No, sir, I haven't seen an admiral. But there was some old guy in coveralls snooping around in here awhile ago."

In his younger days the admiral would on occasion drag a reluctant commanding officer in dress whites "up the stick" [mast] to view a dangerous condition.

At a postinspection briefing, no one in the room escaped his wrath if he was displeased. It could be a very uncomfortable time, especially for the commanding officer of the ship, but I never saw him make a personal attack. His comments were always critical of situations or performance, never directed to, or degrading to, any individual.

Due to the nature of InSurv's mission—detecting and reporting on problems and deficiencies—nearly all of these debriefing sessions were negative in tone. But Bulkeley never failed to compliment the ship's junior officers and enlisted personnel on something that had gone well during the inspection.

CAPT. ALAN S. CABOT, USN (RET.):
As the InSurv board's surface ship senior engineer, I was with John Bulkeley on 244 ship inspections over an eight-year period. During many postinspection debriefings in a ship's wardroom, the admiral would ask a ship's commanding officer to summon Seaman Jones or Petty Officer Third Class Smith into the wardroom. Upon the arrival of the usually bewildered sailor into a meeting with considerable high brass [the ship's squadron commander and deputies to the fleet commander were invariably present], Admiral Bulkeley would request the youth to step forward. Then he would pin either a Navy Achievement or Navy Commendation medal

on his chest and read a personally prepared citation. This addressed recognition of the young sailor's impressive efforts in maintaining a specific ship system or set of ship equipments at an impressive level well above fleet standards.

Admiral Bulkeley was always on the lookout for instances of extremely well-maintained equipment during InSurv inspections and would covertly find out which sailor was directly responsible for the skill, pride, and additional efforts necessary to achieve a superior level of equipment or systems combat readiness. He always carried a number of awards and citation letters to be used to recognize exceptional performance by a sailor at the deck-plate level. The admiral's concern for the lower rated men was always apparent.

Invariably, as Admiral Bulkeley and other InSurv team members left the ship after the inspection debriefing, you could read the long faces of the ship's commander in realization that the inspection would require many additional hours to correct the numerous problems identified. On the other hand, the faces of the crew would reflect admiration for an admiral who was obviously aware of a ship's problems but who gave personal recognition to a job well done.

Not long after Bulkeley had taken command of InSurv, traditionally sacred cages were rattled throughout the Navy. The Sea Wolf quickly discarded many ineffective techniques for determining a ship's material readiness for combat, including what he called "the absurdity of inspecting a ship for its material condition while it lies alongside a pier." So he demanded that InSurv inspections be conducted during three-day power runs at sea under combat conditions and when all equipment and machinery were operational—every piece of gear from anchors to guns to missiles. InSurv's critical inspections soon became dreaded by many ships' skippers.

ADMIRAL BULKELEY:
One thing I was certain of when I took the job was that I would win no popularity contest. But I have never pussyfooted with the facts. This was (and is) our Navy, and it must be ready to fight at all times. If an officer's ship receives a critical report, then only he himself is to blame.

John Bulkeley's sometimes stinging inspection reports to the secretary of the Navy and the chief of naval operations often made him the target of harpoons fired by an array of outraged sources. A swivel-chair, three-star admiral in the Pentagon was nearly stricken with apoplexy when the Sea Wolf submitted a report that was highly critical of this vice admiral's engineer-design experts. Red-faced in fury, the offended gold braid demanded that Bulkeley and InSurv be investigated by the Navy's inspector general for "flagrant abuse of authority."

Vice Admiral John Tyree, the inspector general, probed the complaints and absolved Bulkeley of the "charges." Consequently, the Bulkeley adversary howled publicly that the Sea Wolf "must be a manic-depressive who surely needs psychiatric help!" [1]

A few navy contractors rolled out their heavy artillery and began firing salvos at the new InSurv chief who was rocking their boats. No new ship, submarine, airplane, or piece of equipment would be accepted by the Navy until it had been thoroughly evaluated and approved by Bulkeley. And Bulkeley doggedly insisted that the contractor—who often had hundreds of millions of dollars at stake—meet all contract specifications.

The invective rolled off the Sea Wolf much as water would off a duck's back. "Profits and losses mean nothing in war," he told his staff. "Victory or defeat, life or death for our fighting men, that's the bottom line. And if the contractors don't like that, they can go to hell!"

By the late 1960s, John Bulkeley had become a real pain in the neck to many navy bureaucrats and swivel-chair types. The Naval Ships System Command, for one, was infuriated over the Sea Wolf's penchant to keep harping about ship-design and equipment deficiencies InSurv had uncovered, even after the problems seemingly had been corrected.

ADMIRAL BULKELEY:
What we in the Navy had done was to fall into an old trap—using Band-Aids to correct the *effects* of a problem instead of attacking the *cause* of the problem. Using Band-Aids was a simple way to seemingly resolve a deficiency, but actually they were only concealing temporarily the root cause of the problem. When I insisted on pointing that out, a lot of people got red-necked.

John Bulkeley's role in the Navy's scheme of things was put into perspective by the Sea Wolf himself while testifying before the Seapower Subcommittee of the House Armed Services Committee. A congressman asked: "Your reputation throughout the fleet is one of having horns, is it not, admiral?"

"No, sir," Bulkeley fired back. "I wear a big black hat, sir!" [2]

Some outraged admirals felt that Bulkeley was still saddled with a

''Wild Man of the Philippines'' complex, that he was dashing about helter-skelter firing torpedoes at any target that might pop up. Actually, the InSurv chief was conducting his office with the meticulous planning that had been his hallmark throughout his career. Not only had he served on or commanded nearly every class of ship the Navy had, but since taking over his present post he had burned the midnight oil to study scrupulously the minute peculiarities and construction of nearly every ship in the fleet—more than 600 of them. Often, skippers were startled to learn that when, within minutes of Bulkeley's stepping aboard their ships, the InSurv boss knew as much or more about their vessels as they did.

In early December 1968, Bulkeley took a team of InSurv experts to Norfolk to conduct an acceptance trial of the huge new aircraft carrier *John F. Kennedy*. Not until the InSurv boss had put his seal of approval on the *Kennedy,* the pride and joy of the modern Navy with a mind-boggling array of sophisticated equipment, could she be accepted by the Department of the Navy—and her contractor paid.

For several days, the *Kennedy* was put through her paces on the open sea, then Bulkeley returned to Washington. A short time later a blockbuster exploded in the navy high command. Bulkeley had submitted a damning report on the *Kennedy* to the secretary of the Navy—a shocking list of inadequacies and inefficiencies through the entire process from ship design and construction supervision to test and checkout systems and components.

In some high echelons of the Navy and within contractors' offices, Bulkeley was called every name in the book. Pins were stuck in John Bulkeley dolls. He was symbolically hanged by the neck and left to twist in the wind. However, Adm. I. J. Galantin, chief of naval material, refused to join in the Bulkeley-bashing orgy—nor did Secretary of the Navy Nitze. On December 30, 1968, Admiral Galantin fired off a searing memorandum to the commander of the Naval Ships System Command:

> Rear Admiral Bulkeley's personal letter of 24 December is a grave indictment of NAVSHIPS and the builder. It is shocking. . . .
>
> I direct that you take immediate and vigorous action to put *Kennedy* into condition satisfactory for acceptance, including a correction of all safety deficiencies. . . .

A crash program was launched to correct the *Kennedy*'s deficiencies, and several months later the big flattop took her place with the fleet.

As the year 1970 rolled around, Black Hat Bulkeley and his rejuvenated InSurv had undeniably gained the attention of most of those in the higher echelon of the Navy. But Bulkeley was disturbed by the fact that an admiral on occasion would claim to have been ignorant of a situation after Bulkeley had been clamoring incessantly for months to get a serious ship deficiency corrected. "I'm going to make damned certain that I'll never again hear someone in a responsible position say, 'Well, I hadn't been aware of that,' " the Sea Wolf told his staff.

So Bulkeley adopted a new and greatly expanded communications technique. He had his staff draw up a mailing list that, one wag swore, "rivaled that of the Sears-Roebuck catalog operation." After each ship, submarine, aircraft, shipyard, weapon, or equipment inspection by InSurv, Bulkeley would write a lengthy, detailed, and invariably candid personal letter on the deficiencies uncovered and mail it to the admiral directly involved. He would conclude the letter with the words "just thought you'd like to know." Then copies of the letter would be sent to all admirals, high-ranking officers, and other leaders even remotely involved with that specific piece of navy hardware.

This particular communications technique set off another behind-the-scenes uproar along some sectors of the navy chain of command. A few admirals were especially irate over the Sea Wolf's closing phrase, "just thought you'd like to know." Bulkeley meant that wording to convey a friendly tone, but a handful of flag officers interpreted it to be a sarcastic jab, one inferring that the letter's recipient didn't know what was going on in his own command.

"A pity that some rascals are so insecure," Bulkeley remarked to an aide.

Bulkeley's stream of letters soon came to be a navy "institution," and were known as "Dear Johns."

Despite the storm that often swirled around John Bulkeley's head over his refusal to "pussyfoot with the facts," his contribution to the national defense was widely recognized. In February 1972, the Sea Wolf was decorated with the Distinguished Service Medal, America's highest award for noncombat achievement. The DSM citation read, in part:

> During a period of wartime operations [Vietnam] and an intensely active shipbuilding and conversion program, Rear Admiral Bulkeley brought the standards of ship inspections . . . to an outstanding high level and contributed most significantly toward enhancing the quality of new ships and maintaining a high state of readiness in ships in service. His personal

> stamp of enthusiasm, dedication, and realism, along with his intense personal involvement, is manifest in all aspects of the work of the Board of Inspection and Survey.
>
> Rear Admiral Bulkeley's superb performance in a vitally important assignment has been a strong factor in the improved readiness of the navy's forces afloat.

Early in 1973 Admiral Bulkeley was confronted by an implacable foe that he alone could not conquer—Father Time. His sixty-second birthday anniversary—and mandatory retirement—were looming on the horizon. Only wife Alice knew of the torment that gripped the Sea Wolf about the prospect of being dropped over the side, in navy parlance. He would be separated from the service he had loved for more than four decades on September 1, 1973.

28

The Conscience of the Navy

Faint patches of silver began to line the dark clouds hovering over John Bulkeley's head. On March 15, 1973, Vice Adm. David H. Bagley, chief of navy personnel, wrote a memorandum to Secretary of the Navy John W. Warner, the youngest man to hold that post. Only the president could defer Bulkeley's retirement, Bagley pointed out, and that authority had been delegated to the secretary of defense who, in turn, delegated it to the secretary of the Navy. Due to Bulkeley's towering stature and professional expertise, Bagley told Warner, "his services are urgently required" beyond his retirement date.[1]

Secretary Warner agreed wholeheartedly. Bulkeley had what one admiral quipped was "disgustingly robust health," and his enormous drive, enthusiasm, and dedication were intact. And he knew navy ships like possibly no other man.

On April 16, Bulkeley received a telegram from Secretary Warner: the Sea Wolf would be retired, in accordance with navy regulations, but recalled immediately to active duty. "I know of no flag officer [admiral] who has won such a widespread reputation as a practical, shirtsleeve engineer and seaman, a man devoted to professional excellence," Warner stated.[2]

SENATOR JOHN WARNER:
As a former marine corps captain, I well recall my first meeting, as secretary of the Navy, with Admiral Bulkeley. Having researched him carefully beforehand, I had expected a "blunderbuss" to charge through

> my office door. To my astonishment, he walked in with immaculate professional demeanor.
>
> The old submariners used a phrase ''run silent, run deep.'' John Bulkeley, when it's to his advantage, can do both. He is a legend for walking aboard a new ship and departing, having analyzed the seaworthiness of details from a single bolt in the engine room to the entire complicated combat information center. Countless lives have probably been saved by his careful certification of a ship before it confronts the perils of the sea.
>
> He is a rare combination of professional dignity, humility, tenacity, and firmness. But don't mistake those traits to mean that John Bulkeley cannot mount a typhoon temper if the facts require it. On the whole, he will go down in history as a truly remarkable sailor. He is a sailor's sailor in every sense of the word.

Given a last-minute reprieve from ''death row,'' John Bulkeley figuratively took his inspection coveralls out of mothballs and plunged back into his customary routine: searching for onboard deficiencies. Since 1969, the InSurv chief had been deeply concerned about the intense heat and humidity of boiler rooms, where ''black gangs'' nearly suffocated while toiling around the clock to provide steam to propel ships. When Bulkeley had been inspecting the boiler room of the USS *Farragut,* he had seen one sailor keel over and another one stick his head in an air duct to gain momentary respite.

The admiral pulled out his pocket thermometer; it registered 184 degrees Fahrenheit. Suddenly, Bulkeley was jolted by a shocking thought: ''How in the hell have we navy leaders been so inhumane as to require our men to work in conditions of intolerable heat?''

Back in Washington, Bulkeley began an ongoing bombardment of the navy hierarchy with ''Dear Johns,'' reports and memos focusing upon ''this intolerable and inhumane situation.''

Bureaucratic gears grind slowly, so the months slipped past and no definite action was taken to relieve the heat stress in boiler rooms. The theory seemed to be: ''This is the way it's always been done.'' So Bulkeley decided now that he was back in harness to dramatize the urgent need for remedial action by becoming a human guinea pig.

One morning in April 1973, the Sea Wolf boarded the USS *Henry B. Wilson,* went to the hospital bay, and had his blood pressure recorded. It was normal for a sixty-two-year-old man in superb physical condition.

Then he entered the *Wilson*'s boiler room and began working side by side with the black gang.[3]

Four hours later, Bulkeley felt dizzy and his vision blurred from the debilitating effects of the 190-degree heat. He was rushed to the hospital bay, where medics measured his blood pressure. It had dropped to 100 over 43. More alarming, his heart showed signs of faltering. A medic voiced his diagnosis: the admiral had suffered a heart attack. However, after spending a few hours in the air-conditioned bay, the Sea Wolf's heartbeat and blood pressure returned to normal.

Operation Guinea Pig was a success. Hastily written directives from Pentagon brass went out to fleet commanders: until proper ship-design changes could be made, special attention should be given to crewmen working in heat-stress spaces to guard against excessive and prolonged exposure.

From on high, a green light was given to InSurv to conduct an exhaustive series of sophisticated tests to determine precisely how long a member of the black gang could endure intense heat and humidity before he would be physically endangered. Commander Richard Dasler,[4] InSurv's occupational health expert, was put in charge of the project.

The focus of the testing was in the boiler rooms of selected ships, and the black gang members themselves were involved. Typically, John Bulkeley insisted on being present during the tests. Everyone who went into the boiler room "laboratory" was instrumented—that is, he was outfitted with a special device to monitor his body heat. Commander Dasler suggested that the Sea Wolf should also be instrumented on entering the boiler room, but the Sea Wolf balked, claiming he didn't want to look like "a trussed-up chicken." But when Dasler pointed out that by refusing to comply, Bulkeley would be placing himself "above" those in the black gang, the InSurv chief grumbled and agreed to be "trussed up."

In October 1974, Adm. James L. Holloway III, chief of naval operations, ordered ship-design changes based on a list of recommendations from the Naval Material Command. Bulkeley had won a five-year battle, but refused to take the credit. "All leaders in the United States Navy have been and are vitally interested in protecting the health of all personnel," he said in a memo to the InSurv staff. "These leaders and InSurv engineers were the victors."[5]

As the months rolled past, John Bulkeley continued to let the chips fall where they may. "Bulkeley never worries for one minute about raising people's hackles when need be," a fellow admiral told the *Navy Times* in May 1976. "He has a job to make certain that the navy's ships and aircraft are ready to fight. So he often has to say things that some people would prefer not to hear."

One of Admiral Bulkeley's hackle-raisings occurred on June 17, 1976, when he testified on behalf of Lt. Kenneth M. Knull, who was being court-martialed at Norfolk. The twenty-six-year-old Knull had been officer of the deck when his ship, the guided missile destroyer *Belknap,* collided with the aircraft carrier *John F. Kennedy* off the coast of Italy on the night of November 22, 1975. Eight sailors had been killed and forty-eight others injured.

Bulkeley had sprung to the defense of Lieutenant Knull because he felt the junior officer had been cast in the role of scapegoat for the failure of others in the chain of command to react to a highly critical InSurv report after a *Kennedy* inspection in 1973. At that time, Bulkeley and his engineers pointed out that a montage of red and green lights on the aircraft carrier presented a potentially disastrous situation.

Red aviation lights ran all the way around the *Kennedy*'s flight deck to aid personnel working near the airplanes. InSurv's report had stressed that this could cause confusion to other vessels operating at sea in the vicinity of the *Kennedy,* for red lights were recognized internationally as marking the port (left) side of a ship and green lights indicated the starboard side.

Back in 1973 Bulkeley had strongly recommended that the red deck lights be changed to blue or purple, for the red lights tended to blend with the carrier's port and starboard red and green running lights. That was the heart of Lieutenant Knull's defense: he had not been able to determine her aspect angle and thus her direction of travel due to the maze of red and green lights.[6]

Bulkeley took the witness stand on June 17, 1976. "The famed admiral's appearance electrified the courtroom," the *New York Times* would report. His testimony backed up Lieutenant Knull's contention that the *Kennedy* had altered course and its labyrinth of red lights was bewildering. "Only the most experienced mariner could detect [the *Kennedy*'s] course at night because of them," Bulkeley declared.[7]

"I had long feared that a collision might result from just that type of lighting arrangement," the witness testified in his rapid-fire expression. "However, I felt that the most likely candidates for collision with our carriers were the Soviet ships that harass our carriers in the Mediterranean.'' [8]

On the day following his testimony, the *Washington Post* reported:

> Admiral Bulkeley lived up to his reputation. He interrupted lawyers, offered them advice on what they should ask him, and concluded by commending a prosecutor for having the good sense not to quiz him on the international rules of the road. Bulkeley is regarded as an expert on ship navigation.

Due primarily to Admiral Bulkeley's forceful testimony, most trial observers agreed, Lt. Donald Knull was acquitted. But a short time later he resigned from the Navy.

> ADMIRAL BULKELEY:
> This whole episode was not one of the United States Navy's shining hours. What happened was that, after my 1973 report on the *Kennedy*, people had deferred taking action. A senseless loss of life due to lethargy somewhere along the chain of command. Inexcusable!
>
> But I had learned a valuable lesson. After the *Kennedy-Belknap* collision, never again would I let people nod their heads in agreement when I point out serious safety problems. It's too damned easy to shake one's head yes, and then forget what in the hell we were talking about as soon as I left the room. From then on, I began getting firm commitments in writing.

In 1977, on the tenth anniversary of his taking charge of the Board of Inspection and Survey, John Bulkeley was sixty-six years of age and had grown somewhat portly. But his physical dexterity and enormous endurance continued to astound those around him, including many who were half his age.

> J. WILLIAM MIDDENDORF II:
> As something of a marathon runner and one-time sculling champion, I took some pride in my ability to climb up and down ladders to boiler rooms. And it was more than a hobby for me, for I did manage to visit 351 ships while secretary of the Navy from 1974 to 1977 and present the ''Order of the Golden Snipe'' to those valued men below.
>
> But try as I might, I could never manage to keep up with Admiral Bulkeley, particularly in bounding up those ladders. I finally figured out his secret—he didn't use the rungs, he simply flew.
>
> John was and is a giant among men, always courteous and marvelously inspirational. His men would follow him anywhere.

Periodically over the years, Admiral Bulkeley was called to testify before the Seapower Subcommittee of the House Armed Services Committee, whose function is to monitor the fleet's readiness. The Sea Wolf enjoyed jousting with the one or two members of the panel who were hostile to the Navy, and he never raised his voice or displayed irritation when loaded questions were hurled at him. Privately, Bulkeley would describe the hostile congressmen as "landlubbers who don't know the difference between an aircraft carrier and a rowboat."

> CONGRESSMAN CHARLES E. BENNETT:
> Admiral Bulkeley was such a hero on the American scene and had always been thoroughly creditable in all of his presentations, so that when he had come before the House Seapower Subcommittee I chaired, his word was considered as gospel. He was (and is) a real bulwark of strength for our national defense, and his contribution has not been exceeded by any American in history that I know of.
>
> When it comes to keeping navy ships shipshape, John Bulkeley is truly the conscience of the Navy.[9]

Late in 1977, the Navy Material Command was ready to unveil new-design propellers, whose 40,000 horsepower made them the most powerful

THE SHIP BUILDERS

"One must remember that there are always those people who seldom go to sea that plead cost effectiveness determines design, that if the design is unreliable they specify "band aids" and say that a fix is not authorized or that an alteration will fix the problem if the Fleet Commander funds it. It is too late when war comes. The Board need not add that these same people do not have the responsibility of winning the war, nor facing the enemy, nor the consequence of losing a war that the combat leaders always face in those same ships when war comes."

JOHN D. BULKELEY
REAR ADMIRAL, U.S. NAVY
PRESIDENT, BOARD OF INSPECTION AND SURVEY
24 JUNE 1977

A constant reminder hanging in InSurv offices

variable pitch screws ever built. These propellers were to be installed on yet-to-be-built Spruance class destroyers, and navy brass were quite proud of them. Then John Bulkeley threw a monkey wrench in the proceedings, advising the chief of navy material, four-star Admiral Isaac C. Kidd, Sr., that, as designed, the reversing-pitch propeller would throw a blade.

Admiral Kidd took the warning to heart, even though some top navy engineering officers reportedly scoffed at the Sea Wolf's alarm. Kidd had one propeller installed on the USS *Barbey,* and not long into her sea trial, the *Barbey* promptly threw a blade. Due to the imbalance created by the missing blade, all four blades, in the subsequent words of Admiral Kidd, were shed "like a chicken moulting its feathers."

Design engineers quickly went back to their drawing boards, and some ten months and millions of dollars later, the flaw was corrected and the 40,000-horsepower reversing-pitch propellers were installed on the Spruance destroyers.

During this period, John Bulkeley was in frequent contact with the nuclear genius Vice Adm. Hyman Rickover. The Sea Wolf and Rickover had been junior officers together back in the "China days" prior to World War II, and Bulkeley in the decades ahead would quip that he possessed the "only photograph in captivity of Hyman Rickover smiling."

Rickover, who pioneered in developing the USS *Nautilus,* the first nuclear-powered submarine, was as irascible and painfully blunt as he was brilliant, and at one time or another had crossed swords with nearly everyone in the navy high command and with many members of Congress. He also had a good-sized lobby of influential supporters, who recognized his towering achievements for the Navy.

ADMIRAL BULKELEY:
It had been agreed with Admiral Rickover that InSurv would inspect only the steam end of nuclear propulsion plants—not the reactor—as nuclear power was recognized as Hyman's domain in the Navy. So Rickover and I had to coordinate our activities on occasion.

Rickover was a truly dedicated officer—worked enormously long hours. One time I had just returned from an exhausting 20,000-mile inspection trip to the Far East, so I took Friday afternoon off from my office and was puttering around my house. Rickover had called my office, then phoned my home. When I picked up the receiver, his first words were: "Bulkeley, what in the hell do you mean by taking an afternoon off from work?" I always gave as good as I got when dealing with Hyman.

So I shot back, "And what in the hell are you doing working, Rickover—it's Yom Kippur."

Hyman slammed down the receiver and didn't speak to me again for a year. But he was a great man. When he died at a Washington hospital at age eighty-six in 1986, I was one of the last persons to visit him.

In the first week of August 1977, John Bulkeley and twelve of his InSurv staff were at Subic Bay, the Philippines, on the tag end of a 22,000-mile round trip to inspect, among other vessels, the guided missile destroyer *John S. McCain*. Bulkeley had been to Subic Bay on many occasions over the years, and each visit had been an emotional one. For it had been in these same waters, during the early bitter weeks of World War II, that he dashed to torpedo a 5,000-ton Japanese ship, a feat that had astonished the free world and made the PT boat a household word.

But the Sea Wolf had never taken the short hop from Subic Bay to Corregidor in the mouth of Manila Bay. It had been thirty-five years since Bulkeley's war-weary PT 41 had picked up General MacArthur at Corregidor's North Pier and carried him "out of the jaws of death" in a mad 580-mile dash through a Japanese sea and air blockade. Now, on August 8, John Bulkeley, whose name would forever be linked to the old fortress, was finally returning to Corregidor. At 1:30 P.M. on this hot, sultry day, the warrior they had called the Wild Man of the Philippines, and his staff, stepped from a helicopter onto the sand and jagged rock of the tiny, immortal island.

BRUCE M. BACHMAN:

Admiral Bulkeley didn't ramble, gawk, or stammer. He quickly rattled off many names of gallant men who had remained on Corregidor in 1942—those who had fought and died.

A day earlier, the admiral had asked me, his aide, to locate a wreath and bring it along. Now he walked a hundred yards to a monument that had been erected by the Filipinos in 1949, and placed the wreath solemnly and in silence at the foot of the monument. He took three paces back, came to attention, and made a powerful salute.

For long moments he stood there, motionless. Tears had welled up in his eyes. No doubt his thoughts had harkened back to the death, destruction, and suffering that had ravaged Corregidor and nearby Bataan.

Now a blue and white passenger bus carried the Sea Wolf and his party to Malinta Tunnel, whose confines had reeked with rotting flesh and other putrid odors three and a half decades earlier. Bulkeley leaped from the bus, stood with hands on hips, and peered up at the entrance. Turning to his officers, he broke into a grin and said, "Buster, has this place changed! General MacArthur and his boys would call this a palace if they could see it today!" [10]

The government of the Philippines had indeed turned Malinta Tunnel into a virtual palace. For Corregidor had become a mecca for tourists from all over the world, including aging Japanese parents who tried to find some trace of sons who had never returned from the war. Over the decades, Corregidor had acquired an eerie mystique. Some of the thousands who flocked to The Rock swore that, at night on towering Topside, they could hear the ghosts of Corregidor faintly crying out in anguish.

Admiral Bulkeley and his party walked inside Malinta Tunnel and gazed at the refurbished walls and cubbyhole offices where in the dim long ago of March 1942 agonizing military decisions had been reached. "Over there"—Bulkeley pointed—"was the entrance to General MacArthur's quarters." He paused, then strolled deeper into the tunnel. Gesturing with an arm, he said, "Back in through there was where the men with wounds so severe that only miracles could help them were stacked. They'd run out of morphine. There were days when I would come to see General MacArthur and it was nearly impossible to talk for the screaming."

Again the vibrant Bulkeley eyes were moist, a fact he tried to conceal from his officers by looking away.

There were long moments of silence, then the admiral resumed speaking: "Disheveled, perspiring nurses were constantly at work. Most of them tended patients for seventy-two hours at a stretch. Some nurses keeled over from sheer exhaustion and themselves became patients. All of them were captured." [11]

Next the bus wound down a steep road to the water's edge. Bulkeley leaped out, pointed to a crumbled, broken old dock known as North Pier, and called out, "There it is! No question about it! That's where we took off with General MacArthur and his party!"

A young Filipino marine major, who was serving as escort officer, asked politely, "Are you sure, Admiral Bulkeley? Philippine history books say that it was that other pier over there."

"Well," replied Bulkeley, "your history books are wrong." He grinned, then added: "You'd better have them corrected."

BRUCE BACHMAN:
The emotional peak for the admiral now took place unexpectedly. Ten Filipino children between the ages of ten and sixteen descended on the pier, yelling joyously and holding history books over their heads. ''Admiral! Admiral! Admiral!'' the little ones shouted.

Visibly moved, Admiral Bulkeley opened his arms, and the children encircled him and touched his uniform and body. He had returned, this hero who was part of each Filipino child's history. They had read about this fearless and dashing American naval officer who had waged an unbelievable battle with his wooden boats of lightning, against all odds, in their fathers' and grandfathers' time.

One youngster found in his history book a picture of Bulkeley taken during World War II and excitedly showed it to him. The admiral stared at the photo, then broke into a grin. ''I've changed a little,'' he quipped.

One at a time, the admiral began autographing the youngsters' books, asking each child his or her name and taking the time to personalize each inscription. After each book was autographed, the youngster shook hands with the admiral, stepped back, and saluted. The admiral returned the salute.

As we headed back to the bus, Admiral Bulkeley was quiet and thoughtful. Then the man who had been showered with decorations and honors by America, who had walked with presidents, kings, and princes, said of his encounter with the Filipino children: ''This is one of my proudest moments.''

Most of the InSurv officers had never set foot on Corregidor prior to the current pilgrimage, but they had long known of the dramatic and tragic events that had taken place there thirty-five years earlier and of John Bulkeley's role. Each was gripped by emotion. As they climbed back onto the helicopter to depart Corregidor, navy Capt. Curtis O. Anderson whispered, ''I'm drained!'' [12]

29

The "Show and Tell Bag"

Two years after the nostalgic return to Corregidor, in mid-1979, Congress and much of America were engaged in heated controversy. President Jimmy Carter was planning to hand over to the Panamanian government the canal that the United States had obtained the right to build and operate in a 1903 treaty. Now, seventy-six years later, nearly everyone in America was arguing the pros and cons of the Panama Canal handover.

While in Long Beach, California, on InSurv business, Adm. John Bulkeley received a telephone call from an old friend going back to the Normandy invasion days. Mark Armistead said, "Admiral, the Duke would like to see you." The Duke was John Wayne, who was fighting his final battle, not on the silver screen, but in real life—against a terminal disease.

ADMIRAL BULKELEY:
The mutual respect between John Wayne, a great American, and myself had long taken a priority with both of us. So I went to his mansion in Newport Beach, and I was inwardly shaken by his gaunt appearance and labored breathing. But he was the same old Duke. "How ya doin' admiral?" he roared. "It's been a long time between watering holes, hasn't it? How about a drink?"

I walked into the spacious living room and was pleased to see that the Duke had a large color picture of me hanging prominently on a wall. I was also surprised to see that he had two guests—Ronald Reagan and Senator Barry Goldwater, both of whom beamed at me. It became apparent that these three friends had been arguing vigorously over the Panama

Canal. Wayne was all for giving the canal back, Reagan and Goldwater were for keeping it.

Duke had brought me in to even up the argument, thinking that I would take his side. He was mad as hell when he saw that I was siding with Governor Reagan and Senator Goldwater. He accused us three of "ganging up" on him.

Later that year, the Senate passed a bill that would turn over the Panama Canal to the Panamanians. Gleefully, John Wayne telephoned Bulkeley's aide and roared, "Tell your goddamned admiral that the Senate of the United States *agrees with me!*" [1]

In 1978, Adm. James Holloway, the chief of naval operations, established a practice of having John Bulkeley give a quarterly briefing for him and his deputy flag officers. These briefings were to provide top brass with a synopsis of InSurv inspections conducted during the previous three months and to discuss observed trends for readiness in major areas, such as combat systems, engineering, habitability, medical training, logistics support, aviation, and hull and deck.

CAPT. ALAN CABOT:

Each of the deputy CNO flag officers had detailed briefing papers covering possible responses to the "bad actor" items in each of the InSurv ship inspection reports, which Admiral Bulkeley provided to virtually every flag officer. In many cases, it was apparent to us InSurv board members that the CNO staff preparing the problem responses invariably either didn't have all the facts or simply didn't understand the problems.

After two or three sessions, in which Admiral Bulkeley's perception of a problem was glibly explained away by a Pentagon-prepared point paper, Bulkeley introduced his new creation, the "show and tell bag." This concept consisted of a well-worn seabag full of living-proof samples of failed equipment, bottles of contaminated lube oil, Polaroid color photographs [of defective items or problems], small sections of clogged piping, and other pieces of hard-to-dispute evidence.

I vividly recall the first CNO briefing when the show and tell bag was introduced. At issue was whether a certain shipyard had improperly assembled the oil burner assemblies on the boiler of [a specific ship]. A copy of the shipyard quality assurance report supported the counterargument that this could not possibly happen. Admiral Bulkeley quietly reached into his show and tell bag and placed a large carbon-deposit clinker on the highly polished conference table. (An improperly installed boiler oil

> burner/air register assembly will result in the formation of a distinctly shaped carbon clinker growth on the deck of the furnace.)
>
> With each subsequent quarterly briefing, more and more of the deputy CNO fact folders became thinner and thinner—or disappeared completely. Meanwhile, Admiral Bulkeley's show and tell bag became larger and larger.
>
> About a week before each quarterly briefing for the CNO and his deputies, we [at InSurv] would start getting phone calls from the Pentagon staff attempting to get a heads-up on what would be in the admiral's show and tell bag.
>
> There were numerous instances of a deputy flag officer at a briefing assuring the chief of naval operations that lube oil cleanliness maintenance was being effectively performed on the USS ______, for example, only to be confronted by a bottle of obviously contaminated oil taken from the number two main feed pump of that specific ship.
>
> In essence, what Admiral Bulkeley was doing was helping solve basic fleet problems by laying the facts on the table—literally.

As the decade of the 1970s neared its conclusion, alarming reports reached John Bulkeley's ears. Due to the ships' being crammed with steadily increasing amounts of sophisticated and complex electronic equipment, electromagnetic interference (EMI) was causing problems that threatened to hamper the fleet's ability to fight. EMI is the unintended effect that one piece of electronic equipment can have on another one.

EMI can and has caused a variety of ship problems, from the unintentional folding of an aircraft's wings on a carrier's flight deck to radars failing to see an obvious target, to erroneous readings from electronic fuel-tank gauges. Even worse, EMI can reduce the effectiveness of sensors (which search for potential hostile interlopers) and communications equipment on a ship, as well as causing its fire-control, missile, and gun systems to go haywire.

Bulkeley became especially concerned over the EMI problem when he received word that two American warships had passed each other at 1,000 yards' distance while one vessel was transmitting a simple ship-to-shore message. The transmission caused the other vessel to come to a halt.

The InSurv chief began to suspect that EMI problems were much more severe and potentially disastrous to the fleet than many persons in high places understood or were willing to admit. Bulkeley asked his electronic experts to probe the problem. Their investigation resulted in a report that rocked the navy chain of command and the shipbuilders.

Ship designers had failed to consider the potential adverse effects of EMI, electronic installation practices were sloppy, and shipboard maintenance was lackadaisical, the InSurv analysis declared.

> COMDR. SAMUEL ALEXANDER:
> Initially the results [of the Bulkeley report] were predictable. First, denials that the EMI problem existed. Later, the problem did exist—but it was someone else's fault. And finally, the problems were too expensive to fix.

Admiral Bulkeley continued to hammer at navy brass over the EMI problem. As a result, an EMI research center was created, and far stricter specifications for equipment designers and shipbuilders were issued. Then, to make certain all new guidelines were being followed to the letter, the InSurv boss required that each new ship pass a rigorous EMI test before he would recommend acceptance by the Navy.

Into the 1980s, the Sea Wolf noted with inner satisfaction that countless fleet material deficiencies that InSurv had isolated had been or were being corrected. But he pointed out to top brass that, in the design of new ships, many of the same old mistakes and problems were being repeated. Bulkeley vowed to take drastic action to correct this alarming trend. His solution was simple: InSurv would review each new ship design before construction was actually started by the shipbuilder.

Bulkeley's proposal brought howls of anguish from profit-minded shipbuilders. InSurv, some of the contractors felt, was poking its nose into their business. "I don't give a damn what they think," the admiral told his staff. "What I am concerned about is the lives of our men and the combat readiness of our fleet."

Bulkeley continued to hammer for the right to review ship designs and to recommend needed alterations. Finally, he was allowed to inspect several designs done by commercial shipbuilders and was appalled by what he discovered. Conceptually, the designs were flawed. Gross errors existed in simple systems like piping and electrical distribution. The grave problem of EMI had been given no consideration. Topside, designers had paid minimal attention to maximizing the coverage of antennas or the zones of fire of the weapons.

Bulkeley began bombarding the navy chain of command with "Dear Johns," calling strongly for corrective action. In some cases, it was too late to implement design changes. But in other instances, due to InSurv's preconstruction inspection of designs, changes were made and are appearing in ships being delivered in 1988.

The Sea Wolf's concern for the sailor's safety and welfare never waned. In the late 1970s, when the dangers associated with asbestos became known, he pushed vigorously—and successfully—for the immediate removal from ships and shore installations of all insulating materials that contained asbestos.

Over the years, Admiral Bulkeley had become increasingly concerned about the high accident rate and injuries that occurred when naval vessels had to replenish while underway at sea. Two or three ships steaming parallel courses at a scant 100 to 150 feet apart, and transferring fuel, food, ammunition, or other cargo, was a highly hazardous operation, a hair-raising experience in the daylight, downright frightening at night. Much of this underway procedure had been done the same way for fifty years, except that modern equipment keeps under constant tension the heavy wires that hold the loads being transferred from ship to ship.

Bulkeley and his deck seamanship experts tackled the problem, one that threatened lives and often wreaked damage on ships. They found that accidents during replenishing operations were frequently caused by loads that slammed into the superstructure (above the main deck) of the receiving ship due to severe differences in elevations of the rigs on each vessel. Also, the high-speed connection devices used to hasten the transfer of fuel from one ship to another frequently refused to match up, requiring one or more sailors to engage in the risky business of attempting to "mate" two heavy pieces of machinery.

InSurv's findings zeroed in on commercial designers for the lion's share of the blame, contending that too little attention had been given to the problems of ship-to-ship replenishment at sea.

Again Bulkeley began raising hell and rattling cages, demanding that action be taken to remedy these replenishment deficiencies, particularly those on new ships. Here, he had his greatest clout since the Navy would not accept ships from contractors unless they were approved by InSurv. Shipbuilders were placed under enormous pressure but, to their credit, most of the reputable ones complied happily to correct the problem. Consequently, significant improvement appeared in both the capability of replenishment between ships and the accident and injury rates.

In the last decade, prestigious civilian professional organizations have begun honoring John Bulkeley for his engineering achievements. Kenneth A. Roe of New York, chairman of the American Association of Engineering Societies, informed the InSurv chief that he had been chosen for the group's annual Chairman's Award. In his notification letter, Roe said: ''Although not unmindful of the wide range . . . of outstanding service you have given to our country, many of us feel that your work at InSurv may well have been your most valuable service.''

Then the American Society of Naval Engineers presented Bulkeley with its 1980 Harold E. Saunders Award for his ''enthusiasm and tireless dedication'' while InSurv chief ''that have resulted in significant improvements in the breadth and depth of naval ship inspection.'' And in 1982, the American Society of Mechanical Engineers cited the Sea Wolf with its Outstanding Leadership award. Previous recipients of the ASME award included space pioneer Dr. Wernher von Braun, then Secretary of the Treasury William E. Simon, and Donald C. Burnham, chairman of the board of Westinghouse Electric Corporation.

Sandwiched in between the accolades from the civilian professional sector was a second Distinguished Service Medal presented to Bulkeley in a Pentagon ceremony by the chief of naval operations, Adm. Thomas B. Hayward. The citation spoke of the Sea Wolf's ''highly significant contribution to the quality of new ships and the improvement of the material condition of existing ships.''

ADM. THOMAS B. HAYWARD, USN (RET.):
One of the great early decisions I made as chief of naval operations in 1978 was to have a personal session with John Bulkeley to set the course for tackling a number of engineering problems in need of his particular focus. He never let me down—or the Navy. He has been an inspiration to tens of thousands in the Navy, as well as having scared the hell out of most of them.

In the early months of 1983, Admiral Bulkeley was again butting heads with Pentagon gold braid. The bone of contention was the Black Hat's incessant harping over deficiencies in some of the navy's new weapons, especially the $22.5 million F-18 fighter plane, which Bulkeley had flunked resoundingly after exhaustive operational tests, and the Lamps antisubmarine helicopter.

InSurv's blistering report on the F-18 fighter—Bulkeley listed twenty-seven deficiencies—struck like a bombshell in the bailiwick of Vice Adm. Robert Monroe, the navy's director of research, development, evaluation, and testing. Monroe's department had approved the F-18, so if it accepted Bulkeley's report, it would be embarrassed by having to correct twenty-seven deficiencies in the F-18 fighter. If Monroe challenged the report, he would be accused of trying to foist off a deficient weapon onto navy combat arms.

On May 13, 1983, the heated controversy broke out into the public domain. Jack Anderson, a Washington-based syndicated columnist with a readership running into the many millions, wrote:

> This may be the Pentagon's worst-kept secret—and navy spokesmen deny that it's even happened—but some ambitious admirals are quietly trying to scuttle the Board of Inspection and Survey headed by one of the nation's most respected war heroes, Admiral John D. Bulkeley.
>
> What bothers the brass is that Bulkeley insists on subjecting navy and marine aircraft to rigid testing before turning them over to the pilots. So the admirals have secretly tried to change the regulations—the navy's bible—to keep Bulkeley's experts from evaluating new naval aircraft.
>
> The reason the admirals are surreptitious in their efforts to undercut Bulkeley is that he is a living legend. No swivel-chair admiral in his right mind would openly challenge a man who won the Congressional Medal of Honor, the Navy Cross, two [army] Distinguished Service Crosses, and two Silver Stars in World War II combat.
>
> Medals and celebrity status aside, Bulkeley is known as a gruff, plainspoken navy professional who stubbornly insists on the kind of details that keep ships afloat, planes in the air—and navy men alive.
>
> Among his critics is Vice Admiral Robert Monroe. Sources told my associates that Monroe has been upset about the unkind words Bulkeley's [aviation] board has had for the navy's new weapons and has responded with some vituperative memos directed at Bulkeley personally.
>
> If this was just another personality clash between Pentagon prima donnas, it would rate no more than a couple of paragraphs. But what Monroe and some fellow admirals seem determined to do is get rid of the navy's only effective, independent, incorruptible critic of grandiose weapons systems.
>
> Can the Navy afford to get rid of an old pro by dropping John Bulkeley over the side? [2]

Jack Anderson's twenty-one-gun broadside blasted the lid off the F-18 altercation. The hot potato was dumped in the lap of four-star Adm. William N. Small, the vice chief of naval operations, who convened a convocation of combatants. Battle flags were quickly hoisted. Black Hat Bulkeley manned the deck guns on the port of the conference table, while Monroe and a pair of other three-star types fired salvos from the starboard side.

Bulkeley's adversaries argued strenuously for scuttling InSurv's aviation board, whose findings on F-18 deficiencies had been so devastating. The Sea Wolf, who felt that the true target for elimination was himself, pointed out that if his aviation board were to be abolished, there would be no independent evaluator of navy aircraft.

John Bulkeley carried the ramparts. Admiral Small eventually recommended that the Board of Inspection and Survey continue on course—with all throttles wide open. F-18 deficiencies were corrected, and the sleek fighter plane was put into active service.[3]

Meanwhile, on May 13, 1983, the Navy corrected an oversight—one of forty years' duration—on Admiral Bulkeley's official record. Although for four decades he had been recognized as one of the Navy's foremost authorities on ships and had commanded or served on nearly every type of vessel, he had never been designated a surface warfare officer (SWO). Naval regulations state that the SWO award is to go to "an individual who had demonstrated significant proficiency in the art of surface warfare."

Now, in a Washington ceremony, Bulkeley received his SWO pin. He was in good company. At the same ceremony, retired Adm. Arleigh A. "31-Knot" Burke was also deemed qualified for the award. Burke had gained wide World War II fame as the dashing leader of Destroyer Squadron 23 and was later chief of naval operations.

In mid-1984, the Sea Wolf was in San Diego and renewed acquaintances with an old British friend from the days prior to the Normandy invasion. This friend had been a lieutenant in the Royal Navy at that time, and he and Bulkeley had, on occasion, lifted a pint or two of ale together at the navy officers' club in Portsmouth, on the English Channel. Now this Englishman was Prince Philip, the Duke of Edinburgh. When he married Queen Elizabeth II, he automatically became a five-star admiral in the Royal Navy.

Typically, John Bulkeley was unimpressed by Prince Philip's lofty titles, and remembered him from World War II elbow-bending sessions as simply a witty and personable fellow. So when the Duke of Edinburgh and Queen Elizabeth boarded the USS *Ranger* at San Diego for a luncheon in their honor, Admiral Bulkeley quipped: "Say, Prince, in World War II you and I were both navy lieutenants, we both married English women, and now you are a five-star admiral and the best I could do was two stars. Where did I go wrong?"

Prince Philip grinned broadly and fired back: "You married the wrong English woman!" [4]

Back in Washington later that year, John Bulkeley, Comdr. Samuel Alexander, and three other InSurv officers climbed into a Rockwell Saberliner at Andrews Air Force Base, bound for Idaho Falls, Idaho. It was a cold, overcast day. While the crew prepared to lift off, Bulkeley began reading a book. When the Saberliner climbed to about 100 feet, a loud alarm went off in the cockpit and a warning panel lit up, all of which could be heard and seen by the passengers. A crewman shouted back to the cabin, "We've lost hydraulics, and will land back at Andrews after dumping our fuel!"

COMDR. SAMUEL ALEXANDER:
By the time the fuel was dumped, a snow squall covered Andrews and visibility was almost nil. Our approach was extremely rough, and it looked as though every piece of emergency equipment the base had was lining the runway. Hydraulics were needed for our thrust reversers and brakes, but a hand pump in the cockpit provided enough pressure for stopping.

As we left the plane on the runway, I was shaking visibly. But I noted that Admiral Bulkeley, who had begun reading on the first page prior to takeoff, was now at about page sixty in his book. It had been a close call, but the admiral never missed a word.

On August 19, 1986, John Bulkeley celebrated the milestone of his seventy-fifth birthday by putting in a heavy day of work at his office. A reporter from the *Washington Post* telephoned and asked the Sea Wolf if he had plans to retire. "Yes, I have," Bulkeley responded. "I will consider that possibility when I reach ninety." [5]

Letters and telegrams of birthday congratulations poured in from all over the world. Commander-in-Chief Ronald Reagan wrote: "I am happy to speak for all Americans in thanking you for your dedicated service

THE WHITE HOUSE

WASHINGTON

August 15, 1986

Dear Admiral Bulkeley:

Happy Birthday! Nancy and I are pleased to salute one of our military heroes on this special occasion.

We share your pride in the memories of a rich, full life. I am happy to speak for all Americans in thanking you for your dedicated service to the Navy and your country.

Again, Happy 75th Birthday. We hope that your celebration is filled with happiness and good cheer. God bless and keep you.

Sincerely,

Ronald Reagan

RADM John D. Bulkeley, USN
Quarters "D"
Washington Navy Yard
Washington, D.C. 20374

to the Navy and your country." Secretary of the Navy John Lehman, a former navy pilot, said: "This country owes a debt to you for your sacrifices, foresight, and dedication."

On the frosty morning of January 30, 1987, an aircraft carrying Admiral Bulkeley, wife Alice, and a small group of navy officers sped down the runway at Andrews Air Force Base. A few hours later, the plane touched down at McCalla Field, at balmy Guantanamo Bay, Cuba. It would be a nostalgic homecoming of sorts for Bulkeley, who was back at the locale of his confrontation with Kremlin-backed Fidel Castro two decades ago.

A few months earlier, on August 14, Fidel had turned sixty, and after twenty-seven years as absolute czar, the Maximum Leader still gripped the reins of power. On his birthday anniversary, Moscow had awarded Castro the Order of Lenin for his "great contributions to world peace."

Castro, who had bestowed upon himself the title of president, was still strutting about Cuba in a military-type, 26th of July Movement uniform, packing a .45 Colt and conducting a seemingly endless revolution, replete with time-worn slogans, five-year plans, and periodic attacks on the United States.

Big Iron Bulkeley, as he was still known to thousands of marines who had served under him at Gitmo, would be guest of honor for the dedication of the new Fleet Training Center academic instruction building, which was to be christened Bulkeley Hall. In this case, the sometimes hide-bound Navy had broken with tradition; for two centuries it had been the custom to name ships and buildings after distinguished navy officers who were deceased.

While a throng of thousands—navy men, marines, military dependents, civilians, and Cubans living on base—looked on, Bulkeley Hall was dedicated. The Sea Wolf had been unaware of a number of messages that would be read at the ceremonies. One was from Adm. Carlisle A. H. Trost, the current chief of naval operations:

> At the dedication of Bulkeley Hall, a strong Navy . . . renders its salute to the living example of the American hero who inspires us all.
>
> When, in 1942, his exploits as a PT-boat commander were recognized by the Medal of Honor, for John Bulkeley it was just the beginning of an illustrious career of great service to our country. Twenty some years later, at a critical hour in Guantanamo Bay's history, he and his people

> stood together and defied an adversary who had in mind nothing less than the reduction of this vital outpost to the Communist will.
>
> Since then, in a tour of duty spanning three decades, he has served with utmost distinction as the president of the Board of Inspection and Survey. His outstanding vigor and uncompromising honesty, his technical insight backed by combat experience have had a direct influence not only on the material readiness of the ships he has inspected but on the professional standards of the officers and enlisted personnel who have served in them. Over the years, in preparing for an InSurv inspection, many a sailor has learned that he had better be quick to climb up the mast and check it out before the admiral in coveralls beats him to it.
>
> Today, you men and women of the Guantanamo Bay commands are living the Bulkeley ideal. In the face of a continuing real threat you have not flinched from your responsibility . . . of defending American interests. It is fitting, therefore, that the Fleet Training Group should today occupy a new headquarters named after this national hero, who exemplifies all that you strive for.
>
> I join in the navy's salute to you and to our famous Admiral Bulkeley.

That stirring—and unexpected—tribute from Chief of Naval Operations Trost was followed by the reading of a letter from Mrs. Douglas MacArthur, penned a few days earlier at her New York City home:

> Those of us on those frail PT boats on those fateful days in March 1942 [at Corregidor] owe our lives to John Bulkeley's leadership and skill in running the Japanese blockade. The success of that mission changed the course of history. "My General" would be proud of him today.

Between formal events, Admiral Bulkeley toured the base and renewed friendships with many of the older Cuban civilians. One elderly, white-haired Cuban, tears streaming down his ruddy cheeks, rushed up and threw his arms around the Sea Wolf, calling out emotionally: "Father! Father! Father!" Bulkeley was momentarily taken aback to discover a "son," especially one who was his own age. Then he recognized Frankie Torres.

During the 1964 showdown with Fidel Castro and the Kremlin, following the water cutoff at Gitmo, Frankie had scrambled over the chain-link fence from the Cuban side to seek sanctuary on the naval base. Bulkeley happened to be nearby, and he grabbed Torres and shielded him with his own body from Castro's soldiers, who were making motions as though they were going to shoot the refugee. Since that time, twenty-three years earlier, Frankie Torres had always called his protector "father."

CAPT. JOHN R. CONDON, USN:
From the moment Admiral Bulkeley stepped off the plane until he departed Gitmo, he was the natural focus of all with whom he came into contact, including myself as the current base commander. To be in his presence was an inspiration, to walk in his footsteps, even for a short time, a singular honor.

He spoke for about an hour at a dinner at the officers' club, and the audience was held in rapture. None moved or fidgeted—we could have listened for hours.

The high point of his stay was, for me, not the building dedication, but Admiral Bulkeley's return to the Northeast Gate, where in 1964 he had cut the water pipe to prove once and for all that we were not stealing water from the Cubans. Seeing the sharp, clear-eyed gentleman there telling his story, where I had heard so many others retell it, was simply incredible. It was living history, like having George Washington return to Valley Forge or Douglas MacArthur to the Philippines to tell in their own words what really happened.

On May 17, 1987, a little over four months after Bulkeley's departure from Guantanamo, a seaman was peering through the blackness of the Persian Gulf from his lookout post on the port side of the USS *Stark*'s bridge. It was around 9:00 P.M. Activity in the gulf seemed as placid as the waters. He had no clue that an Iraqi jet fighter less than twenty-five miles away was targeting the American frigate, part of a naval force that was assuring the safe passage of tankers carrying Middle East oil to the free world.

One deck down was the *Stark*'s combat information center, darkened so that operators could see the displays of several sophisticated radar, sonar, and electronic warfare sensors. There Lt. Basil E. Moncrief, Jr., had been tracking the Iraq Mirage F-1 fighter for more than an hour. Around 9:09 P.M. the sensor operators heard the low hum of the jet's scanning search mode transform into a steady high pitch.

"We've been locked on!" the petty officer called out.

The *Stark* radioed a warning on the international military air distress channel: "Unknown aircraft—this is United States Navy warship on your oh-seven-two at thirteen miles. Request you state your intentions." There was no reply. Forty seconds later a similar message was sent. Again no response.

Above, the seaman lookout near the *Stark*'s bridge saw a bright flash split the blackness in the distance, followed by a small blue dot bobbing erratically on the horizon. It grew into a blue fireball as it raced toward the frigate. The sailor shouted: "Inbound missile!" and hit the deck. The projectile pierced the ship's hull about six feet above the waterline and bolted to the starboard side. It was a dud.

Perhaps twenty-five seconds later, a second French-built missile tore through the port hull and exploded, ripping open a hole fifteen feet in diameter. Fires ignited by the missile became so intense that they melted parts of the *Stark*'s superstructure. Thick clouds of smoke filled the maze of compartments below. Thirty-seven of the 221 men on board perished.

Despite the tragic loss of life in the *Stark* missile attack, the death toll would have been much higher had it not been for an earlier hell-raising campaign by John Bulkeley to have EEBDs (emergency escape breathing devices) provided for each ship in the fleet.

Bulkeley had long made it a practice personally to review every accident involving loss of life, and applied the lessons learned to subsequent inspections. His probing disclosed that in several tragic fires at sea crew members not actually in the vicinity of the blaze perished because they were unable to avoid the smoke and toxic fumes. Often they had died when only a few feet from safety. Out of these disasters, the Navy gave birth to the EEBD.

Originally, the design consisted of a small cylinder of air and a hood that provided about three minutes of breathable air with which a person could escape the smoke and fumes. The concept was on target, but the devices proved to be unreliable, difficult to operate in the dark, and prone to lose their air charges.

Bulkeley, over a period of many months, argued, hollered, complained, cajoled, and generally made a nuisance of himself until needed technical improvements were made on the EEBD.

Bulkeley was still not satisfied. Men's lives were at stake. He bombarded the navy hierarchy and division heads with demands that EEBDs be placed on all ships, not just on aircraft carriers, as was the practice. Too expensive, Bulkeley was told. He refused to be silenced. Finally a directive came out of the Pentagon: EEBDs were to be placed on all ships.

Over the years, countless navy men's lives have been saved by the presence of EEBDs on board at times of fire disasters at sea, including large numbers of survivors on the *Stark*. Most were and are unaware that they survived because of a dedicated, tenacious Sea Wolf who refused to take no for an answer.

Epilogue

With the arrival of the year 1988—nearly fifty-nine years after John Bulkeley had strolled wide-eyed through the gates of the Naval Academy—he has shown no sign of slowing down his relentless pace. Doctors say he is a medical miracle; navy brass remain amazed over his unflagging enthusiasm and dedication; associates marvel at his stamina.

In twenty years as chief of the Naval Board of Inspection and Survey, Admiral Bulkeley has traveled 2,500,000 air miles—the equivalent to flying around the world at the equator 100 times—plus perhaps another 500,000 miles on the ground and countless thousands of miles while conducting exhaustive sea trials all over the world. Long ago he lost track of the number of ships that he and his InSurv team have gone over with a fine-tooth comb, but the figure runs into the thousands.

Military experts agree that today's United States Navy is the most combat-ready, flexible, and capable since World War II, a condition in which Bulkeley has certainly played a key, but by no means exclusive, role.

What seething inner forces motivate the ageless Sea Wolf to drive himself so remorselessly, year after year, at an age when most other men have been retired and are taking things easy for a decade or longer? Those who know Bulkeley best are fully aware that his motivational roots were planted forty-six years earlier in the bloody and hallowed soil of Corregidor and Bataan.

"Thousands of American boys lost their lives in the early months of the Pacific war because this nation had stuck its head ostrichlike into the sand and refused to admit that there were predatory forces out there in the world,'' Bulkeley told a New York television reporter recently. ''After taking part in that bitter and tragic experience, I resolved that, once I had gained maturity as a navy officer, I would muster all my dedication and energy to try to make the Navy more effective in the harsh realities of war.''

On June 6, 1988, Admiral Bulkeley flew to France in Air Force 2 to represent President Ronald Reagan at the dedication of the Normandy Battlefield Memorial and Museum. It was the forty-fourth anniversary of the historic D-Day assault in which the Sea Wolf's PT boats formed the tip of the American amphibious spearhead at Utah Beach.

Two and a half months later, on August 25, a ''frocking'' ceremony was held in the Pentagon in the office of Chief of Naval Operations Carlisle Trost. John Bulkeley was promoted to vice admiral. Trost pinned one three-star epaulet on the legendary Sea Wolf and a proud Alice Bulkeley did the honors on the second epaulet.

Then the new vice admiral did some frocking of his own. On Alice, his First Mate and inspiration for nearly fifty years, John pinned a brooch of three stars with diamonds.

At the Sea Wolf's insistence, the ceremony was conducted without fanfare and in the presence of only a handful of guests, an unobtrusive scenario totally in contrast to the flamboyance that had been a hallmark of his lengthy navy career in war and in peace.

With his three stars firmly in place, John Bulkeley then was awarded his third Distinguished Service Medal, America's highest decoration for noncombat achievement. In part the DSM citation states:

> Vice Admiral Bulkeley's operational experience, courage and initiative brought honors to the Navy and victories to his nation. . . . For the past twenty-one years, with an unequaled appreciation for the challenges faced by sailors serving in our men-of-war, he devoted his life to ensuring that they are supported by the best, safest, and most survivable ships.

John Bulkeley took the elevation to three-star rank philosophically. He told a reporter: ''Medals and citations are nice, but what really counts is the inner satisfaction of knowing that I have contributed toward preserving the peace by helping to keep America militarily strong in a volatile and dangerous world. That, to me, is the real payoff.''

Rear Admiral John D. Bulkeley
Decorations and Citations
(Partial Listing)

Medal of Honor (Presented by President Franklin Roosevelt)

Navy Cross (Presented by Secretary of the Navy Frank Knox)

Distinguished Service Cross (Army) with Oak Leaf Cluster in Lieu of Second Award (Presented by Gen. Douglas MacArthur)

Distinguished Service Medal with Two Oak Leaf Clusters in Lieu of Second and Third Awards (Presented by Chief of Naval Operations)

Silver Star with Oak Leaf Cluster in Lieu of Second Award

Legion of Merit with Combat "V"

Purple Heart

Croix de Guerre (Presented by Gen. Charles de Gaulle)

Distinguished Conduct Star (Philippine Commonwealth) (Presented by President Manuel Quezon)

Joint Service Commendation Medal

Army Distinguished Unit Badge

China Service Medal

American Defense Service Medal with "Fleet" Clasp

American Campaign Medal

European-African-Middle East Campaign Medal

Asiatic-Pacific Campaign Medal

World War II Victory Medal

National Defense Service Medal with Oak Leaf Cluster in Lieu of Second Award

Korean Service Medal

Korean Presidential Unit Citation

Philippines Defense Ribbon

United Nations Service Medal

Campaign Combat Stars (8)

THE WHITE HOUSE
WASHINGTON

The President of the United States takes pleasure in presenting the MEDAL OF HONOR to

LIEUTENANT JOHN D. BULKELEY
UNITED STATES NAVY

for service as set forth in the following

CITATION:

"For extraordinary heroism, distinguished service and conspicuous gallantry above and beyond the call of duty, as Commander of Motor Torpedo Boat Squadron THREE, in Philippine waters during the period December 7, 1941 to April 10, 1942. The remarkable achievement of Lieutenant Bulkeley's Command in damaging or destroying a notable number of Japanese enemy planes, surface combatant and merchant ships, and in dispersing landing parties and land based enemy forces during the four months and eight days of operation without benefit of repairs, overhaul or maintenance facilities for his Squadron, is believed to be without precedent in this type of warfare. His dynamic forcefulness and daring in offensive action, his brilliantly planned and skillfully executed attacks, supplemented by an unique resourcefulness and ingenuity, characterize him as an outstanding leader of men and a gallant and intrepid seaman. These qualities coupled with a complete disregard for his own personal safety reflect great credit upon him and the Naval Service."

Franklin D Roosevelt

PAGE 2 RUCKUDI 934 UNCLAS
SHOUTS "COMMANDER IN CHIEF, AT YOUR ORDERS"--ED.), THE FORCES IN THE UNITED STATES ARE BANDING INTO TWO CAMPS, MORE REACTIONARY AND LESS REACTIONARY.

IT COULD WELL BE SAID THAZXUNITED STATES POLICIES ARE DIVIDED UP BETWEEN THE BAD AND THE WORSE. AS YOU KNOW, ON 19 ONENINE APRIL, A CERTAIN TYPE OF EXTREMELY GRAVE PROVOCATIONS DDGAN: CROSSING THE DIVIDQFGSLINENLO GOTANDNUTRAGE OUR FLAG THERE, FIRING AT A SOLDIER AND WOUFUDING HIM, FIRING, BARELY TWO WEEKS LATER, AT ANOTHER SOLDISN, WOUNDING HIM, AND FIRING, IN RECENT DAYS, AT ANOTHER REVOLUTIONARY SOLDIER AND KILLING HIM.

IN VIEW OF THESE EVENTS, WE HAVE GIVEN GREAT EVIDENCE OF MODERATION. WE KNOW WHAT IS BEHIND ALL THIS, AND RAUL EXPLAINED IT. WE DO NOT RPT NOT BELIEVE THAT THE UNITED SHATES GOVERNMENT IS ORDERING THE CARRYING OUT OF THOSE PROVOCATIONS. IT SEEMS TO US SOMETHING SO ABSURD, SO STUPID, AND SO ILLOGICAL THAT WE DO NOT RPT NOT BELIEVE UZ. IN OUR OPINION, THERE ARE ELEMENTS IN THE GUANTANAMGTBASE, POSSIBLY THE COMMANDER, WHO IS A LITTLE GORILLA OF THE WORSE SPECIE--BECAUSE THEY HAVE PLACED THERE A GORILLA COMMANDER WHO IS SAID TO HAVE BEEN IN MACARTHUR'S CLIQUE, WHICH WAS NOTABLY WARLIKE--AND THIS GENTLEMAN, IT SEEMS, IS

PAGE 3 RUCKUDI 934 UNCLAS
DIRECTLY RESPONSIBLE FOR THE BIG PROVOCATIONS THAT HAVE BEEN TAKING PLACE IN THE BASE.

FROM OUR POINT OF VIEW, THE INTEREST OF THAT GENTLEMAN IS THAT WE RETURN THEFIRE, KILL A PAIR OF MARINES, IN ORDER TO USE ~~IT~~ IN THE ELECTION CAMPAIGN AS A POLITICAL LAMPOON AGAINST PRESIDEMV JOHNSON. I DO NOT RPT NOT IN THE LEAST BELIEVE THAT JOHNSON IS A SAINT, BUT, IT SEEMS, THE EXTREME RIGHT, WHICH IS MTRYING TO TAKE POWER FROM HIS IN THE UNITED STATES, IS WILLING TO USE ALL MEANS, IS WILLING TO PROVOKE ANY INCIDENT. AND, OF COURSE, WE DO NOT RPT NOT WANT TO PLAY THE GAME OF THAT EXTREME RIGHT.

WELL, OSAT IS CLEAR. THAT IS LOGICAL. THAT IS REASONABLE. THAT IS INTELLIGENT. THAT IS CORRECT. BUT DOES THISJ PERHAPS, EAN THAT WE, BECAUSE WE DO NOT RPT NOT WANT TO HELP MR. GOLDWATER, WILL HAVE TO BEAR THEIR KILLING OEROUR MEN IN THE GUANTANAMO NAVAL BASE? (CROWD SHOUTS "NO"AAED.) NO! I THINK THAT IT IS NOT RPT NOT ONLY CUBA WHICH HAS

C INTEREST IN THIS PROBLEM. THIS PROBLEM IS OF INTEREST TO THE UNITED STATES ALSO, AND IT IS OF INTEREST OF THE UNITED STATES GOVERNMENT ITSELF. AND ALTHOUGH WE DO NOT RPT NOT BELIEVE THAT THOSE PROVOCATIONS ARE THE RESULT OF ORDERS ISSUED BY THE UNITED ST

NES GOVERNMENT. WE DO BELIEVE THAT UNITED STATES

Page of translated remarks by Fidel Castro in which he called Admiral Bulkeley "a gorilla of the worst species" and the "man directly responsible for the [phony] shootings." The speech was monitored on the base.

Notes and Sources

Chapter 1: The Japanese Ambassador's Disappearing Briefcase

1. Admiral Bulkeley had a much older stepbrother, Frederick Chauncey, who attended Princeton and became an architect.
2. There are other ways to be appointed to the Naval Academy, including by presidential and secretary of the navy appointments.
3. During Civil War, the Naval Academy was moved temporarily to Newport, Rhode Island, because Annapolis was close to battle lines.
4. John Bulkeley's memory of the Naval Academy is so bitter that he has never attended a class reunion, nor does he intend to go to one. However, due to sweeping changes made at the Academy after World War II and beyond, Bulkeley maintains that it is today the finest institution of its kind in the world.
5. *Lucky Bag,* yearbook of Naval Academy, 1933.
6. Captain Stanley M. Barnes, USN (Ret.), who was in command of all PT boats in the Mediterranean, is regarded by John Bulkeley as one of the great combat leaders of World War II.
7. Service academy scholastic rankings had little bearing on combat results. Among famed World War II leaders who graduated far down on the scholastic totem pole were Admiral of the Fleet William "Bull" Halsey, General of the Army Dwight D. Eisenhower, and Gen. George S. Patton.

Chapter 2: A Spy in Shanghai

1. The *Indianapolis* was torpedoed and sunk in the Pacific during the closing days of World War II. Heavy loss of life was sustained.
2. From 1937 through 1939, the United States shipped huge quantities of scrap oil and iron to Japan.
3. Bruce M. Bachman, *An Honorable Profession,* p 159.
4. Many United States military officers believe that Washington's and the nation's indifference to the *Panay* sinking encouraged Japanese warlords to go to war with America.

Chapter 3: "The Situation Is Tense Out Here!"

1. At the end of World War II, the United States had about 100 aircraft carriers.
2. *St. Louis Post-Dispatch,* July 3, 1941.
3. As the Army chief of staff, Douglas MacArthur had been a full general (four stars). But he was recalled as a three-star lieutenant general for reasons that have been obscure.

4. Alice Bulkeley, private files.
5. William Manchester, *American Caesar,* p 179.
6. Torpedoman First Class Charles Di Maio was captured when Bataan fell in spring 1942, survived the war (including the sinking by American planes of his POW ship), and in late 1987, at age seventy-seven, was still working fulltime in the New Haven, Connecticut, post office.

Chapter 4: Disaster at Manila Bay

1. Later in the war, Joseph C. Chalker was killed in action.
2. John L. Houlihan, Jr., survived several Japanese POW camps and eventually returned home.
3. Mrs. Jack (Dode) Fee and her husband were interned by the Japanese at the notorious Santo Tomas camp in Manila, where their daughter was born eight months later. The Fees' daughter left in Cebu was brought to Santo Tomas a year afterward.
4. *Saga* magazine, August 1958, p 84.
5. *American Caesar,* p 212.
6. *At Close Quarters,* the official history of PT boats in World War II, p 7, states that the decision to pull all submarines out of the Philippines was made by Admiral Rockwell and Capt. John Wilkes, submarine commander in the Far East, on December 28, 1941, several days after Adm. Thomas Hart had departed.
7. *At Close Quarters,* p 8.
8. General Douglas MacArthur, *Reminiscences,* p 129.

Chapter 5: A Charge into Subic Bay

1. Jean (Mrs. Douglas) MacArthur would say that the three months she spent on Corregidor seemed longer than the three years she would later spend in Australia.
2. *American Caesar,* pp 225, 226.
3. Sidney L. Huff, *My Fifteen Years With MacArthur,* p 43.
4. Ibid., pp 44, 45.
5. Barron W. Chandler told the author in 1987 that he had talked with a fellow POW at a Manila POW camp who told him that Ens. William H. Plant had swum ashore, been shot by a Japanese soldier, but recovered and spent months working on Manila docks with other American POWs. Late in the war, Ensign Plant was being taken to Japan when his unmarked POW ship was attacked and sunk by American warplanes, apparently taking him to his death.
6. *New York Herald Tribune,* January 21, 1942.
7. Alice Bulkeley, private files.

Chapter 6: "General, It'll Be a Piece of Cake!"

1. *Saga,* August 1958, p 86.
2. Five years later, at the first parade review of Allied occupation troops, General of the Army Douglas MacArthur would take the salute as supreme commander on the precise spot where Tokyo Rose had proclaimed that "war criminal MacArthur" would be hanged.
3. *Saturday Evening Post,* article by Lt. Col. Sidney L. Huff, September 22, 1951.
4. In the old Roman calendar, the Ides was a day near the middle of the month. In March, it was the fifteenth.
5. *At Close Quarters,* p 16.
6. Ibid., p 17.
7. Courtney Whitney, *MacArthur: His Rendezvous With History,* p 49.
8. Admiral Bulkeley told the author in 1987 that General MacArthur planned to use the PT-boat skipper's razor. "With the long beard I had, I wondered where in the hell he thought I was hiding my razor," Bulkeley quipped.
9. *Reminiscences,* p 143.

Chapter 7: ". . . Out of the Jaws of Death!"

1. Of the nine extra PT-boat engines that John Bulkeley had had the foresight to hide in private garages in Manila, three were lost on January 2 when Manila was invaded, and the remaining six were shipped to Corregidor. There two were destroyed on January 9 when the North Pier was bombed, and the remaining four had to be left behind on Corregidor when Bulkeley's boats left for Mindanao in March.
2. Those who made the dash through the Japanese blockade were: PT 41 (Lt. John Bulkeley), Gen. Douglas MacArthur, Mrs. Jean MacArthur, Arthur MacArthur, Loh Chiu (also known as Ah Cheu), Maj. Gen. Richard K. Sutherland, Capt. Harold G. Ray, USN, Lt. Col. Sidney L. Huff, and Maj. Charles H. Morhouse (physician).

   PT 35 (Ens. Anthony B. Akers), Col. Charles A. Willoughby, Lt. Col. LeGrande A. Diller, Lt. Col. Francis H. Wilson, and M. Sgt. Paul P. Rogers.

   PT 34 (Lt. Robert B. Kelly), Rear Adm. Francis W. Rockwell, Brig. Gen. Richard J. Marshall, Col. Charles P. Stivers, and Capt. Joseph McMicking.

   PT 32 (Lt. Vincent S. Schumacher), Brig. Gen. Spencer B. Akin, Brig. Gen. Hugh J. Casey, Brig. Gen. William F. Marquat, Brig. Gen. Harold H. George, and Lt. Col. Joe R. Sherr.
3. *Reminiscences,* p 97.

4. On March 24, 1936, when he was presented a gold baton by Philippines President Manuel Quezon, Douglas MacArthur became the only retired United States general to have held a field marshal's rank.

Chapter 8: A Mission for MacArthur

1. John J. Beck, *MacArthur and Wainwright,* p 120.
2. Ibid., p 120.
3. Theodore Friend, *Between Two Empires,* p 218.
4. Carlos Romulo, *I See the Philippines Rise,* p 113.
5. President Quezon later awarded decorations to torpedomen James D. Light and John L. Houlihan.
6. Admiral Bulkeley told the author in 1987 that his "gut reaction" about the loyalty of Don Andres Soriano had been faulty. "His loyalty was exceeded only by his intense desire to make the mission successful," Bulkeley said.

Chapter 9: Shoot-Out Off Cebu Island

1. *New York Herald Tribune,* March 18, 1942.
2. *My Fifteen Years With MacArthur,* pp 72–74.
3. *MacArthur: His Rendezvous With History,* p 51.
4. When President Roosevelt died in April 1945, Col. Bonner Fellers, an aide to General MacArthur, quoted MacArthur as saying: "So Roosevelt is dead. There's a man who could not tell the truth when a lie would serve just as well!"
5. Barron W. Chandler was taken prisoner on Corregidor, and was liberated nearly three years later when American forces returned to the Philippines.
6. *New York Times,* March 26, 1942.
7. General Eisenhower and General MacArthur did not form a mutual admiration society. Years later, Eisenhower would quip of his time as aide to the flamboyant MacArthur: "I studied theatrics for two years under MacArthur."
8. After the war, Helge and Dorothy Janson moved to the United States. Mrs. Janson in 1987 was living in Stamford, Connecticut. Helge is deceased.
9. PT-32 torpedoman Ned "Colonel" Cobb joined the submarine *Permit*'s crew and made nine patrols. On one of these, the *Permit* sank a five-ship Japanese convoy near the island of Truk.
10. A few weeks earlier, MacArthur had been promoted to full general, the rank he had held when he retired in 1936.
11. This account of the night action off Cebu was pieced together from Admiral Bulkeley's recollections and after-action reports by Capt. Robert B. Kelly and Bulkeley, along with an account supplied the author by Comdr. Albert P. Ross (Ret.), who took part in the fight as an enlisted man.

12. John Bulkeley recommended Lt. Robert Kelly for the Congressional Medal of Honor for his actions in the Philippines, but Kelly was awarded the Navy Cross.

Chapter 10: Summons to Australia

1. *MacArthur: His Rendezvous With History,* p 102.
2. When John Bulkeley prepared to fly to Australia, he gave his binoculars to PT-boater John Tuggle, who fought through the war as a guerrilla in the Philippines. After the war, back in the States, Tuggle returned the binoculars to Bulkeley.
3. *Chicago Herald-American,* July 20, 1943.
4. Actually, in 1956, John Bulkeley got back into the guerrilla business, carrying out a mission for the CIA as part of a cloak-and-dagger group known as the Zulu Team. Bulkeley would never even hint at the nature of the operation, other than to tell the author that it was "very successful."
5. At this time, Alice Bulkeley was still a British subject. She became a United States citizen on December 31, 1942.
6. *San Francisco News* and *Long Island Star,* May 1, 1942.
7. *At Close Quarters,* p 28.
8. John Toland, *The Rising Sun,* pp 310–315.

Chapter 11: A Tumultuous Homecoming

1. John D. "Johnny" Bulkeley, Jr., would become an exceptionally talented musician, and in 1987, and for several years previously, has been the organist at the Washington Navy Yard chapel.
2. In the early 1960s, Anthony B. Akers was President Kennedy's ambassador to New Zealand and also assistant secretary of the Air Force.
3. *New York Journal-American,* May 9, 1942.
4. *Shipworker,* Elco Boat Company newsletter, June 1, 1942.
5. *New York Journal-American,* May 14, 1942.
6. *New York Post,* May 14, 1942.
7. *New York World-Telegram,* May 14, 1942.
8. Ibid.
9. Alice Bulkeley's father, Capt. Cecil Herbert Wood, died in China during the war, but her mother, brother, and sisters survived Japanese internment.
10. *New York Mirror,* May 18, 1942.
11. *New York Sun,* May 18, 1942.
12. *New York Journal-American,* July 11, 1942.
13. *Long Island Press,* June 29, 1942.
14. *New York Herald Tribune,* May 20, 1942.
15. Ibid.

Chapter 12: Lecturing President Roosevelt
1. *New York PM,* August 17, 1942.
2. Ibid.
3. Ibid.
4. *New Republic,* August 17, 1942.
5. *Atlanta Constitution,* August 28, 1942.
6. John Harllee became chairman of the Federal Maritime Commission during and after the Kennedy administration.
7. *Chicago Tribune,* September 5, 1942.
8. William ''Bud'' Liebenow would gain considerable fame a year later when his PT boat would rescue Lt. John F. Kennedy from a tiny Pacific island.
9. Joseph P. Kennedy, Jr., was killed during the war while on a bombing mission in Europe.

Chapter 13: Back to the Pacific
1. Wags called Admiral Nimitz's South Pacific domain the ''Navy Theater of Operations'' and General MacArthur's Southwest Pacific command the ''Army Theater of Operations.''
2. *At Close Quarters,* pp 195, 196.

Chapter 14: Spy-Running for the OSS
1. After the war, David K. E. Bruce became ambassador to Great Britain, France, West Germany, and China, successively.
2. Anthony Cave Brown, *Wild Bill Donovan,* p 524.
3. Ibid., p 525.
4. Officially, John Bulkeley's spy-running boats were designated Squadron 2 (2), indicating that this was a second, or reborn, Squadron 2. The original Squadron 2 had been decommissioned in the Solomons in November 1943. For clarity, the author has used simply Squadron 2.
5. Ray and Winston Guest were said to be related to Winston Churchill.
6. The British called the E-boats S-boats.
7. After the war, Mark Armistead continued cloak-and-dagger missions, this time by conducting air-filming of Soviet-held Eastern Europe. He retired as a captain, U.S. Navy Reserve, and died in the early 1980s.
8. Dan Ford, *Pappy: The Life of John Ford,* p 196.

Chapter 15: Tip of the Invasion Spearhead
1. The author, who made the Normandy D day assault, was in one of the troop transports in the Exercise Tiger convoy, but knew nothing of the mayhem inflicted by the E-boats until long after the war.
2. The 749 American servicemen killed in the E-boat attack were buried secretly in a farmer's field not far from Slapton Sands, the scene of the disaster.

3. John Bulkeley would eventually command sixty-seven PT boats in the Normandy operation, but not all of them arrived in time for D day.
4. After the war, Alan G. Kirk and Arthur D. Struble would rise to four-star rank.
5. Churchill and his chief military adviser, Field Marshal Alan Brooke, were great admirers of General MacArthur. Brooke had written in his diary that MacArthur should have been the U.S. Army chief of staff instead of Gen. George C. Marshall (with whom Brooke had long butted heads over strategy).
6. Samuel Eliot Morison, *The Invasion of France and Germany,* p 71.
7. General Eisenhower was burdened with an avalanche of details. He even had to settle a lower-level dispute over how much toilet tissue should be taken ashore.
8. *The Invasion of France and Germany,* p 79.
9. *Pappy: The Life of John Ford,* p 195.
10. German Naval Command-West war diary, June 6, 1944.
11. In the postwar government of West Germany, highly decorated E-boat flotilla skipper Heinrich Hoffmann became a high navy official in the Defense Ministry.
12. *San Francisco Chronicle,* June 9, 1944.

Chapter 16: Rescues from Two Sinking Warships

1. All times are British double summer time, one hour ahead of German Central Time.
2. General Omar N. Bradley, *A Soldier's Story,* p 206.
3. The disabled PT 505 was finally towed arduously back to Portland and would later get back into action.
4. German Naval Command-West war diary, June 8, 1944.
5. *The Invasion of France and Germany,* p 171.
6. Ibid., p 171.
7. Robert Miller, United Press correspondent, eyewitness report, June 8, 1944.
8. *Rollover,* Defoe Shipbuilding Company newsletter, September 1944.
9. Robert Miller, eyewitness report, June 8, 1944.
10. *The Invasion of France and Germany,* p 172.
11. *New York Daily Mirror,* July 17, 1944.

Chapter 17: A Dash into Cherbourg Harbor

1. *Pappy: The Life of John Ford,* p 195.
2. Ibid., p 195.
3. Many gunnery experts on both sides considered the German 88millimeter gun to be the best artillery weapon of World War II. It was precisely

accurate, had a high velocity, and could be used as an antiinfantry, antiaircraft, or antitank weapon.

4. Navy Historical Center, Washington, D.C.

Chapter 18: Sudden Death for Two Nazi Warships

1. In January 1944, Allied troops stormed ashore at Anzio, Italy, far behind German lines, in the hope that the invaders could dash the thirty-some miles northward to Rome. The Allies got bogged down for months in one of the war's nastiest actions.
2. George Tucker, Associated Press correspondent who covered the Southern France invasion, as reported in the *Elizabeth (NJ) Daily Journal,* June 4, 1945.
3. Brigadier (later Major) General Robert T. Frederick received eight Purple Hearts during the war.
4. After-action report by Capt. Henry C. Johnson, USN, commander of Special Operations Group for Dragoon, August 1944.
5. Ibid.
6. USS *Endicott* after-action report by Comdr. John D. Bulkeley, August 23, 1944.
7. Associated Press correspondent George Tucker's eyewitness report, June 4, 1945. John Bulkeley's discovery of German mine-field charts was kept secret until June 1945. Tucker "sat" on the story, was nervous that other reporters would find out about it and scoop him.
8. Copy of original furnished author by Alice Bulkeley.
9. USS *Endicott* action report of surface engagement with German corvettes, August 25, 1944.
10. USS *Endicott*'s captain's Night Orders Book entry for August 17/18, 1944.
11. After the war, the British hanged Lord Haw Haw as a traitor.
12. General MacArthur used such designations as A day and L day for his Pacific invasions, claiming that Eisenhower in Europe had "monopolized" the term D day.

Chapter 19: Duty Tour With the Nuclear Geniuses

1. *Pappy: The Life of John Ford,* pp 196, 197.
2. Ibid., p 200.
3. At his Field Photographic lodge, John Ford set aside special rooms for the use of John Bulkeley and Wild Bill Donovan of OSS.
4. Several bonafide PT-boat veterans of the Pacific who served as "extras" in the shooting of *They Were Expendable* furnished the author with insights of the location activities.
5. At the insistence of the Russians, a second identical surrender ceremony was held in Soviet-occupied Berlin on May 9, 1945.

6. Peter Wood Bulkeley graduated from the United States Naval Academy, and in 1988 he held the rank of commander and was skipper of the USS *Preble.*
7. *New York Herald Tribune,* August 2, 1945.
8. *New York World-Telegram,* August 2, 1945.
9. The author researched various army, navy, air force, and marine personnel bureaus to determine which American fighting man was the "most decorated" in American history. None kept records in this category, but no fighting man was "uncovered" by the author who had more combat decorations than does John Bulkeley.
10. Navy press clippings, office of secretary of the Navy, February 20, 1951.
11. Two years later, in 1949, James V. Forrestal took his own life. The Navy named a class of aircraft carriers after him.
12. Naval Bureau of Personnel records, Washington, D.C.
13. *An Honorable Profession,* p 60.
14. After thirty-four years, a UN–North Korea peace treaty has never been signed. Technically, the Korean War is still in progress.

Chapter 20: Prelude to a Naval Base Confrontation

1. *An Honorable Profession,* pp 68, 69.
2. During the 1960 presidential campaign, John F. Kennedy quipped to William "Bud" Liebenow: "If I get only the votes of those who have told me that they were on your PT boat when you rescued me, I'll win easily."
3. Operation Pluto planning was done during the final months of the Eisenhower administration.
4. Robert F. Kennedy was shot to death by an assassin on June 4, 1968, while campaigning for the presidency in Los Angeles.
5. Philip L. Geyelin, *Lyndon B. Johnson and the World,* p 4. Not long before President Johnson left office in early 1969, he told television-network anchorman Howard K. Smith: "Here's a shocker for you. Jack Kennedy was out to get Castro, and Castro got him first!" The remark was off the record and never aired.

Chapter 21: "There'll Be No Pearl Harbor Here!"

1. *Life,* December 22, 1963.
2. *Male,* July 12, 1965.
3. Ibid.
4. Declassified intelligence bulletin, United States Naval Base, Guantanamo Bay, Cuba, January 2, 1964.
5. *Time,* January 17, 1964, p 27.
6. Ibid.

7. Declassified intelligence bulletin, United States Naval Base, Guantanamo Bay, Cuba, January 11, 1964.
8. *Newsweek,* February 17, 1964, p 13.
9. *Washington Post,* February 11, 1964.
10. Reuters, February 6, 1964.
11. *New York Times,* February 6, 1964.
12. United States State Department, Office of Public Affairs, bulletin, February 7, 1964.

Chapter 22: Ingredients for Nuclear War
1. Captain Zabisco ''Zip'' Trzyna died in the early 1980s. Reportedly, his good humor and love for his adopted country resulted in the epitaph on his tombstone: ''Born in Poland, Died in the United States, God Bless America.''
2. *New York Times,* February 7, 1964.
3. *U.S. News & World Report,* February 17, 1964.
4. *St. Louis Globe-Democrat,* February 7, 1964.
5. *New York Times,* February 7, 1964.
6. Ibid.
7. United Press International, February 8, 1964.
8. *New York Times,* February 9, 1964.
9. Ibid., February 13, 1964.
10. *Revolucion,* February 26, 1964.
11. Ibid.
12. Ibid.
13. *Memphis Commercial Appeal,* February 17, 1964.
14. *Newsweek,* February 24, 1964, p 24.
15. *Boston Herald,* February 15, 1964.
16. Declassified intelligence bulletin, United States Naval Base, Guantanamo Bay, Cuba, February 14, 1964.
17. Admiral Bulkeley's notes jotted down after radio conversation with Secretary of the Navy Paul Nitze.

Chapter 23: ''Castro Can Go Straight to Hell!''
1. *Time,* February 26, 1964, p 42.
2. Author interview with Michael Infante, Washington, D.C.
3. *Philadelphia Bulletin,* February 20, 1964.
4. Declassified intelligence bulletin, United States Naval Base, Guantanamo Bay, Cuba, February 26, 1964.
5. Ibid.
6. Associated Press story from monitoring of President Dorticós's talk, February 24, 1964.

7. Declassified files, United States Naval Base, Guantanamo Bay, Cuba, March-May 1964.
8. Julia Bates, Reuters, February 26, 1964.
9. The famed, outspoken World War II hero, Adm. William "Bull" Halsey, had also incurred the wrath of some State Department bureaucrats in a similar situation in mid-1943. At a press conference in New Caledonia, Halsey, in "colorful" words, offered his views of Japanese emperor Hirohito.
10. Admiral Bulkeley letter to marine corps commandant Gen. Wallace M. Greene, Jr., March 12, 1964.
11. *Newsweek,* March 30, 1964.

Chapter 24: A $50,000 Dead-or-Alive Bounty

1. *New York Times,* April 30, 1964.
2. Ibid.
3. Ibid., April 25, 1964.
4. Ibid., April 28, 1964.
5. Declassified intelligence bulletin, United States Naval Base, Guantanamo Bay, Cuba, April 24, 1964.
6. Author interview with Michael Infante, Washington, D.C.
7. *Male,* July 1964.
8. Thousands of marines who had served at Gitmo in the mid-1960s still call Bulkeley "Big Iron" in 1987.
9. In 1988, this same marine corps emblem remains on the Gitmo hill.
10. Admiral Bulkeley letter to Gen. Wallace C. Greene, Jr., commandant, marine corps, July 1, 1964.
11. Declassified intelligence documents, United States Naval Base, Guantanamo Bay, Cuba, July 1964.
12. Ibid.
13. Ibid.
14. Ibid.
15. *Columbus (OH) Dispatch,* July 13, 1964.
16. Ibid.
17. *New York Times,* July 21, 1964.
18. *Miami Herald,* July 20, 1964.
19. *New York Times,* July 21, 1964.
20. Ibid., July 22, 1964.

Chapter 25: "A Gorilla of the Worst Species!"

1. Declassified document, translation of Fidel Castro's speech, monitored at United States Naval Base, Guantanamo Bay, Cuba, July 26, 1964.
2. Ibid.

3. Ibid.
4. Ibid.
5. Ibid.
6. *New York Times,* July 30, 1964.
7. *Gitmo Review,* August 3, 1964.
8. *New York Herald Tribune,* August 6, 1964.
9. Ibid.
10. *Philadelphia Bulletin,* August 26, 1964.
11. Ibid.
12. *Norfolk Star-Ledger,* August 29, 1964.
13. *New York Journal American,* August 28, 1964.
14. Author interview with Michael Infante, Washington, D.C.
15. Admiral Bulkeley declined to discuss any aspect of Gitmo's electronic surveillance procedures, presumably because some of them are still being used in 1987.
16. Admiral Bulkeley letter, August 17, 1968, declassified files, United States Naval Base, Guantanamo Bay, Cuba.

Chapter 26: The Great *Viking Princess* Rescue

1. Author interview with Michael Infante, Washington, D.C.
2. Ibid.
3. It required fifteen gallons of saltwater to make one gallon of fresh water.
4. *Gitmo Review* newspaper, December 5, 1964.
5. Edwin Tetlow, *Eye on Cuba,* pp 226, 227.
6. Admiral Bulkeley dispatched the USS *Raleigh* to put out the *Viking Princess* fire. The *Raleigh* stayed there for seven days. Then a Greek freighter, which was hovering nearby, rushed in, hooked onto the *Princess*'s anchor chain, and claimed the hulk as salvage under the laws of the sea. The hulk was said to have been sold for a sizable sum.

Chapter 27: Black Hat Admiral

1. *An Honorable Profession,* p 98.
2. Ibid., p 129.

Chapter 28: The Conscience of the Navy

1. Memo from Vice Adm. David H. Bagley, March 15, 1973.
2. Secretary of the Navy John Warner memo, April 16, 1973.
3. Boiler rooms later became known as firerooms.
4. In early 1988, Capt. Richard Dasler was still with InSurv.
5. *An Honorable Profession,* p 131.
6. Transcript of John Bulkeley testimony, office of the navy judge advocate general, Washington, D.C.

7. Ibid.
8. Ibid.
9. In early 1988, Congressman Charles E. Bennett of Florida still chaired the House Seapower Subcommittee.
10. The author is indebted to Bruce M. Bachman, a former aide to Admiral Bulkeley and in 1987 a businessman in Winter Haven, Florida, for much of the flavor and substance of the Sea Wolf's return to Corregidor.
11. After the war, in late 1945, Mrs. Douglas MacArthur paid a visit to Corregidor. She said that she could "only peek into Malinta Tunnel," for it was filled with "all sorts of things." She said that she could find no trace of the cottage on The Rock where the MacArthurs had lived early in 1942.
12. Captain Curtis O. Anderson, USN (Ret.) to author.

Chapter 29: The "Show and Tell Bag"

1. John "Duke" Wayne (real name, Marion Michael Morrison) died on June 12, 1979.
2. Reproduced by permission of Jack Anderson, Washington, D.C.
3. In 1987, the famed Blue Angels were using derivatives of the F-18 for their intricate-formation flying demonstrations.
4. *Navy Times,* August 6, 1985.
5. *Washington Post,* August 30, 1986.

Principal Interviews and Contacts

Cmdr. Samuel J. Alexander, USN (Ret.)	Fairfax, VA
Mrs. Rose Aloi	Washington, D.C.
Capt. Curtis O. Anderson, USN (Ret.)	Benicia, CA
Donnald K. Anderson	Washington, D.C.
Bruce M. Bachman	Winter Haven, FL
Douglas L. Bailey, Sr.	Pittsfield, MA
Capt. Stanley M. Barnes, USN (Ret.)	New Canaan, CT
Edward W. Barton	Dover, NH
Congressman Charles E. Bennett	Washington, D.C.
Cmdr. Henry J. Brantingham, USN (Ret.)	La Jolla, CA
Joseph Brauneis	Minocqwa, WI
Vice Adm. J. Russell Bryan, USN (Ret.)	St. Leonard, MD
Mrs. Alice Wood Bulkeley	Washington, D.C.
Rear Adm. John D. Bulkeley, USN	Washington, D.C.
Capt. Alan Cabot, USN (Ret.)	Pascagoula, MS
Capt. Lynn C. Cavendish, USN (Ret.)	Mount Pleasant, SC
George Champion	New York, NY
Capt. Malcolm M. Champlin, USN (Ret.)	Oakland, CA
Cmdr. Barron W. Chandler, USN (Ret.)	Gladwynne, PA
Mrs. Juanita V. Cobb	Oxnard, CA
Capt. John R. Condon, USN	Guantanamo Bay, Cuba
Capt. Richard Dasler, USN	Washington, D.C.
Joseph Davis	Danville, IL
Charles Di Maio	New Haven, CT
Joseph R. Ellicott	Alpine, NJ
L. Rumsey Ewing	Ladue, MO
Capt. Douglas E. Fairbanks, Jr. USNR (Ret.)	New York, NY
Mrs. Amelia S. Fales	San Antonio, TX
Capt. William Fales, USN (Ret.)	San Antonio, TX
Paul B. Fay, Jr.	San Francisco, CA
Mrs. Dode Fee	Washington, D.C.
E. J. Garvey	Southport, CT
George C. Gaudin	Newport Beach, CA
Thomas Gooch	Stanford, KY
Capt. Robert R. Green, USN (Ret.)	McLean, VA
Mrs. Alyce Mary Guthrie	Memphis, TN
Russell E. Hamachek	Portland, OR
Rear Adm. John Harllee, USN (Ret.)	Washington, D.C.

E. S. H. Harrison	Taft, CA
Adm. Thomas B. Hayward, USN (Ret.)	Honolulu, HI
Michael L. Infante	Washington, D.C.
Mrs. Dorothy Janson	Stamford, CT
Col. Richard S. Johnson, USMC (Ret.)	New Bern, NC
Capt. Robert B. Kelly, USN (Ret.)	Columbia, MD
Mrs. Elsie La Bar	Wilmington, DE
William "Bud" Liebenow	Edenton, NC
Capt. E. C. Lindon, USN (Ret.)	Lake Park, FL
Mrs. Natalie Lindon	Lake Park, FL
Mrs. Douglas MacArthur	New York, NY
J. William Middendorf II	Washington, D.C.
Paul H. Nitze	Arlington, VA
Robert Parrish	Sag Harbor, NY
William E. Proutt	Aiken, SC
Marcos Ronquillo	Washington, D.C.
Cmdr. Albert B. Ross, USN (Ret.)	Bangor, ME
Adm. James S. Russell, USN (Ret.)	Tacoma, WA
Cecil C. Sanders	Lancaster, KY
Edward W. Slater	New York, NY
Baynard L. Tiegan	Silverado, CA
John H. Tuggle	Lynchburg, VA
Dr. Max A. Van Den Berg	Kalamazoo, MI
Cmdr. C. Joseph Violette, USN (Ret.)	San Diego, CA
Col. Anthony "Cold Steel" Walker, USMC (Ret.)	Middletown, RI
Senator John Warner	Washington, D.C.
Jack W. Watson	Oxford, MS
Alexander W. Wells	Jacksonville, FL
Calvin R. Whorton	Alhambra, CA

Selected Bibliography

Books

Abel, Elie, *The Missile Crisis*. New York: Lippincott, 1966.

Attwood, William, *The Reds and the Blacks*. New York: Harper & Row, 1967.

Ayers, Bradley, *The War That Never Was*. New York: Bobbs-Merrill, 1976.

Bachman, Bruce M., *The Honorable Profession*. New York: Vantage Press, 1985.

Bamford, James, *Puzzle Palace*. Boston: Houghton Mifflin, 1982.

Beck, John J., *MacArthur and Wainwright*. Albuquerque: Desert Press, 1974.

Bonsal, Philip, *Cuba, Castro and the United States*. Pittsburgh: University of Pittsburgh Press, 1971.

Bradley, General Omar N., *A Soldier's Story*. New York: Henry Holt, 1951.

Brown, Anthony Cave, *Wild Bill Donovan*. New York: Times Books, 1982.

Bulkley, Robert J., Jr., *At Close Quarters*. Washington: Naval History Division, 1962.

Casuso, Teresa, *Cuba and Castro*. New York: Random House, 1961.

Colby, William, *Honorable Men*. New York: Simon and Schuster, 1969.

Donovan, Robert J., *PT-109*. New York: McGraw-Hill, 1961.

Draper, Theodore, *Castro's Revolution*. New York: Praeger, 1962.

Dulles, Allen W., *The Craft of Intelligence*. New York: Harper & Row, 1963.

Eisenhower, General Dwight D., *Crusade in Europe*. New York: Doubleday, 1948.

Ford, Corey, *Donovan of OSS*. Boston: Little, Brown, 1970.

Ford, Dan, *Pappy: The Life of John Ford*. Englewood Cliffs, NJ: Prentice-Hall, 1979.

Friend, Theodore, *Between Two Empires*. New Haven: Yale University Press, 1965.

Geyelin, Philip L., *Lyndon B. Johnson and the World*. New York: Praeger, 1966.

Guthrie, Alyce Mary (editor), *Knights of the Sea*. Paducah, KY: David Turner and Associates, 1982.

Hinckle, Warren, and William W. Turner, *The Fish Is Red*. New York: Harper & Row, 1981.

Hougan, Jim, *Spooks*. New York: Morrow, 1978.

Huff, Sidney L., *My Fifteen Years With MacArthur*. New York: Lippincott, 1964.

Hunt, E. Howard, *Give Us This Day*. New York: Arlington House, 1973.

Johnson, Haynes, *The Bay of Pigs*. New York: Norton, 1963.

Johnson, Lyndon B., *The Vantage Point*. New York: Holt, Rinehart and Winston, 1971.
Kennedy, Robert F., *Thirteen Days*. New York: Norton, 1969.
Kirkpatrick, Lyman B., Jr., *The Real CIA*. New York: Macmillan, 1969.
Lansdale, Edward C., *In the Midst of Wars*. New York: Harper & Row, 1972.
MacArthur, General Douglas, *Reminiscences*. New York: McGraw-Hill, 1964.
Manchester, William, *American Caesar*. Boston: Little, Brown, 1978.
Marchetti, Victor, and John D. Marks, *The CIA and the Cult of Intelligence*. New York: Knopf, 1974.
Meyer, Karl, and Ted Szulc, *The Cuban Invasion*. New York: Praeger, 1963.
Morison, Samuel Eliot, *The Invasion of France and Germany*. Boston: Little, Brown, 1957.
Morrow, Robert D., *Betrayal*. Chicago: Regnery, 1976.
Mosley, Leonard, *Dulles*. New York: Dial, 1977.
Nixon, Richard M., *Memoirs*. New York: Grosset and Dunlap, 1978.
———, *My Six Crises*. Garden City, NY: Doubleday, 1962.
O'Donnell, Kenneth, and David F. Powers, *Johnny, We Hardly Knew Ye*. Boston: Little, Brown, 1970.
Persons, Albert C., *Bay of Pigs*. Birmingham: Kingston Press, 1963.
Phillips, David A., *The Night Watch*. New York: Antheum, 1976.
Reid, Ed, *The Grim Reapers*. Chicago: Regnery, 1969.
Romulo, Carlos P., *I See the Philippines Rising*. Garden City, NY: Doubleday, 1946.
Ryan, Cornelius, *The Longest Day*. New York: Simon and Schuster, 1959.
Schlesinger, Arthur, Jr., *Robert Kennedy and His Times*. Boston: Houghton Mifflin, 1965.
———, *A Thousand Days*. Boston: Houghton Mifflin, 1965.
Sorensen, Theodore C., *Kennedy*. New York: Harper & Row, 1965.
Tetlow, Edwin, *Eye on Cuba*. New York: Harcourt Brace, 1966.
Thomas, Hugh, *Cuba: The Pursuit of Freedom*. New York: Harper & Row, 1971.
Toland, John, *The Rising Sun*. New York: Random House, 1970.
Weyl, Nathaniel, *Red Star Over Cuba*. New York: Devin-Adair, 1961.
Whitney, Courtney, *MacArthur: His Rendezvous With History*. New York: Knopf, 1956.
Wise, David, and Thomas B. Ross, *The Invisible Government*. New York: Random House, 1964.

Newspapers

Atlanta Constitution, Baltimore News-Post, Baltimore Sun, Bay City (*MI*) *Times, Birmingham Age Herald, Brooklyn Tablet, Catholic News* (*The*), *Chicago Sun, Chicago Tribune, Christian Science Monitor, Columbus* (*OH*) *Dispatch, Detroit*

News, Elizabeth (NJ) Daily Journal, Gitmo Review, Indianapolis Star, Long Island City (NY) Herald, Long Island Press, Long Island Star Journal, Los Angeles Times.

Louisville Courier-Journal, Louisville Times, Manila Bulletin, Memphis Commercial Appeal, Memphis Press-Scimitar, Miami Herald, Milwaukee Journal, Nashville Banner, National Observer (The), Newark Star-Ledger, New Orleans Times-Picayune, New York Daily Mirror, New York Daily News, New York Herald-Tribune, New York Journal American, New York PM, New York Post.

New York Radio Daily, New York Sun, New York Times, New York World-Telegram, Norfolk Ledger-Star, Omaha Evening World-Herald, Peoria (IL) Journal Transcript, Philadelphia Evening Bulletin, Rolla (MO) Daily News, San Antonio Light, San Francisco Chronicle, Shreveport Journal, Springfield (IL) State Register, St. Louis Globe-Democrat, St. Louis Post-Dispatch, St. Louis Star-Times, Tyler (TX) Telegraph, Variety, Waco News-Tribune, Washington Post, Washington Star, Washington Times-Herald.

Magazines

All Hands, Colliers, Fathom, Fortune, Harper's, Leatherneck, Life, Male, Men, New Republic, Newsweek, Reader's Digest, Saga, Saturday Evening Post, Time, U.S. News & World Report.

Newsletters

Alert: News of the Air Warden Service, 1942–1943; *Catholic Universe Bulletin* (Cleveland); *Full Speed Ahead,* U.S. Navy Department; *Ice Cream Review,* 1942; *Lighthouse,* Elco Employees Association, 1942–1944; *Rollover,* Defoe Shipbuilding Company, Bay City, MI, 1945; *Rotary Club of Queens Borough* (NY), 1942; *Shipworker,* Navy Yard, New York City, 1943–1944.

Oral Histories

Vice Admiral John L. Chew, U.S. Navy Historical Foundation interview; Adm. Robert Lee Dennison, U.S. Naval Institute.

Official Reports and Summaries

Declassified intelligence summaries, U.S. Naval Base, Guantanamo Bay, Cuba, 1964–1966.

Report of Senate Select Committee to Study Governmental Operations with Respect to Intelligence Activities and Alleged Assassination Plots Involving Foreign Leaders (Senator Frank Church, chairman), 1975.

Motor Torpedo Boat Operations of Eleventh Amphibious Force (Normandy), June 1–August 1, 1944.

Role that PT Boats Played in the Invasion of Normandy, 1984.

USS *Endicott* Report of Action With Enemy Surface Vessels Off Southern France (Operation Dragoon), August 1944.

Transcript of Naval Service of Rear Adm. John D. Bulkeley, prepared by Navy Bureau of Personnel, July 1986.

Action Report of CTU 80.4.2 by Lt. Comdr. Douglas E. Fairbanks, Southern France Invasion, August 1944.

Summary of Battle Damage, Rear Adm. John D. Hall, Normandy Invasion, September 1944.

Miscellaneous

Midshipmen's Delinquency Report Log, United States Naval Academy, 1932–1933.

Transcripts of Bulkeley testimony before House Seapower Subcommittee.

Transcript of Bulkeley testimony in court-martial of Lieutenant Knull with regard to *Kennedy-Belknap* collision at sea.

"The Saga of the SS Corregidor, Late of Her Majesty's Navy," compiled by Judge Bert W. Thompson (n.d.).

Lucky Bag, yearbook, United States Naval Academy, 1933.

The United States Mosquito Fleet, by Bob Ferrell, 1977.

German Naval Command-West, War Diary, 1944.

Selected issues of the *Manila Tribune,* Japanese-controlled English-language newspaper, 1942–1943, courtesy of Mrs. Dorothy Janson.

Press releases, office of the United States Assistant Secretary of Defense (Public Affairs), Washington, 1964–1966.

Selected issues of *Hoy* and *Revolucion,* Castro regime–controlled newspapers, Havana, 1964–1966, obtained by author through confidential sources.

Assorted television and radio tapes of John D. Bulkeley interviews and public speeches.

Index